Singing Solo

Singing Solo

In Search of a Voice for Mom

JacLynn Herron

Karen,
    From one author to
another. I have enjoyed
your Peace Fibres book and
have gifted it to a friend.

                    JacLynn Herron
                    2011

NORTH STAR PRESS OF ST. CLOUD, INC.
Saint Cloud, Minnesota

The names of health care organizations, facilities, and providers, as well as the employees of such facilities and residents have been changed to protect their privacy.

First Edition, September 2011

Printed in the United States of America

Published by
North Star Press of St. Cloud, Inc.
P.O. Box 451
St. Cloud, Minnesota 56302

www.northstarpress.com

In honor of my parents,
Warren and Ernestine "Teen" Johnson,
with gratitude for their legacy of love
I dedicate this book
to those who have been silenced by
dementia.

2009

Dementia stole my mother's voice, and sadly, a well-reputed nursing home became an unwitting accomplice.

On many warm days I retrieved Mom from her room in the red-bricked nursing home, bundled her up if the weather dictated, and pushed her in her wheelchair along an outdoor, asphalt path. On a short ten-minute journey, we could circle a small pond, unless we stopped en route to enjoy the scene, which we often did. Unable to speak, Mom enjoyed the rhythmic cadence of the fountain in the center of the pond, and I enjoyed a break from carrying on one-way conversations sugarcoated with fake perkiness, a dismal attempt to mask my sadness at her condition.

Some days I brought cheeseburgers, and we picnicked at a park bench on the water's edge and pretended life was normal. We laughed at the ducks, especially a domestic white one that somehow took up residence with the mallards and their offspring. Like the Pied Piper of the aquatic community, she led the flotilla in small parades around the edge of the pond. Unable to fly south for the winter with her winged comrades, each autumn she was captured and relocated to a warm, safe hobby farm until spring when her caretakers returned her to the pond.

Did Mom feel captured and relocated as well? After strokes and dementia rendered her totally helpless, I received firm direction from the authorities that operated the care system. They said it was time to move my mother to the next level of care away from her friends in an assisted living community designed for people with memory issues. Her next and last home would offer a level of care better matched to her needs, I was told. Mom trusted me to make the right decision, and I trusted those in charge. I dutifully followed the guidelines and moved her to a well-regarded nursing home for the last three years, eight months of her life.

Was this move a mistake? How often I pondered that question as I pulled into the parking space alongside the pond. Daily I arrived to feed Mom her noontime meal. Although stokes and dementia had robbed her of the ability to talk, walk, reason, and care for herself, her medical condition declined at a very slow, undetectable rate. In comparison, the care she received in the nursing home fluctuated wildly from wonderfully compassionate to unacceptable, from competent to downright neglectful, depending on the day's circumstances.

As I walked back to my car at the end of each visit, my gut responded according to the experiences of the day. On Mom's good days, when overworked and underpaid nursing assistants took extra moments to bring her comfort and care, I offered prayers of thanks as I strolled along the pond. Sparkling geysers from the fountain, in tandem with the compassion offered within the red brick walls, eased my worry. On bad days, when understaffing and/or incompetence tainted my mother's care, I cursed the fountain as I passed it by. On those days it was a sham, a misrepresentation of calm, standing in stark contrast to the chaos and neglect that operated inside the building. And on ugly days, after a poison pen letter was added to my mother's laundry or an engagement ring disappeared from her finger, the fountain became a fake. No longer a symbol of "home," I looked upon it as a lowly aerator whose sole job was to keep algae under control, just like administrators who offered lip service to the family to keep dissatisfaction and fear at bay.

Now, three years later, I pondered the fate of the domestic white duck. Had it survived the yearly relocations or did it pass on just like Mom and thirteen of her floor mates during the winter of 2006? *Have conditions improved for current nursing home residents, especially those rendered voiceless by dementia? What are their stories? Who will tell them? Will anyone listen?*

Optimistically, I shut my eyes and imagine the din, muted at first and then louder and louder . . . trampling feet arriving at the doors of nursing homes everywhere . . . in crowds too huge to be ignored . . . expecting the best . . . outraged at the reality . . . unwilling to be placated . . . demanding a new model for eldercare. Voices for change. A full choir, at last! They are coming. Thank heaven, they are coming.

1939 - Teen Young and Warren Johnson announcing their engagement at Hamline University in St. Paul, Minnesota.

1994 - Warren and Teen Johnson enjoying their final trip to Maui before the onset of dementia.

Ten Years Earlier
August 1998

I WAS ANTICIPATING AN EMOTIONAL DAY. Leaving Dad in my parents' new apartment in St. Paul, Minnesota, I picked up Mom and drove her back to their former home, a two-story townhouse located fifteen miles away in the St. Paul suburb of White Bear Lake. Although the sunny, August day beckoned, we entered the townhouse, now empty of furnishings, and descended the staircase to the windowless, unfinished basement. It was time for Mom to retrieve "treasures" from the "stuff" that needed to be downsized now that she and Dad had taken up residence in a one-bedroom, assisted living apartment.

The relocation, necessitated by my father's immediate need for handicap accessibility, was accomplished in three weeks. Left behind were rarely used items, memorabilia, and junk. Now it was time for Mom to decide on the future of each item. How does a person downsize the keepsakes accumulated during fifty-seven years of married life? I was prepared to allow her all the time she needed to accomplish this bittersweet task.

And, I anticipated a morning of storytelling as Mom revisited the memories wrapped around each of her treasures. I had heard these stories before, but my inattention to detail and time's passage had diminished my recall. Now that my parents' mortality was undeniable, I was ready to pay full attention. What was the story behind the antique, chain-mail purse? The felted baby booties? What about those wax Pilgrims, male and female in their customary garb with candlewicks sticking out of their heads? The unmatched pieces of china and glassware, the solid wood tobacco stand, the signed artwork, not to mention the boxes of books, photographs, greeting cards, and memorabilia?

Mom slowly began. Taken aback by the stark emptiness of the main floor, she walked quietly among the boxes in the basement and peeked at their contents. Flexible for her eighty-one years, she bent forward from the waist, reached into a box and fingered one of her needlepoint creations, a framed canvas with red cardinals, relegated to the basement because of an ugly stain. From the back, she resembled a woman half her age. Her yellow blouse was belted neatly into a pair of size two petite cotton pants. Her gray curls were the only giveaway to her advancing years, until she turned around. Then the laugh lines, the frown wrinkles, and the crows' feet were facial clues to life's passage.

"Okay, Mom, here's the plan," I explained. "Let's divide things into keepers, giveaways, and throwaways." Grabbing one of the empty boxes I added, "And, let's set this aside for anything that you want to take back to the apartment today."

I expected some response, but Mom continued her silent walk among the boxes.

"I know there are many treasures here, so I won't throw anything without your permission," I promised.

Still no comment.

"Oh, look, Mom," I said, pointing to a little copper teapot with matching sugar and creamer. "I remember these. Where did you get them?" I asked, hoping to prompt some storytelling. Instead, she simply stared.

"Oh, my! Oh, my!" was all that she managed, and I saw mounting confusion in her eyes.

I tried to calm her rising agitation by grabbing a pressed glass serving bowl, one item with which I was very familiar.

"Remember this, Mom?" I chuckled, remembering my purchase of this bargain. The attractive, straight-sided bowl, offered at the inexpensive closeout price of three dollars, had been perfect to show off a layered salad recipe. Together we had laughed at how "gourmet" the salad looked in this cheap bowl. Perhaps, if I reminded her of this story, I would be priming the pump for other anecdotes.

But before I could comment, she took the bowl from my hands and cradled it in her own. "Oh, my!" she began. "This was my mother's bowl. It's very valuable, you know. She gave it to me many years ago, before I was married, I think." She looked lovingly at the bowl. "It's very valuable," she repeated. "We need to take very good care of it."

"Okay, Mom," I responded. "We'll wrap it and put it over here in one of these boxes for your treasures."

My heart sank as I was confronted with two facts I had been trying so hard to ignore. The encroaching effects of dementia were hijacking my mother's memory. And, my wall of denial of her disability was crumbling. I had seen it coming, hadn't I? Her trouble with making coffee, a simple, daily task; her difficulty with word retrieval, so bizarre for a college English major with a hobby of working crossword puzzles; the nervous laughter, her response to a simple question. How did I deny these messages? A wave of grief overwhelmed me as we stood amidst the pieces of her life in the windowless basement.

I was losing my mother. The stories of her life, the anecdotes, her history, had already bled away. My blurry recollections were all that remained. Why hadn't I been paying attention?

I watched Mom as she walked from box to box, picking up a candlestick, then a china cup. She quizzically examined a broken ceramic trivet that I had created for her in fourth grade, as well as a homemade luminary fashioned by a granddaughter by poking nail holes in the shape of a Christmas tree through an aluminum coffee can. It wasn't that long ago that I had kidded her about holding on to these items. "I'm sentimental," she had said. But today, she saw them for the first time. She walked around and around the boxes, picking up pieces, running her slender fingers through their crevices, and redepositing them in no organized fashion. The confusion in her eyes cut through my heart.

"I think it's time for a break, Mom," I said, hoping for closure after about fifteen agonizing minutes. "Why don't we drive over to Baker's Square and pick up a pie. We can bring it back to the apartment and share it with Dad."

"Yes, let's." Mom brightened and turned toward the stairs, ready to immediately leave the basement and its contents behind.

As I turned the key on the front door of the townhouse, grief descended. My mother's treasures—and their unique stories—were safely and sadly locked away.

The Meadows

I HAVE HEARD IT SAID THAT TIMING IS CRITICAL, such as the turning of a red traffic light to green just as a car approaches an intersection. The lucky driver speeds along without a wasted moment, while a second car in the cross street is forced to slow down and stop. Good timing is, well, good. When everything occurs in synchronicity, the harmony can be so natural that, ironically, it often goes undetected, and people just continue on unaware of their good fortune. Bad timing, on the other hand, screams for attention, just like the slamming of brakes, the squealing of tires, or the disintegration of one's health. The summer of 1998 was marked by both bad and good timing.

Back at their apartment Mom, Dad and I enjoyed slices of French silk pie and avoided the discussion of the recent crash: the collision of Mom's mental and Dad's physical deterioration, the impact that necessitated their move to an assisted-living facility. Instead, Dad inquired into our day's progress at sorting through the remaining possessions at the townhouse. Using my mother's preferred nickname, a shortened version of Ernestine, he directed a question to his wife. "So, Teen, did you get everything sorted? You weren't gone very long."

"Oh, Warren Johnson!" she replied as if he had been kidding with her.

"We did all we needed to do, didn't we, Mom?" I interjected, skirting the question and diverting Dad's attention away from Mom's strange reply.

"Oh, yes," she answered, unknowingly adding to the diversion.

"Good," Dad responded. "Soon we can list the place and get it sold."

I groaned internally. Packing up the basement, stripping wallpaper, replacing carpet, painting, cleaning, touchups—so much work to do before we could even think of selling the townhouse. I changed the subject.

"Things have pretty much fallen into place, haven't they?" Dad added.

It was Dad's simple comment that bolstered my spirits, because in two short months our family had witnessed the crumbling of my parents' independent lifestyle and located the glue, in the form of an assisted-living community, to paste it back together, albeit cracked and weakened.

Ironically, my parents' need for increased assistance occurred within the same month that my husband, Tom, and I celebrated the graduation of our youngest of two children. With one daughter, Krista, already in college and the second, Angela, newly graduated from high school and college-bound at the end of the summer, Tom and I had been anticipating the empty nest with a gleam in our eyes. Parenting had been a great trip, but we looked forward to spending more carefree time as a couple again. The timing of Mom and Dad's crises altered this reality. On the day I turned fifty it quickly became apparent that Tom and I were exchanging one type of caretaking for another. Day-to-day responsibilities of parenting our daughters were ending, just as Mom and Dad's need for assistance mushroomed.

Earlier that summer we had seamlessly shifted gears. Oblivious to the impending transition, I answered the phone on a balmy Minnesota evening in late June. At 10:30 p.m., shortly after arriving home from my surprise birthday party, I heard my mother's voice. Surprised at the lateness (Mom never called anyone after 9:00 p.m.) I stiffened. Mom began the conversation as if she couldn't remember exactly why she had called.

"Hi, hon," she said.

"Hi, Mom. What's up?" I asked, trying to hide the concern in my voice.

She responded with a question. "How's everything over there?"

"We're fine, Mom. What's happening?"

"Well, I don't know," she hesitated.

With escalating anxiety, I asked to speak to Dad. It was then that she remembered the purpose for her call. Dad had fallen in the dining room, and together they had been unable to get him back on his feet. My dad, the gentle giant, a tower of strength, larger than life, now incapable of this simple task. And tiny Mom, helpless and confused.

I had just turned fifty, and my carefree world began shifting ominously, uncontrollably with one phone call. My stomach lurched and seized. It took my brain longer to add up the pieces. The bottom line registered uncertainty, closely wrapped in a shroud of fear.

Following Dad's ambulance to St. John's Hospital that June evening, I sensed that I had begun a maiden journey into a new reality with destination unknown. Mom and Dad, my champions, had always provided a safety net for my family. I had enjoyed the comfort of knowing they were only a phone call away. Many times I had made that call. I sought out Mom's understanding ear or Dad's logical, solution-oriented mind. Now she had telephoned the SOS to me.

It was not their increasing need for assistance that set me reeling, but rather my unease. How could I be only a phone call away, if they had difficulty dialing the number when they needed me? Both eighty-one, Mom and Dad had reached the point where they were no longer able to cover up their own weaknesses or compensate for each other's. This reality was breaking their hearts. And, to see them in this state broke mine.

Mom and Dad, my cornerstones of love and support, could no longer manage life as they had in the past, like two oxen pulling in tandem. They refused to surrender, but they were traveling in circles, and Dad, at least, was well aware of this fact. Mom seemed oblivious to it all, which generated a whole different concern. With my parents' independence diminishing in front of me, I entered the decade of my fifties becoming a parent once again, this time to my own parents.

Perhaps it is a blessing that we do not know the course that lies in front of us. Looking back, my naively positive attitude of the last few years bolstered false hope that life could continue along unchangingly for our family. In hindsight I could now define my simple outlook as basic denial.

Actually, I had been in denial for months. Even though Dad's declining health was documented by doctors at the Mayo Clinic in Rochester, Minnesota, as multiple systems atrophy (MSA), a degenerative neurological disease, I felt that I could provide the assistance my parents needed to keep them safe and content in their townhouse.

Neither of them had been able to drive in over eighteen months. Although this was a huge loss of independence for them, it had been a relatively small inconvenience for me. I enjoyed spending time with them and reciprocating the help that they had showered on me over the years. I expanded my grocery shopping expedition so that one trip to the store stocked my kitchen and my parents'. I became Dad's chauffeur. He rode shotgun during weekly errands around White Bear Lake. Occasionally, Mom joined us when an appointment involved her.

Tom and I drove them to church on Sunday mornings, to a granddaughter's band concert or piano recital, to a family reunion . . . We became their conduits to the outside world. Their only surviving child (my brother Jim had died in 1990 from a brain tumor), I took on the role of chief assistant. Tom, Krista, and Angie provided backup often and without complaint.

Dad had survived a fall earlier that spring that required a three-week stint in a transitional facility before returning to the townhouse with part-time home healthcare assistance. Since then, with his increasing weakness and Mom's memory lapses, erosion of their familiar world was quickening.

After the doctor's evaluation in the emergency room, Dad was admitted to the hospital for further tests. The results were clear: he would be unable to return home without more assistance than my mother would be able to provide. Home health care, although a blessing during the previous two months, was no longer a viable option for my father whose needs had expanded. He was released again to a transitional care facility, and I was advised to find an alternative living arrangement for him before his release in two weeks.

Thankfully, weeks earlier, on the suggestion of the home healthcare staff, my daughter Krista and I had explored assisted living options in the northern areas of St. Paul and Minneapolis.

The search for a perfect assisted-living facility had been an interesting mother/daughter adventure. Since no legal definition for the term currently existed in 1998, each facility defined *assisted living* in its own way. So, Krista and I asked questions, took notes, and compared facilities.

The "acceptable level of health" of a potential resident varied from one assisted-living provider to another. One attractive facility was clearly not interested in renting to someone who might have a health condition that required more than one staff person to assist the resident with transfers to and from wheelchair, bed, or toilet.

Shortly into the tour of this facility I asked, "What happens if the resident's health declines and he needs a two-person transfer?"

"Then that person must move to the adjacent nursing home," the admissions person firmly replied.

Krista looked at me and frowned. We ended our tour at that point, thanked our tour guide and left the building. Our basic goal was to find a suitable home that would keep my parents together for as long as possible, hopefully even after Dad's condition deteriorated.

As Krista and I toured another facility, the Meadows, we asked the same question.

"When a resident's health declines and a two-person transfer is needed, we increase the care," the administrator explained. "Our goal is to delay the move to the nursing home." This was definitely the philosophy we were seeking. The building, under the umbrella of Riverside Homes, a reputable healthcare system, provided everything on our wish list. A care plan could be crafted specifically for Dad and his needs. The apartments, although not huge, had spacious, accessible bathrooms with showers. Meal plans were included. The dining room and sitting areas were beautifully appointed. Little things, like the electrical sockets located three feet from the floor, made life so much easier for the residents. The estimated $5,000 per month cost was daunting, but it included a fixed rate for rent and meals and a flexible rate, known as a cafeteria plan, for customized healthcare that could be upgraded as Dad's disease progressed.

Krista and I felt like we had found the perfect place for "sometime in the future." We drove Mom and Dad over to look at it, and all of us agreed that it was a sound housing alternative. We placed my parents' names on the waiting list with the understanding that once they reached the top and an apartment became available, they could pass until they were ready to make a move. The Meadows would be our backup plan, if Mom and Dad ever arrived at the stage where they were unable to take care of themselves and each other in the townhouse.

After talking to the doctors in the hospital, my wall of denial crumbled. "Sometime in the future" had alarmingly arrived. Dad was discharged from the hospital to a transitional care facility for physical therapy. The doctors, the home healthcare providers, and I agreed that returning to the townhouse would not be a safe option for him, especially since Mom's confusion made her a less-than-competent caregiver.

Dad's MSA had progressed. Now anytime he stood up he was threatened by brownouts. When he rose too quickly, his autonomic nervous system would fail to increase the blood pressure needed to supply oxygen to his brain, and he would keel over. Walking without assistance was no longer recommended for this six-foot, four and one-half-inch, 200-pound man. And, his little five-foot-two, ninety-five-pound wife could no longer provide the support he needed. Clearly, relocating Mom and Dad into a safe, assisted-living apartment needed to be accomplished quickly. My deadline was rapidly approaching.

I quickly called the Meadows and inquired about availability. Good news: there was a one-bedroom apartment opening up. Bad news: Mom and Dad were second on the waiting list.

"I need to offer the apartment to the other couple," explained the admissions person sympathetically after I had detailed my dilemma. "I'll call them right away and call you back as soon as they've made a decision."

Less than three hours later the phone rang.

"The other couple passed on the apartment," she announced. "Your parents can move in after the current occupants move out and we paint and recarpet. It should be ready in ten days."

Ten days—four days before Dad's discharge! I thanked her profusely and smiled, as I pictured her sitting in her office with the phone to her ear and a halo around her head. It was then that I realized that it wasn't only my parents who were unsteady. My world was rocking, and the angel on the other end of the phone had tossed me a lifeline. I hung on for dear life.

This apartment would be my parents' new home. Dad would have assistance, and both of them would be safe. As I hung up the phone, I marveled at the synchronous timing and offered a silent prayer of thanks.

When the apartment became vacant, I visited what would shortly become my parents' new home. Once walls were measured to determine which furniture pieces would fit into the space, Tom and I developed a moving plan and proceeded to carry it out. Meanwhile, Krista and Angie provided transportation and support for their grandmother, who spent each day with her husband at the transitional care facility.

Krista and I memorized the location of each piece of Mom's cut glass collection in her corner display cabinet before bubble-wrapping and boxing it. Then we recreated the same placement in the cabinet after it was moved into the apartment. We did the same with the dishes and glassware in the hutch cupboard.

After spending a full day emptying boxes, setting up the kitchen, organizing the closets, hanging the pictures and trashing the packing material, I arranged a centerpiece on the table and collapsed into a chair. I looked around at the warm, inviting apartment, now clearly my parents' home. The furniture, pictures and décor lent an air of familiarity to the new floor plan. The only missing piece was the presence of Mom and Dad. Both greeted the news of the accomplishment with relief. Dad, especially, knew that a move from their townhouse to assisted living was the best possible scenario, and Mom, tired and worried about Dad, followed along without a whimper.

During Dad's last week at transitional care, the healthcare coordinator from the Meadows visited him to assess his needs and set up a care plan that would be operational the first day of his arrival. She also interviewed Mom and confided in me that Mom's memory loss might present some issues in the future. I pushed those fears to the back of my mind and trudged forward. On the morning of Dad's discharge, Tom and I loaded my parents into our Mercury Villager, collapsed Dad's wheelchair and hoisted it into the back, and drove the short distance to their new home. After a tour and lunch in the communal dining room, Mom and Dad settled in. Dad was definitely delighted, and Mom wore a bewildered smile. Life in their new home had begun, and the entire crisis and resulting relocation had taken place during my two-month summer break from my job at Irondale High School. Perfect timing!

· · ·

"HOW ABOUT ANOTHER PIECE OF PIE?" I asked, as I began to relax after the emotional trip to the townhouse.

"Oh, maybe a sliver," Dad answered with a sly smile, pushing his plate toward me as I cut another slice.

"Mom? More pie?"

"Oh, yes," she said, but instead of handing me her plate she lifted her coffee cup for a refill, another sad reminder that my mother's mental lapses were no longer comical senior moments. Dad, whose hearing loss mercifully prevented him from overhearing the last exchange, shuffled through the day's mail with one hand and glided his fork through whipped cream and chocolate mousse with the other.

Exiting the building at the end of our visit, I stepped into the heat of a humid August afternoon. Confident that health aides would arrive shortly to help Dad to the bathroom before he and Mom descended to the dining room for a dinner that she no longer had to prepare, I drove the few miles home.

With my parents comfortably settled into their new home, the end of my summer break closed in. With only a couple of vacation days to re-claim some feeling of organization in my own life, I turned my attention to the mound of disarray on my desk in the computer room. Two months of neglect awaited me, and I began the task of decluttering. Under a stash of junk mail, I uncovered a forgotten file marked SUMMER. It contained cryptic wish lists for summer activities: books to read, recipes to try, house-hold projects, outdoor concerts at Lake Harriet Band Shell, Minneapolis Aquatennial activities . . . "Wow, I was optimistic," I whispered to no one in particular, as I grabbed a black marker and add the word NEXT before the word SUMMER and filed it away.

Fall, 1998

I HAVE ALWAYS LOVED THINGS WITH A BEGINNING AND AN END. Except when the last page requires severing my relationship with a well-loved character, reaching the end of a book brings me simple joy, as does finishing a knitting project, or pulling into the driveway after a road trip. The task of relocating my parents, an emotionally and physically draining process, had ended. It was time to turn my attention to the beginning of a new school year.

I have always associated late summer/early fall as a time for new beginnings. First as a student, then a teacher, then a mom with school age children, and most recently a staff person at the local high school, my life has always revolved around the school calendar, and this year was no exception.

With an eventful summer vacation concluded, I headed back to work as a ten-month clerical support staff person in the Career Center of Irondale High School, one mile down the road from my home. As I booted up my computer on my first day back, I paused to reflect on all that had transpired in my personal life since I had turned off that computer two months earlier. Although "vacation" had been definitely absent from the summer, I experienced a wave of gratitude that my parents' world imploded during my two-month break. They were safely settled in a lovely new home, complete with needed assistance and hot cooked meals, and I was back to work.

From my perspective, I was overjoyed to be returning to the sane, quiet atmosphere of the Career Center. A summer's worth of dust covered every flat surface. I rolled up my sleeves, and with a bucketful of warm, soapy water, I began washing every flat surface. The housekeeping task was one with a beginning and an end, and progress was visible with each swipe of my cleaning rag. Cleaning was a mundane task, but mundane felt good, productive, and predictable.

Staff members returned from their busy summers and prepared for the onslaught of 1,700 ninth through twelve graders who would storm the school doors after Labor Day. Although certified as a classroom teacher, I welcomed the fact that I worked in a clerical position that required no more of me than the eight hours I was on the job. I gave it my all for that time and then turned the key in the Career Center lock and left it all behind until the next workday.

Normalcy returned to our household, as well. Krista eagerly returned to Concordia College in Moorhead, Minnesota, where, as a junior, she was aiming at a double major in Spanish and history. Since she had dedicated a great part of her summer break to helping her grandparents, I was excited that she could now move forward with her life.

Moving Krista into her campus apartment was accomplished in a single day. A master organizer, she had everything boxed and ready, so driving her the 220 miles, unloading the van, taking her over to the Normandy, the campus canteen, for a bite to eat and returning home were enjoyable tasks.

Returning to campus stirred nostalgic memories of my four years at Concordia College in the late sixties. I cherished the school and the people I met there, especially Tom Herron, a sophomore from Lake City, Minnesota, introduced to me by my roommate during the spring of my freshman year. For me Tom's compassionate, sensitive nature set him apart from the other upper-class students. Grounded and future-oriented, he balanced his earnestness with a love of life. I graduated in 1970 with an engagement ring on my finger, and in December of that year, we married at the tender ages of twenty-three for Tom and twenty-two for me.

Tom and I developed lasting friendships with classmates from Concordia, and now Krista was doing the same. As freshmen she and her Park Region dorm-mates forged a special bond in the spring of 1997 as they stood shoulder to shoulder sandbagging homes threatened by the rising Red River of the North. Ironically, Tom and I had done the same back in 1969.

Still at home, Angie divided her last few days of summer between packing for her freshman year of college and driving over to the townhouse to give

Teen and Warren's granddaughters Angie (left) and Krista (right).

the den a fresh coat of paint, one of the many touchups needed before listing it with realtors.

Angie's move to college was a bit more challenging than depositing Krista in Moorhead. Requiring long-distance travel to the state of Washington, the transition un-folded smoothly and uneventfully during the last weekend in Au-gust. Tom, Angie, and I boarded a Sun Country flight to the SeaTac airport. Her wardrobe and personal items filled our allotted six pieces of checked luggage. Upon arrival we hit a nearby Tar-get store for remaining essentials and helped her move into her dormitory at the University of Puget Sound in Tacoma, Washington. In quick order she settled in for her freshman year.

Even though this relocation spanned half a continent, the relative ease of the weekend surprised me. How different the feeling that accom-panied this move compared to the frenetic insanity of Mom and Dad's re-location. Angie's excitement partially nullified my fears that she might experience long-distant homesickness, or that her dad and I would be struck with overwhelming separation anxiety. Instead, with both my par-ents and our children firmly settled, Tom and I inhaled the first, calm breaths of what I believed to be empty nesting.

Once home, life took on enjoyable predictability. I found each day split between helping students on the cusp of independence in Career Center, and aiding Mom and Dad, who were reaching the end of theirs. On weekdays I awoke at 5:45 a.m., arrived at work by 7:00 and focused on my job until 3:30.

Our black-and-white border collie, Jasper, greeted me daily when I returned home. I changed my clothes, and we set off for a quick walk.

Alert to every sound, smell, and movement, he eagerly chose our route, and I realized that I had him to thank for my daily dose of fresh air and exercise.

Home again, I exchanged Jasper's leash for my car keys and whatever else I intended to take over to Mom and Dad. Bags containing simple groceries like bread, peanut butter, jelly, fruit, or snacks often accompanied me. At other times, essentials such as toiletries, envelopes, paper products and stamps were enriched with the latest letters from the girls or Dad's favorite treat, chocolate-covered peanuts.

The Meadows was an easy drive from my home in New Brighton, a northern suburb of St. Paul. As I pulled into the parking area, steps from the entrance, I recalled my earlier visit with Krista and our positive reactions to our tour.

In the first two months of Mom and Dad's life in their new apartment, the Meadows delivered all that was promised at that first meeting when Krista and I placed their names on the waiting list. "The Meadows is the real deal," my father proudly stated to visiting extended family members as he gave them a grand tour from his wheelchair. I gratefully agreed. I began to relax, no longer fearful that the proverbial second shoe would drop, squashing this period of calmness.

Each afternoon I arrived at Mom and Dad's apartment and knocked on the door. It was rarely locked, but I always waited a few seconds to see if Mom would arrive to open it. Usually she greeted me with a look of delight as if my daily visit was a rare surprise.

Dad, expecting me, was usually in his leather rocker which sat upon a five-inch riser, a wooden box that Tom had constructed to give my long-legged father additional leverage when rising. A remote call button hung around his neck on a cord. Pushing the button activated a small machine that sat on a side table. Through this machine he could speak with staff at the healthcare office located on second floor. Although a constant source of assurance, the communication technology was rarely needed since Dad's care plan already guaranteed assistance with dressing, trips to the bathroom, and help with medications.

Dad, visibly relieved, appreciated the amenities offered by the staff. I finally realized how tired and anxious he had become trying to maintain a normal life in the townhouse as his health failed and Mom's dementia increased. He appeared relaxed, and when Mom disappeared into the bedroom, he quietly shared with me his thankfulness that she didn't have to cook anymore and that the stove in the apartment was unplugged for safety.

Mom and Dad had chosen a meal plan that included breakfast and dinner in the building's dining room. Quickly they both gained weight and strength from their new dietary regimen. Mom's need to putter in her kitchen space was satisfied when she prepared cold lunches, usually a sandwich with chips or fruit I supplied on a weekly basis. The configuration of the apartment allowed Dad to supervise her kitchen activities from his rocker in the living room.

In their apartment, Mom and Dad were surrounded by their favorite things: two comfortable chairs, large for him, small for her; a couch for visitors; their round, glass-top table with four chairs; the hutch cupboard filled with unused china; a corner cabinet displaying Mom's treasured cut glass; Dad's desk; and their queen-size bed, extra long for Dad's tall frame. His wheelchair sat ready for long trips down the hall to retrieve the mail or to the elevator for the descent to meals in the dining room, haircuts in the beauty shop or daily offerings in the activity rooms.

Assisting my father during transfers from rocker to wheelchair or vice versa became easier as his strength and my skills improved. During occupational therapy sessions with Dad at the transitional care facility, I had learned the techniques for correct placement of the wheelchair and the most efficient way to direct and assist the transfer. Now, we began to work as a skilled team.

Just as we had done so often in the townhouse, the three of us gathered around the glass-top table. Only now, instead of Mom perking the coffee, I filled a pot from the machine in the dining room, and while loads of soiled clothes were washed and dried in the nearby laundry room, the three of us chatted about something other than crises, or rather Dad and I talked. The conversations meandered. Grandkids, current events, grandkids, sports, grandkids. Mom uniquely chimed in. Her vocabulary was disappearing into brain files that she simply could not access. Nouns retreated, especially proper nouns. Her use of the pronoun "he" could represent anyone of either sex.

As Mom's communication skills diminished, I found myself forced to play the dementia version of twenty questions.

"Who called, Mom?" I asked, in response to something she was trying to tell me.

"Well, he did, you know," she responded.

"Who is 'he'?" I prodded.

"Well, you know."

"Clay?" I asked, hoping she was looking for the name of her grandson, my brother's only child.

"No," she answered.

And on and on we went until I named every male I thought could possibly be the caller. Finally, she brightened when I asked if it was Uncle Fred, only to spend five more minutes before I arrived at the correct answer. The "he" was Uncle Fred's wife, Aunt Dorothy Ann, my father's sister, who called often to check in on both of them.

At the end of this exchange, I noted fear in Mom's eyes. Perhaps she was afraid that she was treading down the same road as her mother, whose life ended with her mind in confusion. Perhaps she realized that Dad, with debilitating hearing loss and restricted eyesight, could no longer compensate for her cognitive deterioration.

Just as I was about to begin a mental journey to fear-filled recesses of my own mind, a health aide tapped on the door and entered to assist Dad with a bathroom break. With flawless, ebony skin and black hair pulled back from her face, she smiled at us and apologized, "I'm sorry to interrupt."

"Not at all," Dad responded.

"Your timing is perfect," I added. Then turning my attention back to Dad, I continued. "I need to get going, but I'll stop by tomorrow. Is there anything you need?"

"How about some more chocolate-covered peanuts?" Dad responded as the aide unlocked his wheelchair and pulled him back from the table.

"That I can do." Yes, that I could do.

I exited the parking lot and drove the short distance to the nearest grocery store to fulfill Dad's simple request before heading home. Choosing the back roads to avoid rush hour traffic on Highway 35W, I wove through residential streets as if on auto-pilot, my mind contemplating another journey, the one our family had begun, the one brought on by the collision of two long-term degenerative diseases. As I pulled the dusty red van into our garage and turned off the engine, I couldn't help but wonder where, when and how the journey would end.

Winter, 1998

My gut reaction to selling the townhouse signaled a layer of disquietude which lived somewhere below my conscious level of newfound serenity. True, seeing my parents comfortably settled in their new home had reduced my anxiety, and probably my blood pressure. They loved their assisted-living apartment and the simplicity of care that it required. They enjoyed the community of other residents, the food service, the breadth of activities, the healthcare assistance. The move had been perfect. So, selling the townhouse quickly should have been my goal to help them get out from under the monthly association fees and the property taxes that continued to bleed dollars from their checking account. Yet, hesitancy ruled.

First, I blamed fatigue for my reluctance. My schedule, filled with a forty-hour work week, assisting Mom and Dad and attacking my own household chores, left only snatches of time to drive out to White Bear Lake and prepare the townhouse for sale. Thankfully, Tom stepped up both at home and at the townhouse. While I was doing Mom and Dad's laundry at the Meadows, he did ours at home. At the townhouse, after I filled a box with miscellaneous items, he hauled it to its assigned destination. And, once the basement was cleared, he acid etched the floor and gave it a fresh coat of paint, while I polished light fixtures and washed windows.

I declined many offers from kind friends who volunteered to help me clear out the last remnants of Mom and Dad's former life. Instead, I felt compelled to personally examine each remaining item in the basement. Methodically, in no hurry to finalize the job, I proceeded. And finally, with all personal property dispensed with, I surveyed the empty townhouse and confirmed that nostalgia was not the originator of my disquietude.

Mom and Dad moved to the townhouse after their retirements, so none of my childhood memories emanated as I walk from one empty room to another. And, although the girls had blown out many a birthday candle in the dining room, they assured me that their favorite childhood memories occurred at their grandparents' previous home, the three-bedroom rambler on Bald Eagle Lake, only a few miles north. Summer Sundays at the lake often included swimming and fishing. Afternoon picnics of Grandma's fried chicken and potato salad were served on the pontoon while the grandkids took turns helping Grandpa skipper the boat around the island. In the winter when the lake was frozen, picnics moved indoors. Grandma spread huge beach towels on the floor in the den and served the girls and their cousin Clay macaroni and cheese, fruits, and veggies during *Sesame Street*. It was the lake home, not the townhouse, that stirred nostalgic memories for the girls and for me.

Bringing my thoughts back I entered Mom's kitchen, always the center of activity. Now it was empty, quiet, sterile. From this room I stepped through French doors into a cozy, three-season porch. It was Mom's favorite space, a place to commune with her inner thoughts as well as her favorite morning visitor, a brilliant, red cardinal with an incessant song. During all but the most frigid weeks of winter the warmth of the western sun, supplemented by a small space heater, boosted the porch's temperature to a comfortable level. Nestled in the corner, a white, wrought iron table had been my parents' rendezvous point for midmorning coffee.

Then in May of 1989, the table was removed to make room for a hospital bed for my brother Jim. For the last twelve months of his life the porch became his room, as he fought a lethal brain tumor—the worst type, the worst stage. Unable to navigate the steps of his apartment, Jim gave up his independence and lived out his remaining months with Mom and Dad, his chief caregivers. He spent days doing what he loved: writing; reading; watching the sunsets; and spending as much time as possible with his fourteen-year-old son, Clay, who lived with his mother, Jim's ex-wife, Arleen, in St. Cloud, Minnesota.

With the help of hospice, Mom and Dad were able to see that Jim remained at home until the tumor claimed him. On Sunday, May 6, 1990, he quietly passed away. That morning an overwhelming sense of peace filled the porch and blessed those that surrounded Jim during his passing. It was as if his spirit traveled on his last breath, beyond the confines of his cancer-stricken body, to an unimaginable, pain-free destination.

Yet, I do not attach any sentimentality to the room in which Jim died, only gratitude that the weather during his last winter had been mild enough to allow him to comfortably witness each unique, beautiful sunset. The sun's rays morphing in tints and shades will remind me of my brother, not the porch from which he viewed them.

After Jim's spirit peacefully departed, the wrought iron table returned to the porch, transforming it back into a coffee nook. Now, the porch was empty, and the only vestige was my mother's cardinal, who continued to sing outside the window, even in her absence.

I climbed the steps to the second floor with its two bedrooms and two bathrooms. Closets empty, bathrooms cleaned—the upstairs was declared ready. Back downstairs, the fragrance of new carpet emanated from the small den where family members routinely gathered to watch a Vikings football game on a Sunday afternoon, until Mom, with perfect timing, declared at halftime that dinner was served.

The fresh coat of paint in the laundry room gave the space an airy freshness that almost masked a dreaded memory. But glancing at the dryer I recalled the note I had uncovered three weeks earlier, when I moved the bulky machine to access the back wall for my paint roller. A wrinkled small piece of paper torn from a tiny notebook and covered in sticky dryer lint contained written attempts in shaky versions of Mom's handwriting:

Alliss

Allison

Allisson

Allison

Was she practicing the printing of the name in preparation for writing it somewhere? Trying to make sense of my discovery, I sat down with paint roller in one hand and the note in the other. The paper, I surmised, was referring to the only Allison that Mom ever talked about: Allison Cunningham. Mom had been dubbed Allison's "stand-in Grandma," by Allison's mother, my friend Linda. When Linda's mother, who lived hundreds of miles away, was unable to attend recitals and concerts, Mom cheered Allison on. After watching Allison dance with Krista or play piano duets with Angie, she gushed over Allison's accomplishments in addition to her granddaughters'.

Slowly and sickeningly the puzzle pieces aligned. On this small scrap of smudged paper, Mom had been practicing the writing of Allison's name before she placed it, if my hypothesis was correct, on a confirmation card for Allison. I recalled Linda's invitation to my parents for a special gathering following Allison's confirmation. Mom had called me for the correct spelling of Allison's name. Then on Confirmation Sunday she and Dad arrived at the Cunninghams with card in hand.

My dismal conclusion indicated that Mom had been struggling with dementia's attack on her spelling and penmanship at least since that Sunday, over two and a half years ago! Had I been so concerned about Dad's failing health that I had naively overlooked the clues about Mom's? When was the last time I saw anything that she had written other than "Mom" signed alongside Dad's name on greeting cards?

Leaving the laundry room and the sadness it conjured behind, I stepped into the garage and joined Tom, who was placing his toolbox in the trunk alongside painting equipment and cleaning supplies. Tasks completed, the townhouse was ready to sell. But, instead of the immense relief I thought I would experience at finally arriving at this point, I sensed unease, a disquietude whose origin, for the life of me, I could not quite pinpoint.

Grief, Guilt and Gratitude

IT IS SAID THAT FAMILY DYNAMICS CAN BE COMPARED to a mobile that hangs in the air, all parts balancing perfectly until one piece is moved. Then in a domino effect, all the other pieces take on movements in attempts to retrieve that ultimate balance. My parents' deterioration, mental for Mom and physical for Dad, set our family mobile into action. In response to their neediness I jumped to aid them, and in response to the void I left behind at home, Tom and the girls made adjustments. This dynamic, I realized, was universal for all families that experienced trauma. But, I was struck by the overwhelming feeling of imbalance that resulted from something as natural and predictable as parents getting older and frailer. What I was feeling, I decided, was pure, simple grief.

I grieved my loss of parents. Although they were still physically with me on earth, our roles had reversed, and the safety net was held by me, rather than for me. A scary thought! Although I could intellectualize the necessity of becoming my parents' parent, this responsibility began to take on a prominent role in my conscious and subconscious life. I had imagined that inevitably the time would come when I would help one parent take care of the other. Instead, their simultaneous deterioration left me feeling parentless, with a strange and guilt-producing sense of orphan abandonment.

I grieved again for my brother Jim, this time in a selfish way. His death left me an only child with no brother to share the responsibility and decision-making for our parents. I longed for a sibling from whom to seek counsel, someone to relieve Tom and me even for a day or a weekend. I watched friends with aging parents work cooperatively in sibling teams, and I imagined how healthy it would feel to pass the baton of responsibility and worry back and forth. But, I also witnessed bickering and feelings of resentment and frustration among siblings. Having no brothers or sisters to share the responsibilities meant the decision-making was ultimately mine. Period. No arguing. No compromise needed. That was the good news, but even the good news stunk. And when sadness and grief over the loss of my care-free life broke through my façade of control, I was shaken by a hidden yet powerful force, an undercurrent of guilt.

As my world rocked, in response so did our family mobile. Yet, Tom's support was unshakeable. And, the girls in colleges hundred of miles from home supported us with long-distance encouragement and grandparent-focused vacations.

The "in sickness and in health" vow that Tom and I declared at our wedding took on unpredicted and expanded meaning for both of us. As I fearfully witnessed the deterioration of my father's physical health and the gradual fading of my mother's memory and voice, he assisted with the business side of my parents' new circumstances, all the while wrapping his compassionate soul around me.

Weeks passed, and then months. Assisted living proved a perfect solution for my parents' situation. We laughed again. Crises for them involved lost keys or television trouble, both minor. Keys were found, and the TV tuned. I tried to ignore the sadness that the keys had been "put away in a safe place" by Mom, and that Dad had simply been unable to locate the correct channel for the Vikings game.

Dad continued to test his boundaries. Against orders, he attempted solo voyages across the living room without assistance and several times stumbled to the carpet. Thankfully, health aides quickly responded and re-deposited him safely and unhurt back into his chair.

"All athletes learn to roll," he jokingly responded with little remorse when he described the latest accident.

I had no heart to scold him. It was his determined nature that had brought him to this point in life, so I simply encouraged him to wait for help before he attempted to retrieve something out of arm's reach. But, no one except Mom was available to help him most of the day, and she was no longer able to translate his requests accurately. He might ask for a hand-kerchief, and she might return with a toothbrush. Sometimes she simply got distracted in the bedroom or bathroom, both out of Dad's vision, and busily involved herself with "work" that he was unable to oversee. Help came most consistently from the healthcare staff during their visits through-out the day. Dad frequently asked them to check on Mom, and they be-came his eyes and ears as his own failed.

The dining room staff doted on Mom and Dad, too. Clearly, hospitality was a cornerstone of the building's philosophy. For residents, mealtimes ap-peared to be the day's highlights. Certainly they were for my father whose ap-petite rarely failed him. French toast, his favorite, graced his breakfast plate often. And when Mom became too confused to push Dad in his wheelchair down to the dining room, an escort was added to Dad's care plan.

Compared to previous monthly townhouse expenses, the cost of as-sisted living jolted me. The rent and meal plan exceeded $3,000 per month, and added to that was the cost of the healthcare assistance of another $2,200, on average. I was sure that if Dad's eyesight were better, the monthly bill would have concerned him. Assuring him that pensions and Social Security were covering the costs, I acted as treasurer of his finances and paid the bill. Thankfully, we both agreed that the "assistance" part of assisted living was worth every hard-earned dollar.

I shook my head in disbelief recalling my earlier assumption that Mom could help Dad with his medication in the townhouse. What was I think-ing? Surely his failing eyesight and Mom's short-term memory lapses led to medication errors. Dad's occasional loopiness? The drowsiness that caused his head to drop into slumber mid-sentence? Why hadn't I considered over-medication a possible culprit instead of advancing symptoms of MSA?

Now with few hitches, health aides arrived at designated times to dis-pense medications and to assist with dressing and toileting. They became an integral part of my parents' day, and the continuity that accompanied low staff turnover was fertile soil for the growth of special friendships.

•••

"I HAVEN'T FELT WELL ALL DAY," Dad responded when I arrived and asked for a status update. But as I questioned him, it became apparent that his present health status was not what concerned him. Instead, he was bothered by the extra work that his condition required of one particular health aide, who without complaint cleaned up both my father and the bathroom. He raved about her kindness and wondered if we should offer her a financial thank you.

"I don't think so, Dad. The rules don't allow that. No singling out of staff is permitted."

"But she went above and beyond today," he said, unable to quite accept the gift of compassionate care without some reciprocity.

Later that afternoon I spotted the aide in the hallway. "My father told me how wonderfully helpful you were today. He is very appreciate. And so am I."

"I am away from my family, so your family is now my family," she replied. Until that moment I had been consumed with the fear that my parents' world was shrinking. They had given up their home, their neighbors, access to the outside world. But inside the assisted-living building they had found a new community of friends and staff that genuinely cared. And, starting with this aide, I discovered a chain of people who shared my goal of providing my parents with as rich a life as possible as their abilities diminished. Our family was strengthened with each link, and with their help I began to regain my balance. And, in direct response to my new stability, Tom and the girls settled into a redefined level of normalcy.

1999

ONE GLANCE AT MY DATEBOOK REVEALED changes in my mental focus. Now alongside the mandatory doctor and dentist appointments for my parents and myself, the monthly grids displayed leisurely fun for Tom and me. A University of Minnesota Golden Gopher Men's Basketball game, a performance at the Guthrie Theater, a long weekend together at Bluefin Bay Resort in Northern Minnesota or trips to visit our daughters signaled our arrival at a plateau. The slippery slope had leveled off, and Mom and Dad, although experiencing slow and steady decline, were gratefully receptive to their assisted-living arrangement. My average day no longer revolved around their crises.

Special events, like Dad's eighty-second birthday luncheon took center stage. A simple celebration, it provided a pleasant occasion from which to observe Mom and Dad in circumstances that were not governed by their failing health. On May 12, simple arrangements with the dining room staff resulted in a turkey dinner served to a small gathering in the beautifully appointed private dining room available to the residents for special occasions. I watched Dad, fully engaged in his role as host, wryly joking with my aunts and uncle as they enjoyed the tasty repast in this elegant setting. Mom, appearing comfortable, smiled through it all. "Oh, yes" and "You know" were common responses to comments and questions.

My parents had always enjoyed the company of the people around the table, and the afternoon felt like a refreshing return to normalcy, with the only variance being the absence of Mom's witty repartee. Angie, the only grandchild home from college, sat next to her and assisted with little things, like buttering a crescent roll or retrieving a fallen dinner napkin. In the carefree, lighthearted atmosphere of the day, looking beyond Dad's wheelchair and Mom's gibberish was surprisingly easy. Defined by their richly substantive lives rather than their infirmities, two loving and lovable people emerged, and aging took a backseat to living once again.

...

MOM'S TWO SURVIVING SISTERS COORDINATED a long-sought visit in July. Aunt Betty from Indianapolis arrived first, and I met her at her arrival gate at the Twin Cities Airport. Suggesting we stop for a bite of lunch before we headed over to see my parents, I tried to prepare her for the decline she would see in both of them, especially Mom, by describing the mental lapses that she was exhibiting with increased frequency.

Aunt Betty reached out, comfortingly, knowingly.

"Oh, Jacie Lynn," she said in her Indiana accent. Even more petite than my mother, my tiny aunt boosted my spirit by calling me by the pet name that the maternal side of my family had used since I could remember. "I think of you so much and just wish we were closer to help you. I hate that our family is so spread out."

"Me, too, Aunt Betty." My eyes moistened as her kind words instantaneously dissolved the crusty coat of self-protection that I had layered around cracks of vulnerability.

"It is all too familiar, just like Mom." She was referring to her own mother, Margaret Young, my grandmother, whose body outlasted her mind in much the same way that my mother's dementia was progressing. Although Aunt Betty's comments were tinged with sadness, denial was thankfully absent. She had heard the signs during phone conversations with Mom, and written correspondence over the last few years had become increasingly one-way.

Aunt Betty's matter-of-factness about her sister's disease in a strange way lessened its power over me. The strength and attitude of my diminutive aunt shored me up. She had traveled this journey with her own mother, and now she reached out to help me along a similar path.

"Oh, Aunt Betty, I can't bear it. She's slipping away."

"I know, honey," she responded.

She listened. She shared her perspective as a daughter who had lost her own mother to dementia. And, witnessing my aunt's mental clarity, I was reassured that like her, I might dodge this hereditary malady.

Although our lunch together had been my plan to prepare Aunt Betty for changes she would see in Mom and Dad, I was the one benefiting the most from our time together. What comfort to have across the table from me someone with such resemblance to Mom in appearance, size, mannerisms and compassionate response! Almost Mom.

Entering the Meadows, we found Mom and Dad in the dining room awaiting dinner. Dad, outwardly delighted with Aunt Betty's arrival, jokingly asked how I had been able to keep her visit a secret.

"This isn't the only surprise," I confessed. "Aunt Max and Nan are coming tomorrow," I added, referring to Mom's youngest sister and her daughter who lived in Scottsdale, Arizona.

Dad's spontaneous delight brought a smile to Mom's face, but her eyes revealed confusion.

"Well, isn't this nice," Mom said with uncharacteristic formality as Aunt Betty and I sat down at the table. Mom's questioning eyes traveled between Dad and Aunt Betty as they conversed. I watched Mom closely for a sign that she realized that her sister was sitting at her elbow. As Aunt Betty talked, Mom cocked her head, much like Jasper did at home when he was trying to decipher a new noise. Then, a few minutes into the visit, a veil lifted, recognition was made, and Mom interrupted.

"Oh, my, oh, my, I can't believe . . . you're here." Her smile transformed from social politeness to radiant excitement, and the visit truly began.

The following day Aunt Max and Nan joined the reunion. Laughter and storytelling graced their visit. Aunt Max, like Aunt Betty, boosted me up with words of encouragement. In addition, she spoke of dementia as an encroaching enemy and orally attacked it with colorful language by tossing in a "damn" and an "oh, hell," every now and then. For a few days it felt like the family's assault on the disease was winning. Mom, perhaps sparked by familiar voices and stories from her past, enjoyed extended periods of lucidity. Missing vocabulary words returned along with appropriate responses and occasional quips.

Nan offered another diversion. A jewelry salesperson, she had brought samples, and the women spent hours around the glass-top table, trying on rings and bracelets, chatting, laughing and sipping bottomless cups of coffee.

Delivering my relatives to the airport for their return flights, I sensed that I had inherited another family malady: an extreme aversion to saying goodbye. Sadness descended as people who loved my mother and most understood her dementia returned to their homes hundreds of miles away. I softened the loneliness by comparing the sanity of this July to the insanity of a year earlier.

Furthermore, with regained balance I could now objectively view the universality of our situation. Challenges arising during downslides from one plateau to the next were merely the flip side of the gift of having parents live to ripe old ages. Our family was not unique. Many of my generation, blessed with elderly parents who had escaped early death from accident or illness, would eventually find themselves confronted with a transition into parenting their own parents. Only a few lucky ones would have healthy parents who managed to maintain independent lifestyles until they passed away peacefully.

By July 28, Mom's eighty-second birthday, I settled in with grateful heart. For the time being, the current plateau supported us all.

• • •

"I THINK I NEED A LITTLE CASH," Dad informed me during one of my visits.

"Sure, Dad, I'll withdraw some for you. How much?" I asked, wondering why he felt the need for money, since all his living expenses were either billed at the end of the month or handled with credit card or checkbook. Obviously, having an empty wallet was unsettling.

"Oh, about three twenties should do it," he said, "just so I can have a little something on hand."

Until now we had avoided leaving more than a few dollars in cash around the apartment, even though the staff's trustworthiness during the first year at the Meadows had proved unquestionable. Female health aides, consistently compassionate while varying in ages, ethnicity and demeanors, had become as trusted as extended family, and their access to Mom and Dad's apartment was nothing but reassuring. After withdrawing three, crisp twenty-dollar bills from his checking account, I handed them to Dad, and watched as he placed them inside his black, leather wallet.

Dad fought the physical deterioration of his large frame. A superb athlete during high school and college, followed by years as coach and referee, he understood the physical therapy phrase, "Use it or lose it!" During earlier stages of MSA he had conscientiously followed prescribed exercises even though he had found them boring and repetitive. But as the disease progressed, exercise gave way to inactivity after he was given firm direction by doctors and healthcare staff to wait for assistance before walking. Consequently, his legs weakened.

For a man with a reputation of athleticism and strength, his physical deterioration should have been very disturbing. Outbursts of frustration, however, were rare. So, too, were his special requests. So, when he asked me to take him and my mother to Hamline University for the sixtieth class reunion of the Class of '39, I readily agreed, and kept my reservations to myself. Transferring Dad into and out of vehicles had become increasingly difficult, so this adventure required extra help. Plus, the timing of the event gave only a small cushion of time from the end of my workday. Although logistical challenges loomed, I realized that this college reunion might be the last that Mom and Dad would attend. After all the alumni work they had done for their well-loved alma mater, they deserved to return to campus and to spend an evening with classmates, many of whom had become lifelong friends. Dad sent in reservations for the upcoming event, and I tried to remain optimistic that when October arrived, both would be physically strong enough to attend.

Both Mom and Dad considered their college education a gift beyond measure. After graduating from high school in Montevideo, Minnesota, Teen and Warren, high school sweethearts, arrived on the campus of Hamline University in the fall of 1935 during the Great Depression. During the years following their graduation Dad extended the leadership role he was given as senior class president by spearheading an effort to establish a Class of '39 endowed scholarship as a way of passing on the gift of education to future generations. He promoted this dream to other classmates, and together they raised money for the Class of '39 Scholarship.

Thanks to the healthcare staff, Mom and Dad were festively dressed by the time I arrived after work to pick them up for the Class of '39 reunion dinner on the first Friday night in October. Mom was radiant in her red

wool suit with black velvet collar. With a few turns of the curling iron and applications of blush and lipstick, tasks she could no longer accomplish alone, the makeover was complete. Dad, in dress pants, white shirt and tie, handed me four tickets for the evening's dinner. Tom and I would be their guests. With Dad seated in his wheelchair and Mom on his lap they posed for photos to commemorate the event before we departed. Two aides who had carefully assisted them with preparations for their special evening accompanied us to the front door and transferred Dad, too weak to do much assisting, into my minivan. Mom, with a hint of anticipation, climbed into the back seat with the ease of a youngster, handicapped only by the narrowness of her skirt.

Teen and Warren before they depart for the sixtieth reunion of the Hamline University Class of '39.

As we drove to the nearby campus, I uttered a quiet prayer that Tom would be waiting for us. If he was able to leave work early, he would meet us in the handicap-designated parking area to help me transfer Dad from van to wheelchair. Otherwise, I would need to accomplish Dad's transfer solo, an increasingly difficult task. As I turned into a parking space, Tom pulled up nearby, right on cue, and together we easily transferred Dad.

With Tom by my side relaxation began as the four of us headed to the reception area for the Class of '39. Dad, from his wheelchair, greeted classmates by name, introduced Tom and me, and struck up animated conversations with old friends. Mom, clueless with names and faces, appeared surprisingly relaxed and hardly embarrassed at her mental lapses. As I watched their interplay with fellow classmates, I imagined them as Hamline seniors strolling the campus, attending classes and preparing for a world they could not envision. The senior class president and the winter carnival queen. Young, vibrant, strong. Sixty years! My parents, attending possibly their last college reunion.

Dinner was followed by short speeches from Hamline personnel and class representatives. Then surprisingly, Dad was presented with a special commendation acknowledging his work on the class scholarship. The inscription read:

Spring, 1937 - Warren and Teen during their dating years at Hamline University

As the elected president of our class, the Class of 1939 expresses its appreciation for the more than 60 years of service and guidance you have given us. We honor your partnership with us and Hamline University in organizing and building the exemplary Class of 1939 Scholarship Fund which now serves as an example for more recent classes. We celebrate your years of service and your generous spirit. Presented on this 1st day of October, 1999.

Dad received the framed commendation with his usual humility. Mom, although unsure of the reason for the applause, looked over at her husband with a look of pride so characteristic over the years. Tom and I, stunned at the turn of events, leaned into one another.

"Oh, my gosh, am I glad we got them here," I whispered.

"You didn't know this was planned?" Tom asked.

"Not a clue. But isn't it cool?"

At evening's end we returned Mom and Dad to the care of the night staff.

"It was a great evening for your folks," said Tom in his understated way.

"I couldn't have done it without you," I replied, repeating a statement I have made so often during the last sixteen months. "You arrived just in time. I envisioned a possible repeat of last winter's trip to the dentist."

A few months earlier in sleeting rain and darkness, I had attempted to transfer Dad from his wheelchair to the minivan after his dental appointment. During mid-transfer with one foot inside the vehicle, his other foot, along with one of mine, began to slide under the van on a thin layer of ice. Holding on to my quivering father as my legs split and he began to collapse, I called hopelessly to a security guard who stood sheltered between the double doors of the medical building about twenty feet away. Miraculous help arrived in the form of my tiny mother, whom I had reluctantly allowed to accompany us to the evening appointment. With Herculean strength she grabbed Dad's belt and steadied him, stopping his slide, just long enough for me to regain my footing. Finally, all three of us, drenched and cold, were again planted firmly inside the vehicle. It was that evening when I vowed never to take Dad anywhere alone, especially after dark, when the exhaustion of the day and his impaired eyesight increased his vulnerability.

"Remind me tomorrow, to show Dad's commendation to the women who dressed him for the occasion," I said. "It sure took a lot of us to pull off this evening. Getting them spruced up. Transferring. Transporting."

"All those things we take for granted when we're healthy," Tom succinctly stated.

"Too true," I added before offering a silent prayer of thanks for the successful completion of one of Dad's few requests.

...

MOM AND DAD FOUND THE CONSTRUCTION of a one-story building on vacant land right outside their living room windows a source of entertainment rather than annoyance. Certainly it was a welcome distraction from the latest calamity. Dad's wallet had disappeared, and when I found it between folded sweaters in his closet, the three twenty dollar bills were disappointingly absent. This time he asked for only one bill to replace them and vowed to keep his wallet locked in the small fire safe next to his rocker, the perfect perch from which to observe the construction of the building next door.

During each visit Dad gave me a status report as an empty hole becomes a U-shaped building that surrounded a yet-to-be-planted garden area with concrete pathways. One afternoon he pointed out a scale model of this building displayed under glass in the activity room.

"They tell us it is specifically designed for people with memory issues," he said. "It will be connected by tunnels to our building."

Studying the model, I agreed. "Looks great, Dad."

I noticed the fence that closed off the garden to unwanted visitors, and then uttered an audible "Duh," as I realized that the fence had been added primarily to keep residents in. Thanks heavens Mom didn't wander. She stuck to Dad like glue, her knight in shining armor, the cliché that described their relationship so perfectly.

Mom and Dad's partnership had been forged by love of life and Midwestern work ethic. The celebratory nature of their engagement and graduation from Hamline University was followed abruptly in June of 1939 by the sudden, accidental death of my mother's father, Ernest Young. Mom needed to help her mother financially, and, since married women back in 1939 were not allowed to teach, her only option was to remain single temporarily. She began her teaching career in Milroy, a small Minnesota town. At the same time, Dad taught and coached three sports in nearby Long

June 29, 1941 - Warren and Teen's wedding day.

Prairie. Finally, two years later in June of 1941 they wed, only to have their married life interrupted like so many others by an induction letter from Uncle Sam following the bombing of Pearl Harbor. Back together for good in 1945 they expanded their family with the birth of their son, Jim, followed three years later by my arrival on their seventh wedding anniversary.

As much as Dad loved teaching and coaching Minnesota high schoolers at Long Prairie, Crookston, and St. Paul Harding, he found his lifelong calling with the Minnesota Department of Corrections (DOC). He began as a parole agent in Crookston, a small town in the northwestern corner of Minnesota. Later in 1963 he moved his family to White Bear Lake when he became instrumental in developing the educational program at Lino Lakes Reception and Diagnostic Center just north of the Twin Cities. Years later he served as superintendent of the facility. He finished his career with the DOC as director of adult field services for the Twin Cities metropolitan region.

Through the years, Mom loved her roles as wife and mother, substitute teacher, and eventually reading specialist for the White Bear Lake School District. But her role as grandmother trumped them all. It was the presence of grandchildren Clay, Krista, and Angie that was most apt to penetrate the fog of dementia. Their voices called her back to the enjoyment of the present. Three grandbabies, now adults, continued to exchange with her the unconditional love that had flowed seamlessly between these two generations.

...

"HE'S HERE AND HE'S HEALTHY!" was Mom's memorable report over the phone as she relayed Clay's arrival, gender and health status in five excitedly spoken words back in 1975 before jumping into the car that Dad had idling in the driveway for the trip to the hospital.

And when Tom and I were encouraged by our adoption agency to inform extended family about our plans to interracially adopt an infant from South Korea, Mom's reaction confirmed our belief that no barriers would exist.

Teen and Warren with their first grandchild.

"Oh, a granddaughter!" she squealed. "How soon will she arrive? Do you have pictures?" The many questions about Krista's arrival were repeated two years later with the adoption of Angela, "my little Angie" to Grandma.

Through the years Grandma was the demonstrative one, the one whose verbal expressions of praise and awe could not be topped, the one whose knitting needles clicked away tirelessly while producing outfits for grandchildren, Cabbage Patch dolls and favorite stuffed animals. Grandpa, more reserved, sat for hours reading Dr. Seuss and Golden Books to whichever grandchild settled into his comfortable lap with a loaded book bag.

During one birthday party, Angie, still a preschooler, was given a unique, yet typically creative gift from her grandparents.

"Now you can have a book read by Grandma anytime," explained Grandpa as Angie unwrapped a new, six-book set of Sesame Street adventures. She popped the accompanying tape into her tape recorder, hit the "play" button and listened to her Grandma's voice reading the script of each book, complete with impersonations of Bert, Ernie, and the rest of the Sesame Street characters.

"Hear the bell?" Grandma asked, directing Angie's attention to the occasional tinkling in the background. "When you hear that sound, it is time to turn the page."

...

ALTHOUGH GRANDMA STUMBLED over her grandchildren's personal names, she inquired daily about the latest news from each of them and listened intently as I read lengthy emails about college classes and campus activities.

On one particular visit, Grandpa proudly handed me a newspaper clipping with a picture of Clay being sworn in as a police officer with the Shakopee Police Department. After a stint in the Navy and a four-year college degree in applied psychology followed by police training, Clay was establishing himself in a career in law enforcement in a town on the southern edge of the Twin Cities, and Grandpa's pride radiated.

"I just wish Jim could be alive to see what a fine adult Clay has become," he said with a whisper.

"He sees," said Mom matter-of-factly with spiritual clarity that defied her disease.

...

PICKING UP MY JOURNAL, cast aside long ago like other contemplative activities crowded out of my busy daily routine, I started again.

1999. It has been a very good year. My trusty journal, you have been so neglected, but I vow to begin again, at the end. The end of a year, that is. The end of a very good year, a year filled with nostalgic journeys, sadly poignant, yet unmarred by crises and runaway fear.

Yes, it has been a very good year.

2000

THE MILLENNIUM! A NEW YEAR, A NEW DECADE, A NEW CENTURY BEGAN. Tom, a director of Investment Systems Development for American Express Financial Services, breathed audible sighs of relief when legacy computer programs, never originally designed for a century change, transitioned smoothly with the start of January 1, 2000. After years of contingency planning, all went well.

It was my lack of contingency plans for Mom and Dad that unsettled me. My goal was to keep them together for as long as their health allowed. But, just as surely as time passes from one century to another, there was an inevitability that at some point the plateau beneath them will crack, and one or both will fall through. And then what?

Our two-story home with bedrooms at the top of a full flight of steps and handicap-inaccessible bathrooms limited the possibility of bringing my parents home to live with us, even with home health care assistance. As I pondered housing alternatives, the mystery over my reluctance to sell the townhouse finally unveiled itself. The finalization of the sale of their townhouse made my parents one crisis away from homelessness. This reality had been understood on some subconscious level for months.

Perhaps Dad, too, felt some of the same anxiety, because he tempered his desire to see the townhouse sold. He was visibly relieved when I informed him that after unsuccessful sales attempts, it had been temporarily taken off the market. Yet, we both knew that returning to their former home was a fantasy rather than a viable contingency plan.

Continuum of care was the assurance my parents were offered by the large health care system that oversaw the Meadows. Mom and Dad did not have to fear being thrown out on the street. Perhaps in the future, however, they would be asked to move to another facility within the system. As I inquired about what health conditions would require a move, I was informed that certain healthcare procedures could not be accommodated at the assisted living level.

"Such as?" I asked.

"Tube-feeding, for one. We can handle most things, but a person needing that level of nursing care would have to move to a facility that provides more than we offer here," the administrator explained. "Don't worry," she added, sensing my anxiety. "Your folks are doing well here. We can continue to increase the care for your dad, and even though your mom has memory-related concerns, she doesn't wander and appears in no danger of leaving the building. If that becomes a problem we can address it." Then she described a bracelet device that automatically locked the front doors when a wanderer approached.

With those kind and straightforward messages, I was reminded that my parents were in the perfect place. And, for a woman whose anxiety was usually quelled only by the knowledge that the future has been mapped out with contingencies to cover all possible scenarios, I began a relationship with the concept of taking life one day at a time.

A phone call from Angie on Sunday evening, February 13, confirmed that futures can never be predicted, must less prepared for. Having transferred to the University of Maryland Baltimore County after her freshman year, she was now living on the East Coast, and her phone call originated from a hospital room in Baltimore. She had been admitted for a serious blood infection, a complication from a kidney infection inadequately treated by an antibiotic that turned out to be a poor match for the attacking bacteria. The following day I flew to Baltimore and spent each day by her bedside. She vacillated between periods of relative comfort and attacks of wretched pain caused by firestorms of bacteria. Improvement would be forthcoming, the doctor told us, if the antibiotic that was dripping into her veins was a correct match. By Wednesday she was significantly better, and by Friday she was discharged with oral antibiotics and doctor's orders to refrain from attending classes for an additional week.

Two days after my return from Baltimore, another crisis surfaced, and Dad was admitted to St. John's Hospital in Maplewood. Aspiration, resulting from his inability to swallow, the latest MSA development, had led to pneumonia. A last ditch effort to provide lifesaving sustenance came with the insertion of a gastrostomy tube that delivered food directly to his stomach. Its insertion, I realized with sickening clarity, closed the possibility of his return to The Meadows. For me, living a day at a time had melded into living a moment at a time. But Mom, registering no hint of worry, sat silently by his bedside and communicated with the loving touch of her hands.

Medical professionals nickname pneumonia "the friend of the elderly," since it often takes sufferers out of their misery. Yet, not one member of our family was comforted by this disease. It attacked quickly and, in collusion with the disabilities associated with Dad's advanced stage of multiple systems atrophy, took his life in a sub-acute unit of a nursing home less than thirty-six hours after his release from the hospital.

On that final day, Dad was surrounded by family: Mom, Clay, Krista, Angie, Dad's brother Wayne, and sister-in-law Harriet, Tom, and me. We decorated his tiny room with small family photographs and a huge poster made from a blown up photo of Dad and Mom leisurely walking along one of their favorite Maui beaches. Most of the afternoon was spent alternating between group viewing sessions of homemade family vacation videos and individual, private talks with Dad.

On the March evening of what turned out to be the last day of my father's life, I reassured this gentle man of almost eighty-three years that "no matter what" I would take care of the love of his life, my mother. At about eight in the evening, concerned about Mom, who appeard tired and disoriented, the girls and I brought her home to spend the night with us. With reluctance to leave Dad, I checked in with the nurse on duty and expressed my fears. She assured me that he was showing no "end signs," so Krista, Angie, Mom, and I drove home together, while Tom lingered a while longer with Dad. At home the girls pampered their grandmother with a bubble bath and tucked her into bed in the guestroom.

Tom arrived home shortly after 10:30 p.m., and exhausted, we all turned in. The phone rang shortly after 1:00 a.m. waking everyone but Mom. Tom took the call. The message was brief: Dad had passed.

Hearing the telephone, both girls exited their bedrooms. I joined them in the upstairs hallway and confirmed their fears. Then the three of us entered the guestroom and gently woke Mom to tell her about Dad. She smiled at us and nodded as if she already knew. She exuded a peace that broke through the confusion of dementia, and her empathetic expression gave assurance that all was well.

"Do you want to go back to the nursing home and see him one last time?" I asked.

"No," she answered smiling.

Not sure she understands what has fully happened, I added, "Tom and I are going back to see Dad. Would you like to come with us?"

"No," she repeated, again with a peaceful smile on her face.

The girls remained with their grandma, while Tom and I quickly dressed and headed out to the car. As we backed out of the driveway, I quietly commented, "I'm not sure why we're going to the nursing home. Dad's body may be there, but I know his spirit is in that room." I pointed to the only lit window in our home, the upstairs bedroom with Mom and her granddaughters curled up together on the bed.

After Dad

In the days following Dad's burial and memorial service, I sorted through his belongings as Mom quietly puttered around the apartment. The emotional trauma of the previous weeks had taken a toll on her, and I yearned to blame her detached demeanor on grief rather than the insidious signs of encroaching dementia. But now weeks later, it had become undeniably clear that without Dad's assistance, Mom was becoming hopelessly lost in a confusing world.

Help came in the form of my new extended family, the staff at the Meadows. They responded by designing a care plan specifically for Mom's emerging needs and by monitoring her wanderings via the hall cameras. Thankfully, she made no attempt to exit the building. Yet, the hallways beckoned and led her on perplexing indoor journeys away from her familiar apartment.

Ironically, without dementia my mother would have been the picture of health. Shortly after Dad's death, with strong heart and able body, she easily accompanied me up multiple flights of stairs to the top of Old Main in the center of Hamline's campus to deliver contributions to the Class of '39 Scholarship in Dad's memory.

"Why didn't they tell me that you were here?" the Hamline representative apologized. "I would have met you downstairs. I'm so sorry you had to climb so many steps," he said, directing his comment to the eighty-two-year-old woman in front of him.

Mom smiled, and I assured him that my mother had maneuvered the stairs with no difficulty. I didn't mention that although she responded to each of his questions with a laugh, she probably had no clue what he was asking.

Not encumbered with a heavy wheelchair or even a walker, Mom was very portable and easily accompanied me on short excursions. She loved walking outside as long as she had a guide, so often we strolled the short distance to a nearby restaurant for afternoon pie and coffee. Other days she gladly climbed into the passenger seat of my van for jaunts to Como Park Conservatory, where we ambled through tropical flowers and ferns, or to Fairview Cemetery, the resting spot of generations of my father's family in the nearby river town of Stillwater. Mom's non-emotional response to the two names on the stone marker, Dad's newly etched below Jim's, added another dimension of loss to an already painful cemetery visit.

"Oh," Mom said, as she momentarily paused at the gravesite before sidestepping to a planter filled with red geraniums and a green spike. Instinctively she deadheaded the flowers and poked her finger into the soil. Then she meandered to the nearby water faucet and filled a plastic watering jug provided by the cemetery. How could her mind compute that plants need water, yet be oblivious to the burial site of people who were central to her world?

Perhaps Mom, like me, held little sentiment for cemetery visitations. After Jim's death she often commented that she felt his presence in her heart, not at Fairview Cemetery, yet several times a year she and Dad traipsed out to the family plot to make sure the summer urn or the winter wreath were in place and maintained. I wanted to imagine that in Mom's current, day-to-day reality she felt Dad's spiritual presence, just as she did the night of his passing. Perhaps that explained how my mother, with a well-earned reputation as a master worrier, surprised everyone by greeting each day with a sweet calmness, even though the love of her life had transcended his earthly existence. Perhaps dementia softened the worry as it scuttled the memory. Perhaps—perhaps—she was no longer capable of discussing spiritual matters, so I was left to ponder. Whatever the reason for my mother's serenity, I was grateful that as her memory faded, so too did her stress and anxiety. Once more, I was struck by the uniqueness of dementia.

Excursions with Mom always transported me to an introspective place. Uncomfortable with silence, I carried on one-person conversations with her, since she could no longer participate. She was not totally silent, but her voice, her ability to state her wishes, to share her story or to advocate for herself, had disappeared somewhere within the tangle of brain pathways. Gone were the intelligent insights, the witty comments, the curious nature, the affirmations, all replaced by a sweet passivity for which I knew I should be grateful, but the loss of "mom" weighed heavily on my heart.

Krista with her grandmothers, Donna Herron and Teen Johnson, after graduation ceremony at Concordia College in Moorhead, Minnesota.

Two months after Dad's passing Mom and Tom's mother, Donna, accompanied Tom and me to Moorhead for a weekend celebration highlighting Krista's graduation from Concordia College. A milestone for Krista, her graduation marked the best thing that had happened to our family in the new millennium, and both of her grandmothers enjoyed the occasion.

Donna, a widow since 1992, the year Tom's dad passed away after a year-long battle with cancer, empathetically reached out to Mom. Over the weekend Donna regaled her with entertaining stories about life in Lake City, a picturesque town on Lake Pepin in Southeastern Minnesota, where she and her husband LaVern raised four children. The anecdotes required little conversational response from Mom, who listened intently. Donna provided not just a welcomed diversion but another set of hands to assist Mom with her special needs throughout the weekend festivities.

As long as Mom was in the company of family, such as her weekend in Moorhead, new settings were surprisingly non-threatening. Another gift of dementia, perhaps? But each gift was accompanied by another downturn.

During each getaway with Mom I found myself seeking out lavatory locations much as I did when the girls were first potty-trained, just in case with little warning one was required. Mom had reached the stage

Teen with Jackie and Tom

where she needed frequent reminders to attend to bodily functions, such as eating, drinking, and going to the bathroom. She simply forgot.

For the second consecutive year, I spent my summer break readying the townhouse for sale. Diana, a good friend and reputable interior designer, offered fresh eyes. She toured the empty home and offered simple suggestions: brighten the entry, the stairway and the kitchen by exchanging clear glass light fixtures for the current ones that cast dark shadows through smoked glass; prime and paint over textured wallpaper in the master bedroom. The effects were stunning. The townhouse felt open and bright, and once it returned to the market, it sold in five days. Signing the papers at closing brought a welcomed finality. With Dad gone, the emotional security of owning property was superfluous, and I happily turned over the keys to the new owners. Mom's awareness of the transaction, if present at all, was short-lived.

The letter from Mom's doctor declaring her incompetent to handle her own affairs, my power-of-attorney designation, and the original trust document that named me trustee to handle the details of my parents' living trust were bundled together. This file accompanied me to all legal and financial dealings to which I had complete control, a role for which Dad had done his best to prepare me.

•••

"LET HER DRINK HER COFFEE. She doesn't want to go down to the basement yet," Mom chided.

"She can take her coffee with her. We won't be long," Dad responded.

These conversations always took place as if I wasn't sitting right next to them at the table in the kitchen of the townhouse.

"Let's do it," I interrupted as I rolled my chair back, grabbed my coffee cup and headed for the stairs. Dad followed me down and pulled the cord that switched on a single blazing light bulb that dangled over a metal five-drawer file cabinet in the unfinished basement.

"Just so you'll know," he began, as he pulled a file from the top drawer, "here's where I keep the insurance policies and the phone numbers you would need to call."

This scenario was reenacted before each vacation, in case the plane went down, Maui was swallowed up by a killer hurricane, or one or two of them dropped dead from sunburn or the ingestion of too much fresh pineapple. Not wishing to consider the worst-case scenario, I hated these "what you need to know in case we die on our vacation" tutorials. Account numbers, codes, safety box keys, contact information, specifics of a living trust, all neatly accessible to make my life easier if they didn't return.

Then in later years, even when Mom and Dad could no longer enjoy quiet Maui vacations, Dad periodically sat me down for expanded tutorials that included details of his retirement hobby, financial investing. His portfolio's expansion correlated with the prosperity of the eighties and nineties. He was the teacher, and I was the reluctant student, stuck in denial that I would ever have to access his system without his guidance. Slowly, as his eyesight diminished and his fingers lost the dexterity required to write checks and bank deposit slips, I became Dad's financial secretary with a cursory understanding of my parents' fiscal situation.

•••

HOW OFTEN I FELT WAVES OF GRATITUDE for those trips to the basement. They allowed me to transition slowly into my present role as financial manager instead of having Dad's complicated system suddenly dropped into an untrained lap.

Dad's financial investments, even after his death, continued to augment healthy retirement pensions, so thankfully, Mom's needs rather than their costs determined her living arrangements. This was especially comforting when, eight months after Dad's passing, an administrator at the Meadows asked if I would like to consider moving Mom to the more expensive memory care facility that was now completely built and operational next door.

"We're noticing that your mom is becoming increasingly lost outside of her apartment," she said, as she pointed to the monitors in the health-care office. Thanks to the discreetly positioned hall cameras the monitors displayed the activity in each hallway. "The Gardens is designed to be less intimidating," she continued, "and staff are specially trained in issues related to memory loss."

"I know Mom would benefit from more supervision and interaction," I responded.

"Would you like a tour to see what the facility has to offer?" she asked.

My mind returned to thoughts of Dad and his keen interest in the construction of the building outside his window. Did he somehow know that this facility might become a giant safety net, a contingency plan, for a time when he would no longer be able to watch over his wife?

"Yes, for sure," I answered.

Connected by a tunnel to the Meadows, the Gardens was specifically designed for people like Mom. A tour of this one-story, state-of-the-art building quickly convinced me that any setbacks Mom might experience from relocation would be offset by the supportive environment. She no longer would have to wander long hallways in search of human interaction, because in this memory care building residents and health care assistants were highly interactive. *Perfect* was the word that popped into my head during my tour, and before it was over, I selected an empty apartment in the Orchid Wing.

During the last weekend in February 2001, the family moved Mom through the tunnel and into her small studio apartment. In the Orchid Wing she joined seven other female residents, each with a small studio of her own.

This relocation was a major downsize, but many of Mom's treasures, like her cut-glass collection and the corner cabinet that housed it, found a new home in her studio apartment. After the move-in was accomplished, I culled through items left behind in the assisted-living apartment and discovered evidence of Mom's increasing dementia. As I sifted through the contents of her bureau, I quickly realized that I needed to scrutinize everything. What looked like a wrinkled ball of discarded tissue in actuality was Mom's hiding place for a Black Hills gold bracelet, a precious anniversary gift from Dad. Socks contained earrings and Dad's white handkerchiefs housed rings tied in the corners.

I found silverware everywhere, not Mom's kitchen flatware, but knifes, forks and spoons from the communal dining room, enough to fill two gallon-sized plastic storage bags. Occasionally, at the conclusion of a meal Mom had wrapped a piece of silverware with her paper napkin and attempted to carry it back to her apartment. Perhaps she was helping, in her own peculiar way, to clear the table of what remained after the servers removed the dishes. But looking at the stash in the Ziplocs, I finally comprehended the regularity of her action. Sheepishly I returned the overflow of silverware to the food service personnel in the kitchen.

Once more I found myself sadly sifting through the pieces of my mother's life. Her jewelry drawers had been her playground, I surmised, as I struggled to separate gold chains from cheap beads, all the time searching for three special, valuable mementos: engraved ten-carat gold, miniature basketballs that had been awarded to my father for his all-conference honors as a Hamline Piper basketball player back in the 1930s. Now the small glass-covered case, that through the years had housed these treasures, contained nothing but velvet fabric. Finally, after searching through every drawer, I turned my attention to the cubbies in the roll-top desk. Tucked into the left mail slot jammed against a folded up envelope was a wad of tissue. Unwrapping it, I uncovered five more balls of tissue and continued to carefully peel back each one. Three contained gold basketballs with an "H" and a different year on the front and Dad's name engraved on the back. The fourth held a small gold football and the fifth a gold track shoe.

The last two I had completely forgotten about. But as I set them back on the velvet fabric I remembered the first time that Mom opened the case and allowed me to hold each piece and read the engravings.

"Daddy must have been proud to get these," I said, examining each golden treasure with my ten-year-old eyes.

"Your daddy was proud just to play on a basketball team coached by Joe Hutton," she said, invoking the familiar name of my father's coach and mentor. "And I was so proud of your dad. So tall and handsome, and such a fine athlete." Then she explained how as soon as he received a golden award, he quickly passed it on to her so she could wear it on a necklace or bracelet. Their courtship as high school and college sweethearts was my favorite fairy tale.

"Someday you and your brother can split them up," she continued, referring to the gold all-conference honors, "to help you remember what a great athlete your daddy was."

"But there are five," I said, already starting to worry about the logistics of the division.

"Well, that will be something you and Jim will have to negotiate," she added.

Warren Johnson (Number Eleven) and Coach Joe Hutton with the 1939 Hamline University basketball team.

...

AS I RETURNED THE GOLD PIECES to their velvet home, a suffocating wave of grief, grief for Jim, for Dad, for Mom's disappearing memories, crushed in, until I forced myself to continue the task at hand. I turned my attention to the remaining item in the mail slot, a blank, white envelope folded over and over into the shape of a flattened cigarette. Unrolling it, I carefully unsealed the flap and pulled out the contents: three, crisp twenty-dollar bills.

The bills confirmed what I had suspected. Mom had been the culprit. She had hidden Dad's cash, right along with other precious possessions. Did she fear the type of thievery that her mother experienced in a nursing home during the last years of her life back in the eighties? I recalled Mom's harangues about Grandma Young's missing personal items. Before a trip to Nebraska, Mom shopped for hand cream, a bed jacket, or a special memento and delivered her carefully chosen purchase to her mother, and then returned on her next visit to find no sign of it. Many things disappeared from the nursing home, even Grandma's dentures and glasses. With anger and tears Mom grieved each of her mother's losses.

Unlike Grandma Young's nursing home, the Meadows maintained a stellar, trustworthy reputation, as the three bills in my hand attested. To my knowledge, nothing belonging to Mom or Dad disappeared into the pockets of employees. In fact, for two and a half years the Meadows had surpassed all expectations that Krista and I had cautiously set during our initial visit.

Finally, with the trash discarded and the last box of my mother's treasures in the van for the trip home, our family closed the door on assisted living and moved to memory care, the next and perhaps last stop on Mom's journey.

The Gardens

AFTER THREE MONTHS I CONFIRMED that Mom's new home at the Gardens was, in ways I never first imagined, uniquely perfect. With warm hospitality it wrapped her in quiet comfort. Her transition appeared seamless. Some aides from the Meadows also worked in the Gardens, so they already knew Mom and her unique needs. Others, like the building itself, were new and ready to offer their best. A job in this state-of-the-art memory care facility was a coveted placement, and workers' positive attitudes and smiling faces uplifted the residents.

After signing in at the registration desk and punching in a numbered code on the security door, I entered for a visit with Mom. Obviously, great thought had been invested in the layout and interior design of the three wings of the Gardens. New, impeccably clean tile, carpet, upholstery and wallpaper provided decorative cohesion throughout the building. Yet each wing was distinctive. The purplish hues of the Orchid Wing provided chromatic clues as Mom sought out her apartment after daily strolls around the building.

The Orchid Wing housed the fewest residents, eight. Small studio apartments encircled a short hallway at the end of the wing. Each door was personalized with photos, wreathes or memorabilia as unique as the person who occupied the private space beyond. On Mom's door hung a small wooden ornament, a cottage decorated with two overlapping hearts. "Teen" was neatly painted on one and "Warren" on the other. This was the first home since World War II that Mom had not physically shared with Dad, but for me his name on the door was more than symbolic. In some form was he here with her? Looking skyward she often communed with what I liked to think was his spirit. Those one-sided conversations, which seemed to be gibberish to outsiders' ears, were psychic possibilities to mine.

Mom's apartment was craftily designed to optimize space. Her single bed occupied one corner next to a convenient bathroom and two small closets. The remaining area was large enough for her favorite chair, a loveseat, dresser, corner cabinet, the glass-top table and two of its four chairs. Running along one wall, a small kitchen provided visual reminders of "home": sink, refrigerator, counters, and cupboards. It became useful as storage space, since no food preparation was necessary.

Stepping into the Orchid Wing was like entering a group home. Communal living room, dining room and kitchen areas buzzed with activities that drew residents, including Mom, out of their apartments. Assistance from the staff was only a few steps away because the multipurpose kitchen also served as a nursing station.

Teen with her companion, "My Little Angie."

When Mom strolled out of the wing and into the bright, indoor courtyard, it was as if she were taking a walk around town without stepping a foot outside. She passed entrances to one small room after another, each with an open door. One housed a tiny worship center, another a library, another a nursery of sorts filled with dolls and cradles, another a beauty shop, a craft room or an office. Park benches and rocking chairs provided resting spots as she traveled the oblong route around the center of the facility before veering off for a side trip into one of the other wings then returning to the center once again.

Mom walked laps around the facility with her precious companion, a small, stuffed teddy bear, a birthday present from Krista.

"I thought maybe she would like something to talk to now that Grandpa is gone," explained Krista at her grandmother's celebration.

None of us anticipated the degree to which Mom would adopt this cuddly bear. She named this creature My Little Angie, a gesture that perplexed her family. Perhaps the tiny bear symbolized a far-off memory of the last baby in her life, her youngest granddaughter, now a junior in college. Yet, Mom referred to her bear as a "he" which confused us even further. But, we ignored the pronoun and simply appreciated the joy that this stuffed animal brought to a sweet little lady who had lost so much.

Mom and her bear were usually inseparable. Together they traveled around and around the indoor courtyard of the Gardens, until she set him down in an unlikely place, like a corner of a bookshelf or in the base of a huge, potted plant, before ambling away. When the bear's disappearance eventually registered, she fretfully grieved for her companion. When a kind soul, often another resident, but sometimes a nursing assistant or staff person, returned him to Mom, she held out her arms and welcomed her little one back home with a mixture of relief and excitement.

Misplacing My Little Angie had become so commonplace that Krista and I feared the possibility that the wayward bear would someday remain lost. To avoid the consternation that scenario might cause, Krista purchased a matching bear, which we immediately dubbed the spare bear, and stashed him under extra bedding on the top shelf of her grandmother's closet. On rare occasions he emerged to provide solace until his bedraggled brother returned home.

Although loss of the bear created distress in Mom, all other aspects of life in the Gardens had become predictably secure and enjoyable, thanks in great part to the other residents of the Orchid Wing. Within this family-like atmosphere eight women, each with unique memory challenges, enjoyed each other's company throughout the day. In heartwarming displays of solidarity they advocated and assisted each other as best they could.

Mom and the other ladies unknowingly offered outsiders a crash course in the effects of memory loss. Mom, whose brain disease had attacked her ability to retrieve words, stumbled over vocabulary and sentence structure. She communicated increasingly with facial expressions and short one-liners like "Oh, wonderful, wonderful" or "I don't think so." "Please" and "thank you" and other polite responses sometimes found their way into appropriate usage, but complex sentences were rarely begun and even more rarely completed.

One attractive, well-dressed resident spoke eloquently with a full vocabulary. However, she repeatedly told a story about growing up in St. Paul and "sliding down snow-covered Ramsey Hill." Over and over she related the same story, with the same characters, the same dialog, the same punch line. Wonderfully, in the Orchid Wing no resident rolled her eyes. In fact, a woman with short-term memory loss always appreciated the story. This gray-haired, grandmotherly type listened intently to the story and laughed wholeheartedly over and over as she heard the details as if for the first time.

Another resident of the Orchid Wing carried on well-versed conversations about almost any philosophical subject. Yet, at the conclusion of each meal, she asked the same question: "Now, where is my apartment?" Then she waited for either a resident or an aide to point to a door that stood less than fifteen feet from her position at the dining table. "Of course," she responded each time before standing up, repositioning her walker and heading off.

None of the eight residents in the Orchid Wing exhibited belligerent or aggressive behavior. Together they cooperatively participated in the activities of the day or huddled around the television for some evening relaxation. Not unexpectedly, while some of Mom's friends sang along with Julie Andrews, "The hills are alive with the sound of music . . ." she munched popcorn and laughed instead.

Witnessing Mom with these women warmed my heart. She was no longer alone like she had been for most of the day back at the Meadows, and the staff had increased her care to keep abreast of her increasing needs. Each morning someone assisted her with dressing and daily hygiene before escorting her to the dining area for breakfast. Throughout the day nursing assistants supported her with prompts for bathroom breaks, mealtimes and bedtime routines. Mom had entered the stage of her disease in which she was unable to function without round-the-clock aid and supervision. The Gardens provided both. If there was a model for quality care of people with memory issues, the Gardens set the bar, and I pondered the synchronicity of Mom's increased needs and the opening of this new facility. Once more I offered up a silent prayer.

Well-trained staff members impressed me with their dedication, skill, patience and concern. The first time I saw Paul, a tall, African immigrant enter Mom's apartment to help her in the bathroom, I cringed. How would my modest mother accept toileting assistance from this young, male aide? I listened for signs of distress from my position on the loveseat in the sitting area of her apartment as the two of them disappeared behind the bathroom door. But all I heard was muffled conversation. A few minutes later Mom emerged without a hint of embarrassment or discomfort.

"I'll be back later, Teen. Have a nice afternoon," Paul commented as he opened the apartment door and stepped into the hall.

"Thank you," she replied with a lilt to her voice.

Daily I observed and marveled at the comfortable interaction between this tall, young man and my petite and proper mother. When I described the relationship to Tom, we wondered if perhaps Paul reminded her of all the other tall and gentle men in her life: Dad, Jim, Clay and now Steve, the special guy who has won her granddaughter Krista's heart.

Along with Paul, aides at the Gardens were an impressive group. Several were hired directly from a nursing assistant training program, and they brought to their new jobs enthusiasm and a tireless work ethic that they sustained month after month. Louisa, June, Jen, Zippy and many others joined Paul on the pedestal of compassionate caregivers who offered Mom a special human connection along with their skillful assistance.

Round-the-clock skilled nursing care was not provided at the Gardens. But since Mom's body (apart from her brain) was strikingly disease-free, this absence was a non-issue. Supervision provided by part-time nursing staff plus routine visits from Mom's nurse practitioner fostered Mom's health. In this caring and supportive environment, my mother and her new friends maintained their dignity as their memories failed. Transition to this uniquely perfect "home" appeared effortless for Mom, as if she grasped that she would be surrounded by compassionate caregivers as her memory fades.

I found this assurance extremely comforting. It allowed me to breathe, to refocus on other family members, and to fulfill a dream that Tom and I had held since our daughters' arrivals from South Korea: traveling as a family to the country of their birth. Krista, who was now working at Children's Home Society of Minnesota (CHSM), the agency through which we adopted both girls, described a CHSM tour specifically organized for adoptees and their families. We registered for a trip that would commence immediately after my job at Irondale High School wrapped up for the summer.

Purposely I waited to share the news of our upcoming three-week journey with Mom. Perhaps she would not comprehend the magnitude of this trip, but if she did, would she register excitement over the significance of such a trek, or anxiety over the fact that most of her family would be halfway around the world? She had always dreamed that we would take her granddaughters back to their homeland to fill in missing pieces of their lives, but now dementia had robbed her of the joy of seeing that dream realized.

One afternoon after work, I snagged Mom who was tirelessly walking with My Little Angie around the interior courtyard of the building and suggested we go back to her apartment where we could talk.

"Mom, I have great news," I began, as I described our Korean tour. Her eyes never left my face, and her smiles and affirmations of "yes" and "good" reassured me, but in actuality I was unsure that my words entered her brain in a comprehensible fashion. Perhaps she was simply reading my excitement and responding to it much like an infant who giggles at her cooing mother.

One month before the start of our trip, a call from a nurse at the Gardens reminded me of the fragility of Mom's situation. "Your Mom has fallen," she informed me. "An aide found her on the floor in her apartment. Her eye is bruised, and we would recommend that her shoulder be X-rayed."

"I'll be right over," I replied.

I found Mom sitting with her arm in a sling and listening intently to musicians who were wrapping up the afternoon's entertainment. Then she turned her head. Even though alerted, I was taken aback by the iridescent shiner that covered what seemed like a quarter of her face. Without Mom's ability to describe what happened, the details of the fall remained a mystery.

X-rays and a visit to an orthopedic specialist confirmed a broken shoulder. Thankfully, no surgery was required, but Mom appeared shaky and hesitant to walk without assistance. Attempting to pinpoint the scope and severity of her injuries, we played a guessing game. Was she sore? Afraid of another fall? Experiencing weakness, a side effect of a possible mini stroke?

I watched as Louisa, a strong and comforting aide, orally encouraged Mom to walk. She simultaneously wrapped one arm around Mom's waist and stabilized her with the other. Mom responded to Louisa's strength and took a few jerky steps before regaining a small measure of confidence. But each time she sat down, she reverted back. And, when she did not feel the same level of firm, physical support from other aides that Louisa was able to provide, she balked completely. Dad's wheelchair, although too large for my mother, took up residence in the corner of her apartment so it could be called into service if needed.

As the date of our departure to Korea approached, Mom's eye turned from shades of black and blue to green and yellow, and her shoulder pain subsided. Her ability to move around independently, however, did not improve.

Meanwhile, Tom, Krista, Angie, and I packed for our much-anticipated trip. Our suitcases were loaded with an assortment of customary gifts for the many people who would be assisting our family and sharing their lives with us: caseworkers from the girls' South Korean adoption agency, unwed mothers, orphaned infants and toddlers, and a South Korean host family. When I described all the exciting details to Mom, she listened attentively, but sadly, and uncharacteristic of her in healthier days, she offered few comments and asked absolutely no questions.

Many people stepped up, easing my worries about leaving Mom behind. Clay promised to visit his grandmother while the rest of her family was out-of-touch. Familiar with the role of supporting their elderly mothers, three of my friends, Linda, Cindy, and Joann, volunteered to visit mine. Nursing assistants offered to be extra vigilant.

With back-ups in place, we began our three-week trip and quickly discovered the life-altering significance of returning the girls to the country of their birth. The emotional whirlwind of events trumped any residual fears I had about leaving Mom behind.

Once our plane touched down on the tarmac of the Incheon Airport and we passed through customs, our tour group was greeted with a huge banner, "Welcome to Your Motherland." This simple message set the tone for the entire trip. With open arms the country welcomed back the children that had left so many years earlier. The word *hospitality* did not begin to describe the outpouring of thoughtfulness and the degree of care taken with each detail of our visit to the girls' country of origin. Although Krista and Angie were immensely disappointed that searches for their birth families hit dead ends, we celebrated with the fortunate adoptees in our tour group who were rejoined with birth mothers, families, or in one unique case, a birth family that included an identical triplet.

On the return trip our tour group escorted three babies to waiting families in Chicago and Minneapolis. Krista and Angie witnessed for the first time exciting airport arrivals similar to theirs. Emotional puddles, we returned to our New Brighton home and our former lives.

Although numb from jet lag, before we collapse into bed, Tom headed up to Anoka to pick up Jasper from the Armstrong Kennels, while I headed over to the Gardens for a quick check on Mom. I found her much like I left her, with two slight changes. The whitish-pink skin around her eye showed no sign of injury, and, instead of relaxing in a comfortable chair in the Orchid Wing's living area, she was sitting in Dad's wheelchair. Answers to my inquiries revealed that she was becoming increasingly dependent on the use of the chair, a reality that I witnessed myself in the days and weeks that followed.

When I compared Mom's current condition with her abilities only a few months earlier, it became apparent that she had been knocked off a comfortable plateau. Before her fall she had been walking laps around the interior of the building. Now she sat quietly and passively in the wheelchair. Before her fall she had silently connected with others through eye contact and short phrases. Now she periodically drifted into mental seclusion. Before her fall she had eaten like a Trojan, enjoying the tantalizing concoctions of the new chef. Now a fork mystified her, and she did not know how to proceed when an aide placed it in her hand. Slowly, her weight dropped under eighty pounds.

By the end of summer, Mom exhibited increasing evidence of a major retreat from life. Dementia caused by either Alzheimer's disease or vascular strokes was the culprit, and for the first time I heard the words *end stages* when medical people described my mother's condition.

I mentally prepared to lose my mother. The administrator of the Gardens had informed me that under normal circumstances, Mom, now wheelchair-confined, would be asked to move to the nursing home, the last stop in the continuum of care. But since she had no acute need for round-the-clock skilled nursing care, she was allowed to remain in her home at the Gardens for what appeared to be the last few weeks of her life. Mom's nurse practitioner ordered a wheelchair that fit Mom's petite frame and supported her hyper-extended neck and rigid right leg, two new and restricting conditions.

The label, *end stages*, conjured the need for an immediate response, so I phoned Mom's sisters with the latest update. Again they headed for the Twin Cities. This time Betty's daughter Deb accompanied her and Max's son-in-law John joined her and Nan. Three days into their visit, Mom, mostly silent until this point, uttered her first decipherable words after I introduced our relatives to Zippy, one of my mother's favorite aides.

"Zippy, this is Teen's baby sister Max," I said with a wink as I gesture to my aunt, "her daughter Nan and Nan's husband John. And," I continued as I gestured to each one, "this is another younger sister, Betty, and her daughter Deb."

"And I," Mom emphatically added without prompting and with inflection that shocked us all, "am the big sister!"

With these six words my mother reconnected with life. Suddenly, she had a renewed interest in food, even though she was no longer able to negotiate a forkful from plate to mouth. For the rest of their visit my aunts and cousins took turns re-introducing foods to my mother who eagerly munched away while others chatted. Too soon, the end of their visit arrived, and I taxied everyone back to the Twin Cities airport for return flights to either Indianapolis or Phoenix. It was September 10, 2001, the last day of carefree air travel, one day before jets, commandeered by terrorists, flew into the World Trade Center and the Pentagon. Death came quickly for so many.

Back at the Gardens, Mom denied the specter of death, at least for the time being.

With mealtime assistance, slowly she became stronger as she gained weight ounce by ounce. I began a nightly ritual of visiting her later than usual so I could feed her dinner.

Quickly I learn that mealtimes at the Gardens were unusually quiet as dementia-stricken residents focused on the food in front of them rather than the company next to them. To break the monotony of carrying on monologues directed to Mom, I often chatted with aides who were assisting other residents. It did not take long to realize that if there was a blessing resulting from my mother's debilitating illness, perhaps it was the insight I gleaned from engrossing dinnertime conversations with the young women and men working as health aides. Hardworking and compassionate, many were immigrants, well educated in their homelands. They shared stories of life in Africa and courageous trips to America in search of education and work. Many also juggled college coursework which was preparing them for futures in nursing, law enforcement, business and many other fields. Mom responded to their compassionate care, and over the months I developed close relationships with many staff members.

Mom developed an unusually strong connection with Zippy, a young woman from Kenya with an uncanny ability to break through the wall of silence created by my mother's increasing dementia. I watched their interaction closely. Was it Zippy's smile and upbeat attitude, her soothing voice or her mixture of efficiency and compassion that retrieved Mom from some faraway dimension? Perhaps it was a mixture of all the above. But, most miraculously, Zippy manages to draw out my mother's voice. She began each conversation by looking directly into Mom's eyes and waiting until they locked gazes. Then with a blend of firmness and encouragement she asked simple questions and pried responses, often appropriate ones, from Mom. Her technique was a tutorial for me. I was reminded to slow down and be intentional with simple questions instead of throwing out rhetorical ones in an attempt to fill the silent void.

I wondered when the breakdown in Mom's communication process occurred. Was it immediate with an inability to understand the words addressed to her? Did she understand the message but become incapable of formulating an appropriate response? Did she mentally formulate a response but lack the ability to communicate it verbally? Where along Mom's communication highway did she hit road deconstruction?

As I watched Mom interact with Zippy, I witnessed the benefits of calmness and patience. Zippy gave Mom the time and prompting she needed to function to the best of her ability, whether that was to speak, to lift a glass of milk by herself, or to raise an arm for its insertion into a sleeve. Where and how did someone so young as this radiant twenty-something learn such fine-honed skills? Were they cultural byproducts of her upbringing in Kenya?

Zippy appeared tireless. She studied at St. Paul College to be a licensed practical nurse and dreamt of studying further until she became a registered nurse and possibly a nurse practitioner. Plus, she worked as many hours as possible to support herself in a country half a world away from her parents and the customs and culture of her homeland. I jokingly encouraged Zippy to keep studying, because I wanted her to be the nurse that worked in whatever memory care facility I ended up in if I followed the path of my mother and grandmother.

At support sessions for family caregivers, people of my generation voiced similar fears that they were destined to experience the memory losses that were decimating the lives of their parents. I listened as speakers, authorities on issues related to Alzheimer's and dementia, threw out statistics that over fifty percent of people over eighty-five have serious memory-stealing maladies.

One speaker in particular picked up on the unspoken fears that permeated the room.

"How many of you have experienced a momentary blip while driving somewhere? Your mind's wandered, and you look back to a road marker and for a split second wonder where you are, or if you've passed by your exit."

Slowly, many hands rose, mine included.

"This is normal brain aging," he assured us. "If, however, you drive along and somehow find yourself in Rochester," he said, referring to a town in southeastern Minnesota, "and wonder how you got there—that's Alzheimer's."

In my mind, I continued to revisit that scenario. Every time I momentarily misplaced something, found it difficult to remember a new ten-digit phone number, or unsuccessfully searched my brain files for a simple crossword puzzle answer, I reminded myself that at least I was not in Rochester. Yet, between Jim's brain cancer and Mom's dementia, my family's track record with healthy brains caused trepidation. Plus, I knew that stress exacerbates memory difficulty, and anxiety only increases stress. Finally, after fruitless worry about all the things I could neither predict nor control, I said a simple prayer and continued with my day.

One afternoon, however, I arrived and heard with consternation that Mom had offended an aide by calling him or her a racially unacceptable name. My heart dropped with fear that Mom's dementia was following a dreaded condition of Alzheimer's that manifested itself in strange behavioral changes. Name-calling of any sort, especially racially biased name-calling, would have been a monumental shift in behavior for my mother. I raced off to find Zippy to get the lowdown on Mom's infraction.

"One of the aides is upset that your mom called them 'my little monkey'," explained Zippy without naming the injured party or giving a clue to the person's gender.

With an outpouring of relief, I burst into laughter, leaving a startled Zippy wondering about my sanity and my own racial bias.

"Zippy," I tried to explain as I regained my composure. "'My little monkey' is an endearing expression that Mom has used with her grandchildren all of their lives. She's referring to Curious George!"

"Who?" Zippy responded, still confused.

"Curious George, from the Curious George books. The mischievous monkey that is always getting into trouble and pulling pranks."

"Oh," said Zippy, clearly unacquainted with Curious George but happy that there was a plausible explanation for my mother's comment.

"Any time the girls would kid with her, or hide from her, she would say, 'You're a little monkey—MY little monkey.' Only people she loves get that designation."

Relieved that Mom had not exhibited unexplainable, nasty behavior, the fact remained that offense at Mom's comment had been taken, and I was sickened by the thought that this misunderstanding had injured someone's feelings and my mother's reputation.

"It's okay. I'll talk to them," Zippy said, still keeping the offended party's identity confidential.

On my way home after helping Mom with dinner, I detoured to the closest bookstore and picked up one of the many Curious George books on display. The following day I read the story of the curious monkey and his mischievous antics to Mom before I presented the book to Zippy.

● ● ●

CURIOUS WAS MORE THAN AN ADJECTIVE for an enterprising monkey who found himself in one predicament after another. *Curious* was also a fitting adjective for the circular path that this children's book had taken in my mother's life. First she read it to Jim and me back in the early '50s, then to her grandchildren in the early '80s. Now in 2001, I was reading it to her. Curious, too, was Mom's journey backward to a childlike state that now required of me the patience and guidance that she so willingly bestowed on her children and grandchildren.

Entering the World of Oz

Mixed news was delivered at a care conference, an omen for the year to come. Although Mom has gained weight and death was no longer imminent (the good news), she had also reached a plateau and was not likely to improve any further (the bad news). Our previous agreement that allowed Mom to remain at the Gardens for the last few weeks of her life was no longer operable because Mom was not actively dying. Instead, I was informed by administration that my mother must become a candidate for the next and last step in the continuum of care, the nursing home. After a quick self-tour of the floor designated for Alzheimer's residents at the nearby nursing home, I requested another meeting for Tom and me with the administrator of the Gardens, a sharply dressed woman who had always impressed me with her concern for my mother.

"So, you have gotten a chance to tour the Alzheimer's floor of Riverside North?" she asked, framing her statement as a question. "What did you think?"

"It was awful," I blurted out tactlessly. "So dismal and overcrowded. So many people sitting in wheelchairs, doing nothing. Mom will simply get swallowed up there."

"Is there some way we could negotiate a continuation here?" Tom asked. "We would be willing to pay for additional staffing."

"Possibly. I would have to take it up with corporate," she replied. After further discussion her final response was, "I'll get back to you."

A few days later she shared the good news that Mom could stay temporarily for an additional fee. "The option will be reconsidered in three months," she added. "We'll see how it goes."

But at the end of three months the agreement was rescinded.

"I'm afraid corporate is unwilling to extend your mother's stay here any longer," she reported.

"Wasn't it working? Mom is so much better than she was," I replied.

"There is a concern about precedent setting. Plus, the nursing home is a better fit for your mother's needs." Sensing my reluctance she added, "We recommend that you put your mother's name on the waiting list. Otherwise, if she has a medical setback and needs immediate nursing care, you will have to take whatever space is available and that might be far away. But," she added, "she can continue to stay here as long as necessary to secure a room."

"I can't bear moving her to that floor," I said, my mind grasping for other alternatives besides the overcrowded floor designated for residents with Alzheimer's disease.

"Your mother is in no danger of wandering off now that she is confined to her wheelchair, so there is no reason why she needs to be on a secure floor. You could request a room on one of the other floors."

It was with a fair amount of trepidation that I agreed to place my mother's name on the nursing home's waiting list. After the care conference, I located Mom, sitting in her wheelchair in the Orchid's living room. I watched her, verbal skills almost gone, interacting through smiles and laughter with the other women. Heartbroken, I could hardly believe that those relationships would be severed by a phone call announcing availability of a bed in Riverside North. Selfishly I prayed for all the residents in the nursing home, hoping that Mom's name traveled slowly up the list. I also silently petition God for the emotional strength to uproot Mom again, this time to a facility that was structured more like a mini-hospital.

Basically I retreated into denial, hoping that Mom could continue at the Gardens until she took her final breath. Weeks passed, summer break began, and I continued to assist Mom at dinnertime at the Gardens.

On Monday, July 29, the day after we celebrate Mom's eighty-fifth birthday at a Johnson family picnic in Stillwater, the admissions person at the nursing home left a brief message on my answering machine. Mom's name had reached the top of the waiting list. Two rooms were available and the family had a twenty-four-hour deadline to choose one of them. Out of options, I scheduled an appointment for a guided tour of the facility.

I felt a bit like Dorothy entering the world of Oz as I tromped through the nursing home the following morning. Like an obedient child I followed an admissions staff person around as she proudly pointed out the amenities of the first-floor commons area. I had passed through this area before on my brief trip to scout out the Alzheimer's floor. But now I allowed each sense to gather information. The lounge area, patio with gardens, gift boutique and snack shop provided a quiet ambiance. But the atmosphere quickly changed as we ascended by elevator to upper floors that housed residents. We meandered down long cluttered halls and around rolling carts containing residents' records. My guide stopped to reprimand a nurse for leaving an important room unlocked, and the nurse replied defensively. I was not sure what made me more uncomfortable, this exchange or the sight of three residents sitting in their wheelchairs, lined up in the hall like train cars on a track.

Where was the "home" in this nursing home, I wondered? Third floor alone housed sixty residents. Several were sitting in wheelchairs in the dayroom, staring at the back of the wheelchair in front of them or at the small television set at the edge of the room. Some were sleeping; one woman was screaming, "Help me, help me!" as unconcerned staff members passed her by. Embarrassed, my guide spoke to the resident and assured her that someone would be helping her soon. I was skeptical. I knew I was not in Oz, but I definitely felt like I wasn't in present time either. Had I stepped back—two, three decades? Hadn't nursing homes changed since my grandmother's experience in the '80s?

But this was one of the best nursing homes I was told, so I hoped my tour had been an anomaly. What wasn't an anomaly was the pressure to move my mother in on Thursday, and it was now Tuesday. I pleaded for an extension over the weekend so I could gather family assistance but was informed that extra time was unlikely.

Finally, a compromise was reached. On Friday, August 2, 2002, Mom would be moved into her third-floor private room at the end of the hall. Sadly, she would leave many friends behind, exchange her studio apartment for a much smaller single room and substitute an institution for her present home, all for a daunting price tag of over $72,000 per year, payable by Mom.

The Final Move

"THE ONLY CHANGE I ENJOY IS THE LOOSE CHANGE IN MY POCKET!" Where had I hear or read this? On some radio talk show or television program? Perhaps it rose from the recesses of my inner nature. Anyway, after being instructed to move my mother to the nursing home, I related to the very essence of that message. Life changes were hard, especially the ones made for us by others.

Some people thrive on change and the excitement and new expectations that accompany it, especially moving to a new locale. I moved from St. Paul to Crookston, a farming community in the northwestern corner of Minnesota, when I was three years old, too young for any recollection of the move itself. Just like the sugar beets that grew in the Red River Valley soil, I flourished in this town of 8,000 inhabitants where, during the 1950s, a genuine spirit of neighborliness melded with civic pride. I was too young

1953 - Teen and Warren with children JacLynn and Jim in Crookston, Minnesota.

and naïve to question the lack of cultural diversity or to be bothered by the fact that everyone knew everything about everyone. Instead, the security and constancy of life in this town provided a comforting backdrop for my early years.

Then in 1963 in the fall of my tenth grade our family moved three hundred miles southeast to White Bear Lake, a suburb of St. Paul, Minnesota. I traded a small town for a suburb, a school's class size of 180 for one of 500 and my narrow view of the world for an expanded one. I realized then that when one moves, one loses many valued bits of the past, but an exchange is made and new treasures are unearthed. White Bear Lake in the early 1960s lacked a small town feel, but its location which included White Bear and Bald Eagle lakes offered serenely beautiful water, perfect for water-skiing, fishing and swimming. In addition, the Twin Cities of St. Paul and Minneapolis and all their amenities were only a short drive away.

Although I was excited about moving and beginning anew in my school, insecurity and self-doubt accompanied me through the first few weeks. My sophomore class at White Bear High rivaled the number of students in the entire high school at Crookston, but new friends welcomed me into their hallowed circle. Enthusiastic teachers tapped my excitement for learning, and shortly, I was once again in the groove. White Bear Lake was not Crookston. Not worse, not better, just different.

So, what had I learned? Simply, when change comes, and it will, things will be different from the past; some benefits will be sacrificed and others gained. The lesson, I guess, was simple. Be thankful for what was, and be open to the future, because change is much easier if one keeps a flexible spirit.

It did not take me long to comprehend that a flexible spirit was a necessity during the summer of 2002. Again Angie and her grandmother were relocating during the same summer. Newly graduated from college in Baltimore, Angie loaded up her car and independently moved to the West Coast. A few weeks later her grandmother left her friends and trusted caregivers behind and began anew at Riverside North. The mere size of the complex reminded me that she was moving from a small setting to a much larger one.

Would her new home have the intimate feel of the Gardens? Probably not. What strengths would compensate for this change? Time would tell.

I felt so rushed. On the eve of Mom's arrival at her new home Tom and I moved a dresser, TV and wingback chair into her private room with assistance from Rebecca, the third-floor receptionist, who led us through the bowels of the building to find a flatbed. We filled Mom's closet and dresser with clothes and necessities and hung some family photographs on the walls. We hoped that when she arrived at her new home, the pieces would breathe a bit of familiarity into her new surroundings and would offer a measure of comfort.

I held on to the promise that Mom had been asked to move because, according to corporate, her needs would best be met at the nursing home. This was the message that was relayed by the administrator of the Gardens. But, I was struck with several questions.

Who was corporate? I knew that Riverside Homes was a nonprofit corporation headed by a CEO and a board of directors. But, who actually made the decision regarding the best placement of my mother? Wasn't she enjoying a high quality of life at the Gardens? During the last few months she regained her lost weight and rebounded from what we thought was a total withdrawal from life. Who benefitted from uprooting her at this stage? Once wheelchair-bound, had she simply become too much work?

Somewhere within administrative hierarchy, people gathered to create and assess the "Continued Stay Criteria" at each facility within the care system. Mom had been asked to leave the Gardens, so obviously she no longer met the criteria listed in the contract that I had signed seventeen months earlier. I located the contract and reviewed the criteria.

Which of these did Mom no longer meet? The one that jumped off the list was the sixth: *has personal needs that are manageable with staff intervention, for example: bathing, dressing, grooming, incontinence, nutrition.* The words "manageable with staff intervention" were open to variances of interpretation. Mom was totally dependent on staff for her activities of daily living. Were her time-intensive needs placing undo burden on the staff and therefore considered unmanageable? If so, staff members had been wonderfully patient with my mother and with her family. Zippy, Louisa, Paul, June and so many others had allowed her to live a dignified, happy life, but now she was leaving them and her friends behind.

Friday arrived. At 7:15 a.m. over a cup of coffee and a bite of breakfast, Tom and I finalized the morning's schedule for picking up Mom and delivering her to her new home. Our conversation was interrupted by a phone call from a nurse at the Gardens, who informed us that a health aide had found Mom on the floor beside her bed. There was no obvious sign of injury, she informed us, but a medical checkup was advised. Tom and I arrived at the Gardens shortly after the paramedics. Mom appeared at ease, even smiling from her position on the gurney as they wheeled her past us and into the ambulance. One hypothesis was that Mom may have slithered to the floor while attempting to get up. One more time I wished she could talk and tell me what happened and if she was hurt and where.

After a visual exam and X-rays the attending physician at the emergency room of St. John's Hospital gave Mom a clean bill of health. Nothing was broken, and no bruising appeared.

A young nurse replaced the bedclothes Mom wore to the hospital with the sweater, knit pants, socks and shoes that a thoughtful aide had passed to me as I exited the Gardens. "She will want to look nice when she arrives at her new home," she had said.

Mom's rigidity was no match for the nurse's skill. Before I could even offer my assistance, she managed to steady Mom on the examining table with one hand and to thread arms and head through the sweater with the other. Then she lay Mom down on the table, placed one leg in each pants leg, and rolled her from one side to another as she simultaneously raised the waistband of the knit pants to the proper position.

"Wow, you are skilled!" I commented.

"You learn fast around here," she responded with a smile as we each grabbed a sock and a shoe and secured them on Mom's feet. Then addressing my mother she added, "Now, how 'bout we comb that hair of yours. Gotta look good when you leave here."

Mom responded to the warmth of the nurse like a kitten to the sun. Smiling, she appeared to have thoroughly enjoyed the whole emergency room experience. Oh, the subtle gifts of dementia!

Finally, at 1:00 p.m., four hours later than scheduled, Mom arrived at Riverside North. The first day in her new home began with introductions to an array of people with various roles in her care. While Mom napped in her new bed after a bit of lunch, the floor's mild-mannered social worker painstakingly reviewed a stack of paperwork with me that included the mission statement of the corporation. Descriptive terms, such as "highest quality," "innovation" and "compassionate and highly competent care" jumped off the page. I learned about the practice of using designated nursing assistants, people assigned to Mom's care on a regular basis. This continuity would be critical, I thought, because my mother was now totally unable to communicate any of her unique needs. Her caregivers would have to anticipate all of them.

Mom was asked to move, I had been told, because she needed the services that the nursing home provided. So, here she was. I looked for positive additions to her care and quickly found two. She would be under round-the-clock nursing supervision. Plus, occupational therapy was available within the building. I began to relax while I answered questions, filled out forms and fleshed out medical history and personal information that might be of value to those responsible for my mother's care. I described my eighty-five-year-old mother's health apart from her dementia: that she took no medication stronger than a multivitamin and low-dosage aspirin, and that although stroke-disabled, her body housed a healthy heart, a full set of strong teeth, a renewed, hearty appetite and a strong constitution. This information garnered a look of surprise from my mother's new social worker.

Before I left at the end of Mom's first day in the nursing home, I wrote a note of thanks to the people who would be entering her room to care for her. I briefly described her and added some information that might prove helpful in her care—how she startled easily and became apprehensive in new situations, how she stiffened when fearful, how she loved being spoken to and how she responded well to quiet voices and gentle ways. After a final statement of appreciation for the care that she was about to receive, I taped it to the wall and left her for the night. How I wished that Mom could speak! How much easier it would be to leave if I knew she was capable of depressing a call button or asking for assistance. As I departed I felt a bit like an apprehensive new mom leaving her infant in a crowded daycare for the first time.

"Goodbye, Mom." I kissed her and received a warm grin in return. "I'll be back tomorrow."

A wave of grief descended, as I poured out my fears in my journal, a ritual that was becoming an integral part of my day:

> I am quite aware that the move to the nursing home requires great changes, and that change can be challenging. But if Mom can receive better care here than at her previous location then this is where she belongs. But how do I communicate Mom's humanity to people who never have had the opportunity to know her before her dementia? How will I explain that, before she could no longer speak coherently, she majored in English and taught it for many years, performed both comedy and drama in thespian performances, loved great books and read to her children and grandchildren?
>
> How can I describe the previous active lifestyle of this petite lady, now confined to a wheelchair and unable to even wiggle herself into a more comfortable position? I wish the staff could have known her before dementia trapped her vast interests and abilities behind its impenetrable wall of darkness. Those who will become her caregivers may never know that until she turned eighty, she often walked two miles each day, knit intricate sweaters, cooked special family dinners and delivered pies to church visitors. They will soon discover, however, that her family adores her, especially her grandchildren who will be frequent visitors. And, they will learn that she greets each day with a smile on her face. Dementia has graciously left that intact.

...

THE FOLLOWING MORNING I TIMED MY VISIT purposely so I could spend some time with Mom before I fed her lunch. As I stepped off the third-floor elevator into the reception area, I stopped for a moment and wondered which direction to go to find her. There was no one at the third-floor desk to ask, so I peered around the corner into the drab, windowless dayroom and spotted Mom sitting in her wheelchair behind several other residents. Did she look even tinier than usual? Wheelchairs of other residents were lined up in rows around a diminutive TV set positioned so low that only the first row of residents enjoyed an unobstructed view. Few seemed engaged in the activity. The room was eerily quiet.

I circled in front of Mom, knelt down beside her chair and whispered in her ear. "Hi, Mom. It's Jackie!" She looked at me and smiled. What was going on in that head, I wondered. Did she know where she was? Did she miss the familiar surroundings and people of her previous home? For a brief moment I considered Mom's dementia somewhat of a friend, a buffer between the reality of her loss and her comprehension of it.

But there was timidity about her demeanor that caused me to question whether the confusion in her brain could truly protect her from the uncertainties of her changing life. There was no visible or audible panic, just the look of caution, much like the behavior of an animal that strayed from the security of its lair. This was the adjustment period, right? I reminded myself that as Mom began to trust, she would relax, and so would I.

"Let's explore, Mom," I said as I unlocked her wheelchair brakes and slowly pushed her around the perimeter of third floor. Private and semiprivate rooms, posted with names and youthful photos of the residents, lined the exterior, while offices, storerooms, the dayroom and the dining room occupied the center.

I was confused by the atmosphere on a Saturday, so different from the bustle of the day before. Except for the murmur of an occasional television or radio, the hallways were eerily quiet, and no employees appeared. I surmised that the floor's clinical coordinator, social worker, community coordinator, and recreational therapist must be Monday to Friday staffers who enjoyed weekends at home with their own families. I made a mental note to ask about the staff/resident ratio on weekends.

The most enjoyable part of the day's visit began in the dining room when I met Mom's three tablemates at her assigned dining table. Two, Pearl and Mary, were very talkative, entertaining and enlightening. The third, Esther, like Mom, was quiet and needed help with feeding. A gracious woman, Esther responded to our introduction but then dozed off again while she awaited her meal. It was a great table! Mary's daughter Luann was also visiting. She had pulled up a chair and was helping her mother cut her meat. Luann knew the ropes of the dining room and felt comfortable getting whatever her mother needed from the serving line and refrigerator. I waited patiently with Mom and Esther until a staff person set their meals in front of them. As I fed Mom, a young, female nursing assistant pulled up a chair to assist Esther. Laughter, the first I have heard all day, punctuated the table conversation.

In short order I realized that Mom's relocation had not affected her appetite. With my help she polished off her entire main dish, and most of her tossed salad and steamed vegetables and then turned her attention to dessert, a square of apple crisp with a dollop of whipped topping. As Mom happily chewed, Pearl and Mary filled me in on the community of residents and staff. Mom responded with smiles and laughter. During this first noontime meal I learned a valuable lesson: To get the straight scoop on the realities of life on third floor ask a resident, and Pearl and Mary would be two able and willing resources.

Halfway through lunch, Zippy appeared and pulled a chair up to the other side of Mom, who greeted her with a smile of recognition and a laugh. Zippy's arrival was a delightful surprise and a special gift on a day when everything else around Mom looked and sounded unfamiliar. Not employed as an aide in the nursing home, Zippy had no responsibilities here. Her visit was simply a welcomed gesture of friendship. She and Mom, no longer aide and resident, were now simply two friends. Connecting. Laughing.

After lunch Zippy departed, and I pushed Mom back to her private room and attempted to add homey touches to the small space that contained a bed, a chair, a bedside table and a small TV with stand. I hung a familiar picture of Dad alongside those of the three grandchildren, and refreshed the water in the cut flower arrangement. Shortly, Mom's designated morning aide appeared. Mildred, a diminutive woman considerably older than the other aides on the floor, reminded me of Aunt Betty in appearance. Unlike my aunt, however, the style of my mother's aide was abrupt.

"Your mom is very hard to dress," she said matter-of-factly.

The bluntness caused my stomach to lurch.

"I know she can get very stiff when she's fearful," I defensively responded. "I hope that as you get to know each other, things'll get easier."

"I hope so" was the response. "I need to put her down for her nap now," she added.

I offered to help with the transfer as I had done so many times at the Gardens, but Mildred politely declined. Yet, she made no attempt to begin. Instead, she stood her ground and waited for me to leave. Feeling shooed away, I said a hurried goodbye to Mom and walked down the long corridor to the elevator. With each step the insecurities about Mom's future regained a foothold in my stomach. It was just a matter of time, this adjustment period, I reminded myself. The elevator delivered me down to the first floor, and I left with resolve to return again in the morning.

On my way to the Gardens, I stopped at Byerly's and pick up a fruit tray and a selection of goodies and then set them out for the staff alongside a handwritten note of thanks. Slipping back into Mom's studio apartment I finished packing the treasures that had not accompanied her to the nursing home. Each sparkling piece of Mom's cut glass collection was bubble-wrapped and carefully nestled into cardboard boxes. Then, silently I waited for Tom, and together we moved the boxes home.

New Lessons

AT SUMMER'S END, I EXCHANGED MY FULL-TIME CLERICAL POSITION in the Career Center for a part-time teaching position in my field, Family and Consumer Science. The move excited me. I was back in the classroom again teaching subjects I loved and still able to arrive at noon to feed Mom her dinner, the largest meal of her day.

Labor Day arrived, and so did the students of Irondale High School. Flocking through the doors, they filled classrooms to overflowing and exhibited educational attitudes ranging from boisterous enthusiasm to aloof detachment, with a few cases of overt belligerence mixed in.

Thankfully, my two interior design classes were filled with great kids. As I observed their demeanors, I found myself searching for the quiet, undemanding students, the ones with the greatest possibility of falling through the cracks, just like Mom at the nursing home. She could not speak or request anything, and each night as I left, I asked myself the same question: Will she be overlooked when overworked nurses and aides tend to more vocal residents? At school I asked a related question: Can I provide a positive educational environment for all the students in my classroom, even the silent, unassuming ones? Two different environments for people at opposite ends of the spectrum of life, yet so much correlation.

The school year was underway, and so was Mom's transition to Riverside North. I found myself teaching at Irondale in the morning and learning tough lessons at North in the afternoon. As my students wrestled with new concepts, I struggled to understand my greatly expanding role as daughter/advocate in Mom's new environment.

Understanding the nursing home system was a frustrating process. Knowledge built slowly, first through observation. Some families deposited a loved one in a nursing home bed and bid farewell for an extended time;

others visited on a weekend afternoon and whisked their family members off the floor and down to the snack shop for a treat. Surprisingly, few residents had daily visitors.

After a few weeks I deduced that witnessing firsthand the interaction between residents and staff, residents and residents, and staff and staff was critical to obtaining an accurate picture of life on third floor. To glean the most knowledge I varied my visiting times and days as often as my schedule permitted to observe Mom's care during p.m. shifts and weekends. But the more I saw, the more confused I became.

Asking questions was essential to unraveling the confusion. Besides speaking to the staff in charge, I learned quickly that a resident's take on a situation was eye opening and certainly worthy of consideration.

Eventually, basic protocol became evident.

Lesson number one: There was a place for me to address my mother's care concerns. It was called the care conference. At the nursing home the care conference took on a more formal role than in assisted living. A conference was held for each resident every three months, and families were invited to participate. Each conference included a status report on the resident's condition followed by a sharing of concerns between family and staff. Because of my mother's inability to communicate, she napped in her room while I conferenced on her behalf with a care team that included a nurse, community coordinator, dietary technician, recreational therapist and social worker.

Lesson number two: Mom's care plan was an all-important document enumerating her problems/conclusions and the approaches/interventions used to accommodate her needs. Her care plan was discussed at the care conference.

Lesson number three: If necessary changes were not spelled out in the care plan, no changes in my mother's care would occur. Therefore, hearing the words "we'll put it in her care plan" was a good thing.

Lesson number four: Once changes were agreed upon there was a substantial lag time before they were communicated to those responsible for providing the care, in Mom's case, the aides. Changes needed to be entered into the computer before aides received updated plans. Then, hopefully, aides spotted the changes and proceeded accordingly. Patience was required.

But, I was also learning that too often intention did not mean execution. The disconnection between what was discussed in the care conference and the reality of care on third floor confounded me. I chalked up many of my concerns to the bumps of transition and patiently waited for Mom's care to smooth out.

I tried not to dwell on the negatives and desperately sought and found many positives in Mom's new life at Riverside North. The staff was friendly. Mom's tablemates were delightful. Residents seemed to enjoy the comfort foods that graced their tables every meal. Volunteers were plentiful. They visited with residents or transported them to Mass, the beauty shop, and the dentist, all within the complex. When family members visited, the snack shop was a tasty destination, and the small gift boutique rivaled any in the nearby malls in selection and price.

But, I was flummoxed by the reduction in quality care that Mom experienced after leaving The Gardens. Her needs had not changed, yet the condition in which I found her, day after day, rarely measured up to the worst day in her previous home. And, most disturbing was the unspoken message that the reduction in quality was simply business as usual. Nothing better illustrated this phenomenon than my inability to bring about a change in the uncomfortable positioning of Mom in her wheelchair. When I arrived for a visit, rarely did I find her sitting erect with her hips square and her head fully supported by the headrest. And, since she spent the majority of the day in this chair, proper positioning was critical to her quality-of-life.

A shining star in my mother's new home was the occupational therapist, who retrofitted Mom's wheelchair with side pads and leg rests to support her tiny frame and rigid right leg. The weakest link, unfortunately, was Mildred, Mom's morning aide, who seemed unwilling or incapable of correctly lowering Mom into her improved chair. I believed that *incapable* was the better term, since *unwilling* implied malicious intent, but either way, the result was the same. Mom suffered day after day from poor positioning, leaving her uncomfortable and ripe for pressure sores.

Daily, as I stepped off the elevator onto third floor, I often found Mom in what was becoming her usual position: sitting cockeyed in her chair with her body shifted precariously to her weakened right side. All too often her head and shoulders sloped to the side at such a degree that the wheelchair's back and headrest were no longer supporting her. Distressing was Mom's inability to wiggle around and change position on her own. Equally troubling was the staff's blindness to her problem as they routinely passed her by on their way to more important matters.

My observations revealed a distinct pattern reflecting two extremes: excellent attention to positioning two days a week and dismal results the other five, and there was a direct correlation between Mom's posture and the caregiver on duty.

Mom was transferred between bed and wheelchair with the help of a mechanical apparatus called a Hoyer lift. Using the Hoyer to transfer a resident from a wheelchair to a bed was a fairly simple procedure. It involved the use of a sling resembling a rectangular tarp with four looped straps, attached to each corner of the sling, plus a mechanical conveyance from which the sling hung. The sling was placed behind the resident, the top two loops were placed on one horizontal bar on the Hoyer and the two bottom straps were crossed between the resident's legs (to prevent the person from slipping through) and looped on a second horizontal bar. A button was pushed and the Hoyer slowly raised the metal bars and, consequently, the sling with the resident safely cupped inside. The resident was then positioned over the bed or wheelchair and slowly lowered onto it. Then the sling was detached from the bars of the machine and removed from under the resident. After the resident was placed in the bed, it was easy to reposition him or her to a comfortable position. However, extra vigilance was needed to insure that the resident was lowered into the wheelchair with healthy posture intact. Aides could take advantage of the two additional handles on the back of the sling to align the resident so his or her back was straight and hips were square as the descent was made.

Some aides accomplished Mom's transfers with ease. After the transfer an additional boost was often needed with one person on each side lifting her quickly up and settling her back comfortably into the chair. Mom's petite frame made this lift quite easy. When the simple procedures were followed, her comfort improved drastically, but my frustration with the habitual lack of follow-through in this regard grew with each passing day.

Unfortunately, once Mom was transferred into her wheelchair, the Hoyer sling often remained underneath her after it was detached from the machine. Too often I arrived to find the bottom straps wadded up in a bumpy, canvas package and pushed under her rump to get them out of the way. On those days she balanced uncomfortably on top of this mound like a sled perched at the crest of a hill, until the weakness of her right side caused a gradual slide in that direction. Some days I arrived to find that Mom had slipped off her perch into an uncomfortable lean over the side of her wheelchair. Few staff members seemed to notice or care. On those days I stopped the first helpful person who walked by and asked him or her to help me give my mother a boost to straighten her hips. On other days I found her with straps still crossed between her legs, wedged into her crotch and cutting off circulation. One afternoon I arrived to find her hog-tied with her right arm caught in the tangle of dangling Hoyer straps. Although nurses and aides were always willing to remedy the situation once I brought it to their attention, the repetitive need for this adjustment discouraged me.

From what I observed with Mom and other residents needing mechanical assistance with transfers, there appeared to be no protocol regarding what to do with the sling once the transfer was accomplished and the loops were removed from the Hoyer bars. Sometimes the sling was removed completely. Sometimes it remained under the resident with the straps pulled to the back of the wheelchair and secured. Some aides left the bottom straps crossed and between the legs of unfortunate residents creating a front side wedgie. The variance of the aides' techniques was confusing and discouraging.

Most distressing, few staff members noticed and remedied an uncomfortable situation for a resident, especially for someone not under their direct responsibility. Mom's nurse, the one responsible for supervision of her care, was busily involved in more pressing health concerns of other residents and oblivious to Mom's poor positioning. In her defense I reminded myself that she was one of three nurses on a floor with sixty residents. Mom and nineteen other residents were under her direct car and many had serious health issues that required the attention of a nurse. Mom did not. So, why was she here, I asked myself, if nurses had no time to attend to her simple needs? Mom, leaning cockeyed over the right side of her wheelchair, was a human billboard that sent a dire message: POOR CARE! POOR CARE! And, if this obvious situation was overlooked by the nurse responsible for overseeing the work of the aides, what other not-so-obvious care concerns, I wondered, were being ignored?

Business as usual on a floor with sixty needy residents meant that quality-of-life issues, like timely and correct positioning, sometimes disappeared off the radar of harried staff. Advocating for a loved ones appeared not only necessary, but critical. The theory of the squeaky wheel getting the grease was tested as I began to squeak.

Using the protocol of the care conference I set about formally addressing my mother's need for proper positioning and shared my frustration about the daily condition in which I found her. After I addressed my concerns, the care team changed her care plan to instruct staff to fold and tuck the straps to the sides of the wheelchair.

Patiently I waited for Mom's leaning tower of Pisa routine to change. Eventually, I saw some change. Some mornings the straps were pulled out of the way and tied behind the chair. Unfortunately, many days I found her in any of the previously described uncomfortable positions. More squeaking resulted in more assurances that change was coming. The reality was more of the same.

Another care conference. Another adjustment to the care plan. Andrea, the new third-floor clinical coordinator (a registered nurse responsible for the care of all residents on the floor), solved the problem (or thought she had) by radically changing the care plan to state: Hoyer sling will be completely removed after use. No sling meant no more mounds to sit upon or to slide down from, no more hogties, no more wedgies.

Problem solved? Not really.

Some days the sling was removed. Too many days the sling was agonizingly present. I wondered if the care plan was read at all, or just ignored. Like a tiny pebble inside a shoe, this simple but neglected procedure caused severe festering.

Weeks passed, but Mom's positioning did not improved in any sustained manner. Although her care plan stated that she was to be repositioned every two hours, often time flew by with no change. Unable to wiggle herself into a more comfortable pose, she was often forced to endure for hours a slouched position that had me concerned about the possible development of pressure sores on the skin covering her tailbone.

Once more my journal became a place to reflect on the lessons I was learning each afternoon in the nursing home:

> *Mildred, the aide that consistently ignores the new care instructions, now avoids me as well. I have voiced my concerns at the care conference, and I now find myself at odds with the person assigned to care for my mother five mornings a week. Paying attention, spotting a problem and trying to rectify it through the correct protocol demands a price. Although the care team delivers a message that my concerns for Mom are legitimate and as a team we will work to solve them, the person missing from the discussion is the one causing the distress, Mom's designated morning aide. I have identified the weakest link in the chain of Mom's care, and unfortunately, this link is the one person who has the greatest responsibility for her wellbeing.*
>
> *I have learned one more disappointing lesson. Lesson number five: Having something spelled out in the care plan doesn't translate to problem solved.*
>
> *How should I proceed when Lesson 5 trumps the other four?*

Paying Attention

Does the desire to teach run through one's veins along with all the other chemical components of the bloodstream? Is it inherited like a strong heart, fine hair or thick ankles? Mom loved to teach, and her example inspired me. And because I loved to learn, I thought teaching would be a welcomed, straightforward procedure whereby I would sprinkle students with knowledge and their sponge-like brains would eagerly and easily absorb every droplet.

But, students are as different as their brains and their circumstances. Some see their worlds holistically with "big picture" creativity and excitement. Others are structured, logical and organized. Some have learning disabilities; others are hungry or homeless, or both. Some are gifted with skill sets that, like square pegs, don't quite fit into educational round holes. Others suffer from depression, anxiety, addiction or a host of other obvious and not-so-obvious diseases and manifestations. Each needs tending in a unique way.

As I exited the Irondale High School parking lot each weekday afternoon and drove to the nursing home, I moved from one classroom to another. In one, I was the teacher. In the other, a student. And, try as I might, I was failing to raise Mom's quality of care to the level that she had enjoyed at the Gardens. Mystified, I felt like I had dropped her into a very confusing place, an institution with the reputation of a round hole and the reality of a square peg. Something just did not seem to fit.

During my youth Mom taught me a great lesson: trust your instincts. Sometimes your gut knows the truth long before your brain, she explained. During my daily visits at North, my instincts told me to pay attention, because it was a very confusing world in which Mom lived.

What would reveal itself in Mom's new home if I truly payed attention? Hoping to answer that question, I created a word document on my computer, named it "Mom's Journal" and dedicated it specifically to issues involving my mother. It became a chronological record of my visits and her daily condition. I resolved to include care conference summaries; notes regarding conversations with doctors, nurses and other caregivers; documentation of health-related issues and my attempts to correct them. When days were good I recorded in my journal the evidence of compassionate care and kind gestures offered by both staff and residents. When those days followed one upon another, I felt especially grateful.

Easy to document were the facts; elusive were the confusing undercurrents that I was unable to ignore once they bubbled to the surface and demanded my attention. As I documented these conundrums, disturbing patterns surfaced that gratingly soured my hope and trust that the organization hired to care for my mother could live up to its lofty mission statement. My journal became the depository for difficult questions:

> *Critical observation can be painful. Troubling realities surface when one fully pays attention. Once a person uncovers a problem, it becomes a challenge to be dealt with, and often, convincing others there is a problem is the first obstacle. Putting on blinders or living in denial is much less stressful, temporarily at least. So, I start with simple questions. Do I have the emotional constitution to honestly scrutinize my mother's quality-of-life within this home that I have chosen for her? And how do I proceed with the knowledge that is revealed?*

With an uncertain future I continued to journal daily, and over time the pages began to reveal a disturbing pattern that emerged once I truly started paying attention.

The Poison Pen

A PEN IS A CURIOUS INSTRUMENT. Somehow ink from its slender tube glides over a tiny ball and leaves a thin path of intricate lines and curves on an absorbent surface. My brother was a writer. In the last year of his life while the brain tumor grew uncontrollably, Jim refused to trade his pen and pencil for a typewriter or tape recorder, even when the writing of words became arduous. "It is like it's an extension of my arm," he explained to me one afternoon as he directed my attention to the writing utensil in his hand. "The thoughts flow from somewhere here," he said, tapping his head, "down my arm, out this point and onto the paper."

I liked the idea that such a simple tool could be a conduit of inner thoughts. But each night, instead of picking up a pen or pencil, I opened up "Mom's Journal" and typed in the daily account of my mother's care. I recorded a clinical report. Often the undercurrents were too wearisome to resurrect, so I left the internal messages in my head and in my gut and stuck to the facts. Nonetheless, the daily entries overwhelmed me with sadness and frustration.

In addition to the issue of correct positioning of my mother's stroke-disabled body, I found myself at odds with her morning aide on another basic issue. I wanted Mom to wear her own clothes. For ease of dressing Mildred wanted Mom to wear snap-up-the-back adaptive dresses. I had seen other wheelchair-bound residents in this drab and unflattering garb. Too often the dresses remained unfastened except for a snap or two at the neckline, leaving the residents vulnerable to both cold drafts and indignity when the rest of the garments fell open.

Instead, I looked for loungewear, shirts and sweatpants in stretchy fabrics, and gradually changed over the last garments of Mom's wardrobe. In her healthy days she preferred tailored outfits cinched in around her tiny waist with belts of all colors and widths. "Elastic waistbands are for old people and I'm not there yet," she'd laugh as she searched sale racks for hidden bargains during mother/daughter shopping excursions. During her early years with dementia, when Mom's ability to dress herself waned, buttons and zippers gave way to elastic and Velcro, and woven pants and cotton blouses were gradually replaced by knits and fleece wear. Nothing in Mom's closet resembled the petite classic styles she would have chosen for herself. But at least her stretchy wardrobe was colorful and neat.

A cause of friction between Mom's morning aide and me centered on our conflicting definitions of "appropriate dress" and our inability to find common ground. Once, I arrived at noontime and found Mom sitting at her seat in the dining room with a cardigan sweater on backwards with the top button fastened behind her neck. Disgusted with the look and Mildred's insistence that Mom have back-opening garments, I took two of Mom's sweatshirts home, cut them up the back, finished the raw edges and applied Velcro fasteners so at least she could wear something warm with the front side facing front. But after a few episodes of finding Mom in these adapted sweatshirts with nothing but the top Velcro fastener secured, and the skin of her back exposed and sticking to the wheelchair's plastic, I took them back home and set them out for a charity pickup.

The adaptive sweatshirt fiasco reminded me of a September conversation with Kent, the third-floor clinical coordinator who oversaw my mother's care until he moved on and was replaced by Andrea. When I asked for his thoughts regarding adaptive clothing, he discouraged me from buying anything with too many closures. "They won't get fastened," he had said. So, witnessing the inability of Mildred to close the back of Mom's adapted sweatshirts, I gave up attempts to alter Mom's wardrobe and continued instead to search for readymade garments constructed from stretchy fabrics.

One day I arrived and found Mom sitting in the dayroom in a washed out, cotton dress that would have snapped up the back if the snaps had been secured, which they weren't. Mildred rushed up to me and explained that she has found the dress in the laundry room, a leftover from a prior resident. She thought she would try it on my mother, she explained, because Mom had experienced some diarrhea earlier and changing her was difficult.

"Won't you consider this type of dress for your mom?" she asked expectantly, with a smile of satisfaction that she had outfitted her charge easily. "Pants are just too difficult," she added.

Looking at Mom, I fought back tears. Sitting in a dress several sizes too big, legs and arms bare and exposed to the winter drafts, she had never looked so sad, so cold, so uncomfortable, so unkempt, so old, so unlike my mother.

"She needs her legs and arms covered" was all I can mumble in my state of dismay.

"We can cover them with a blanket," she replied, as she grabbed one from a nearby storage area and draped it over Mom's knees.

Right, like tha'll stay on, I muttered internally as I wondered who would bother to replace it once it slipped off. *Would anyone notice if it did?*

Not wishing a confrontation in the middle of the dayroom, I wheeled Mom up to her place in the dining room and whispered to her, "I'll be right back," before heading off.

I sought out Eleanor, Mom's social worker. She confirmed that, yes, Mom should be allowed to wear her own clothes and that the practice of throwing a cover over a person's legs as an alternative to long pants was a throw back to the way things were done in the "olden days."

"There was a time," she said, "when even men weren't allowed to wear pants, so a blanket was draped over the lower extremities."

But, she assured me that the dark ages were over, and Mom would not be asked to wear dresses from the laundry.

Returning to the dining room, I fed Mom dinner and wheeled her back to her room. The gravity of my mother's change in appearance was made all the more startling when I compared her current condition to the one in the framed photo that sat on the shelf under her window. The photo captured her, sitting upright in her wheelchair with her birthday cake in front of her. Ironically, the picture was taken the day before we received the telephone call that a room was available at North. Dressed in a red and blue knit outfit that fit her trim figure, she smiled for the camera. Early on in Mom's stay at North, Mildred culled out this outfit and tossed it and many others into the "clothes to take home—too small" laundry basket after she informed the family that too many of Mom's clothes were too difficult to maneuver over her rigid right side.

Some had become tight, thanks to much-needed weight gain after months of mealtime assistance at the Gardens. But, as I took home the majority of her wardrobe I couldn't help but wonder if the nurse in the emergency room would have had half the trouble Mildred seemed to have with many of Mom's outfits. The size six pants the young nurse had so deftly placed on my mother in the emergency room quickly joined the castoffs in the basket. Simultaneously, Mildred instructed me to buy nothing smaller than a size twelve for my mother who weighed in at 108 pounds.

Mildred and I definitely were coming at this situation from different perspectives. My issues with Mom's dress concerned her dignity, warmth, and comfort, and although fashion was not a prime concern, I wanted her to look presentable and to reasonably fit into her clothes. Understandably, Mildred wanted ease of dressing, because she had many residents to attend to each day.

My compromise was to shop in loungewear departments for colorful, stretchy knit garments. French terry tops and matching pants in aqua blue and butter yellow became some of Mom's comfortable wardrobe additions.

• • •

NONETHELESS, DRESSING ISSUES CONTINUED. Some days I found Mom sitting in a loungewear outfit with the pants so twisted that the outside seams ran between her legs. Other days she was neatly dressed in the same pants. The only difference I could see was the aide who had dressed Mom. *How can there be such a discrepancy, and why doesn't anyone besides me notice or care?* With increasing paranoia my mind wandered to more sinister motives. Was Mom a victim of passive aggression aimed at me in retribution for the continued dissatisfaction that I voiced during care conferences?

Each night my journal recorded the discrepancies between the quality of care that Mom received on her final day at the Gardens and her first and subsequent days at North:

Adapting to change and moving forward is difficult, especially when high quality care has been left behind.

Andrea, the floor's clinical coordinator, assures me that Mom is at the nursing home because she requires extra care, so the family's request that she be appropriately dressed is not out of line. Here is the message once again, the reason for moving Mom in the first place. According to the powers that make these placements, the nursing home is the place within the care system that can best provide for my mother's needs. Yet, the disconnection between the message and reality is striking. The issue of dressing overshadows everything, and I wonder if Andrea's message to me regarding the validity of my concerns over Mom's appropriate appearance is communicated to Mildred. Or, is Mildred so entrenched in her old ways that she is just too stubborn to change?

After haggling with this issue for months, I became enlightened on the morning of Tuesday, April 29, 2003, when I stopped Mildred near the reception desk and explained that I had cleaned out Mom's closet and had added summer-weight pajamas. Without commenting about the night-clothes Mildred declared a need for stretchier undershirts. She assured me that she could "find" some unclaimed undershirts in the laundry that opened up the back. My first reaction was one of exasperation at the revisitation of the open-backed clothing option.

But then my frustration turned to anger when she suggested that I visit in the morning and watch my mother being dressed, so I could see firsthand how much pain she was experiencing because I was unwilling to let her wear adaptive dresses. I could not believe what I was hearing. She spoke as if I had never changed my mother's clothes. Yet, every week, when I found Mom sitting in the dayroom soaked to the skin after her beauty shop appointment, it was I, not Mildred, who returned her to her room, stripped off all the wet clothes and dressed her in a dry undershirt and top. And now, to hear her say that my insistence was the cause of her pain . . . I seethed.

I did not seek out Eleanor to communicate for me this time. I shot back, "Mom is not easy to dress, but dressing doesn't have to cause pain." I wanted to add "if done skillfully" but bit my tongue and instead, with a measure of my own passive aggressiveness, I said, "I see Mom in pain when she's forced to sit for hours on those bunched up Hoyer straps."

"That's why the straps are being put to the side," Mildred replied.

I was stunned. She spoke as if this technique was her solution and routinely done. Then she added, "But you should know that she experiences pain when the straps have to be re-placed under her legs."

Here it was, the "Gotcha!" That my care conference request was creating pain for my mother was Mildred's not-so-subtle message.

I could not believe I was hearing that justification for making Mom sit on canvas straps. Clearly this conversation had veered away from Mom's care and had turned into a power struggle. To bring things back to center, I ignored her comment and returned to the issue of dressing.

"I know Mom is more difficult to dress when she's rigid, and rigidity gets worse when she's afraid or rushed. Slower approaches seem to work better." As soon as I finished the sentence I realized by the look on Mildred's face that I had committed the unpardonable sin: telling her how to do her job.

"I have ten to twelve people to get up for breakfast. I can't take any more time with your mother."

Unbelievably, Mildred then returned to the issue of the undershirts and asked again if she could find some back-opening ones for Mom.

Once more, my temper flared.

"A care conference is coming up in two days. I'll talk to Andrea about the dressing issue," I replied, and then to make my intentions perfectly clear I added, "But, I'll be the one who provides the clothing for my mother." *And I better not find her in any more castoffs from the laundry.*

"Good. Talk to Andrea," Mildred answered ignoring my last spoken comment. "She'll tell you how difficult it is with your mother."

I entered the elevator and continued down to the first floor. Seething with anger, and distressed with grief that I had left Mom in the care of this woman, I questioned again my decision to move her to North. I had heard all the right things from the care team who administered from afar, but had seen and heard all the wrong things from the one person who was so critical to my mother's care. The reality was chilling. I could no longer naively assume that problems with Mom's care were issues of transition that would eventually work themselves out. She was an innocent victim in the midst of it all.

The next day I arrived to find Mom sitting in the dayroom. As I passed the reception desk, Rebecca, jack-of-all trades and compassionate to boot, stopped me to say that Mom's Hoyer straps were giving her trouble again. This time they had been left unsecured and her hands were getting caught in the loops. She offered to fix them after Mom was finished being examined by her doctor.

The doctor was here! I found Mom with her medical doctor, and asked to sit in on the examination that was taking place in a closed off area next to the dayroom. I inquired about the possible pain during dressing that Mildred had reported.

"Well, let's see how that shoulder of yours is working," he said as he lifted and guided first one arm and then the other through a full range of motion.

Instead of wincing she smiled.

"She doesn't seem to be registering any pain, but a Tylenol given one hour before dressing might be helpful." He made a notation in her file, and I naively assumed that her care plan would be adjusted. It wasn't until months later that I discovered that this was not the case.

At the end of the exam, I inquired about the cause of my mother's debilitating conditions (Alzheimer's verses dementia verses stroke, or a combination), and his response was simple: "We will never know, but it really doesn't matter, because the treatment would be similar in all cases."

For a person who liked definitions, causes, effects, and timelines, I was slowly accepting the ambiguity of my mother's disease.

The exam ended on a positive note as the doctor commented on the rest of Mom's general health. He rarely saw someone like my little eighty-five-year-old mother who required no prescription medication, and when he commended her on this, she looked up at him and flashed a smile. Could she comprehend his remark or was she just responding to his gentle demeanor? In a strange twist of fate, except for the effects of dementia, Mom was a picture of health.

Dinner was underway in the dining room. As I pushed Mom past Rebecca, she dealt with the troubling Hoyer straps as promised by removing the entire canvas.

Kate, the recreational therapist, was filling a dinner tray for a resident over at the steam tables. Her appearance in the dining room meant that one or two lucky residents would enjoy mealtime assistance embellished with conversation and laughter. Since Mom's arrival at North, Kate had impressed me. Young and enthusiastic, she showed no signs of burnout, and during care conferences, her summarization of Mom's needs was always spot on. She had rightfully earned my trust. I asked if we can talk, and we agreed to meet in Mom's room at the conclusion of dinner.

When Kate arrived, I shared my latest frustrations over the adverse situation with Mildred that was affecting my mother's care. As a timely confirmation Mildred, without knocking, opened the door and entered. Then, after spotting Kate and me, she abruptly turned and exited, leaving an icy tension in her wake.

Kate assured me that it was okay to advocate for my mother, that Mom was here because she needed help, and that she should not be accused of being too difficult or time-consuming. Kate's support improved my spirit and eased my apprehension about the care conference that was scheduled for the following afternoon.

The next day I arrived after work and found Mom in her room with an aide who occasionally was assigned to her care. The window was open, and the room felt chilly. Had Mom spent the night in a cold, drafty room? I walked over to the window to shut it. I couldn't.

"You'll have to get a crank at the reception desk," the aide informed me. "They've been removed from the windows in all the residents' room," she added, as she positioned Mom's wheelchair for a Hoyer transfer.

I borrowed a crank from Rebecca, closed the window, and pushed Mom down to the dining room for her noon meal.

Concerned about the situation with Mildred, Tom took off work in the afternoon, and together we located the room that was being used for the care conferences. Since Mom's initial move-in, Tom had been my listening ear and problem solver, but up to this point I had handled the day-to-day interaction with the nursing home staff. However, time had arrived for him to hear what the care team had to say. The latest flare-up with Mildred baffled both of us, since it was so incongruous with Mom's caregivers in the past.

The care conference began, and unexpectedly so did my tears as I described my fears. I cried for Mom and the situation in which I had placed her. I cried because I was tired of fighting for her dignity while supervisory nurses just passed by her. I cried because for the first time since Dad's death I had encountered a vitriolic reaction from one of Mom's caregivers. And, I cried because I could not comprehend why all of a sudden, things were just so difficult. Tears of grief, of sadness, of frustration, of anger flowed uncontrollably. Thankfully, everyone appeared sympathetic and ready to work with Tom and me and to move ahead in a positive direction.

First, we received an apology for Mildred's behavior from the clinical coordinator. Andrea assured Tom and me that Mildred's suggestion that I witness the pain that I was forcing my mother to endure during dressing was directly opposed to the nursing home's philosophy of respectful treatment of residents and family members. But, an apology was not what I was seeking, especially when it was delivered by a third party. I just wanted my mother's care to improve.

Concerning the dressing issue, Eleanor and I agreed to select and order stretchy undershirts from a mail-order catalog that targeted people with limited mobility. Interestingly, she discouraged the open-back variety for the same reasons I did. Andrea agreed to act as intermediary with Mildred and to evaluate Mom's wardrobe for feasibility. Movement forward.

To avoid chilly temperatures in Mom's room, Eleanor volunteered to put a note in Mom's window to ask staff not to open it. I assured the care team that if Mom could talk, she would opt for stuffy and warm over chilly and drafty. Andrea closed the discussion with a reminder that I could obtain a crank from the third-floor receptionist and air out the room whenever I wished.

Tom and I left the care conference, and another family took our place.

"So how are you feeling?" he asked as we walked out the front door and down the asphalt path to the parking lot.

"Guarded," I responded, commenting more on the outcome of the conference than my internal exhaustion. "We heard all the right things."

"Andrea will be evaluating your mom's wardrobe. That's a good thing," Tom said.

"I doubt that Mildred will be happy with the analysis," I replied, bringing us back to the crux of the problem. "She's pretty entrenched."

"Yeah," he responded. "But management should know that the reputation of their care system is only as good as its weakest employee. Before the bar can be raised, there will have to be adjustments. The care team is responsive; now they just have to get Mildred onboard."

• • •

THE NEXT DAY ELEANOR AND I LOOKED at undershirts in a catalog, decided on a style that did not snap up the back, and ordered two as starters to see how they fit. On my way out, having opted to do my mother's laundry, I grabbed the laundry bag of soiled garments from her closet and brought it home. Not having enough for a full load of wash, I set the bag aside in my laundry room.

It had been a long week.

• • •

WEEKENDS IN THE NURSING HOME were eerily quiet, and as I arrived on Saturday I found the halls of third floor deserted. Mom, dressed neatly, sat squarely in her wheelchair in her room. Perhaps we had turned the corner and Mom's care was improving. It was a bit early to transport her down to the dining room for her noon meal, so we chatted, or rather, I talked, and

Mom smiled. The window was open again, and although the room was cool, it was not yet chilly. Tracking down a crank became a fruitless challenge. I found no one at the nurse's station, in the reception area or in the hallways, but I did see Mildred entering the room of another resident. Before I transported Mom down to the dining room, I grabbed a pencil and paper and jotted a quick note to her and left it on Mom's bed:

> Mildred,
> Would you please close the window? Mom gets chilled very easily and doesn't like sitting in drafts.
> Thanks,
> Jackie

Slowly the dining room filled with residents. Most arrived in wheelchairs. One buzzed by in her motorized scooter-like conveyance. A few shuffled in alone. Aides escorted the remaining residents. Two of Mom's tablemates, Mary and Pearl, were already eating when we arrived, thanks to Mary's daughter Luann, who had fetched meals served up by dietary staff behind the steam tables. I delivered Mom her dinner tray and then returned to the serving line to gather a dinner plate and side dishes for Esther, Mom's other tablemate.

Simultaneously feeding Mom and Esther I chatted with Luann, who assisted her mother. Laughter punctuated the table conversation, and I watched Mom's eyes light up with enjoyment of the interaction. I kept frustrations over dressing issues to myself as I marveled at the women in front of me. Mary, who suffered from chronic pain, and Pearl, who never seemed to have a visitor, had forged a special friendship. Housed on opposite sides of the floor, they relished mealtimes, their opportunity to share the gossip of the day interspersed with tales of their pasts. Luann and I were kindred spirits, two daughters wishing our mothers' lives did not have to wind down under these circumstances. I envied her ability to clearly voice dissatisfaction. Firmly and with emotional detachment she confronted the culprits who tardily answered call lights or forgot to give Mary her medications. My emotions ran too close to the surface. I hated confrontation and usually avoided it, unlike my verbal exchange with Mildred. I considered disclosing the whole miserable encounter to Luann, but the opportunity for a private conversation didn't present itself.

Perhaps it was best to keep things to myself. "Keep your own counsel," my mother used to say. I looked at Mom and wondered what advice she would have for me now, if only she could communicate.

If Mom's appearance was any indication, hopefully we had turned the corner Perhaps after a nine-month struggle Mom could finally enjoy two simple improvements in her care: the dignity of being appropriately dressed in her own clothes and the comfort of being positioned squarely in her wheelchair. I was dumbfounded at the effort and time that I had expended on these simple goals.

The following day after church I located Mom already in the dining room with Zippy. Mom, dressed neatly and munching away, was already well on her way to polishing off her tossed salad. At the end of the meal Zippy left, and I pushed Mom back to her room and found the window open and the room chilly. Again down the hall I went seeking a crank. A trained medication aide (TMA), a compassionate man from Kenya, handed it to me from behind the reception desk.

"Thanks, William," I said. "There's a cold wind today."

"Windows are open all over the floor," he said. "When you are done with the crank, return it to me. I'll check other rooms before I leave."

On the way back to the room I passed Mildred in the hallway. Her few words were crisp and direct: "Just so you know, I don't have your mother on the weekends." Then she continued on, leaving me wondering the motive for this odd remark. I chalked it up as her response to my written request to close the window. Obviously, I had offended her again. This time I brushed it off. But, as I was leaving for the day, an unsettling conclusion was reached: today's improvement in Mom's dressing and positioning was not the result of adjustments made by Mildred.

On Monday, the third floor bustled again as weekday staff returned from their weekends. My visits were brief on both Monday and Tuesday, just long enough to feed Mom. Then I raced home and spent hours on preparation for teaching as I geared up for the final month of school.

On Wednesday my routine continued with one addition. I grabbed a small bag of laundry, brought it home and combined it with the other bag from the previous Friday. Sorting and pretreating, I placed one item after another into the washing machine. Near the bottom of the laundry basket an unlikely piece of paper poked out between two wadded up pairs of stained sweatpants. Probably trash that someone had inadvertently thrown into Mom's laundry bag, I surmised, as I bent over to weed it out.

The paper was actually an envelope strangely trimmed as if to eliminate a return address in the upper left-hand corner. In distinct, large uppercase lettering the word "DAUGHTER" was emblazoned across the front. Scotch tape secured the left edge and the side. Shaken, I abandoned the laundry and took the envelope upstairs. Sitting down in the computer room I broke the seal and removed a folded up sheet of paper, cut in a crude circle that eliminated the letterhead that previously must have run across the top of the page. Uppercase letters delivered the message: YOU HAD TROUBLE AT SOUTH—NOW HERE—GO BACK THERE.

Shock, anger, fear . . . I was not sure in what order, but I experienced them all, first one at a time and then jumbled together as the reality sank in that I had left Mom in a building with a demented person that detested our family. Ten minutes later, Tom returned home from work and found me in a state of despair. Together we scrutinized the poison pen note before calling Andrea, the clinical coordinator who was ultimately responsible for all third-floor residents.

"Oh, no," she groaned after I read the note's message over the phone.

We agreed to meet immediately. Tom and I duplicated the note and envelope on our copy machine and then drove over to North with the original. By the time we arrived, Julie, the community coordinator, and Eleanor had joined Andrea, and the five of us crowded into the tiny office that Andrea and Julie shared. Tom and I produced the note. Their reactions were much like ours: shock, disbelief mixed with anxiety, questions.

I stressed my concern for Mom's safety. The first verbal response was from Eleanor, who firmly stated that we must not tell anyone about the note, that it must be handled confidentially. Tom and I disagreed. We asked for open discussion among the staff, since Mom would be safer with more people on alert. Furthermore, we argued, the incident negatively affected all of them and the reputation of their workplace. Before any decision was made, Andrea informed us that she had contacted Audrey Jorgenson, the administrative head of the facility, who was waiting to speak with us in her downstairs office. All five of us headed for the elevator.

Ms. Jorgenson introduced herself and quickly offered an apology for the family's experience. Then she ushered us to a nearby conference room. Asked if I had experienced any poor treatment from staff, I responded that people were very kind with one exception, and then I described my recent unsettling interactions with Mildred.

In response, what Tom and I heard from the woman in charge of the facility was:

1. Mom's safety was of utmost concern.
2. An investigation would begin immediately.
3. A hidden camera would be installed in my mother's room.
4. Two aides would be assigned to my mother.
5. Few people would be told about the note at this point. (We were asked to tell no one.)
6. Riverside North would not tolerate this behavior and would sort out who was responsible.

The incident was ill-timed for Ms. Jorgenson, who informed us that she was flying to Europe the following day. Yet, she insisted that she would check in with me in the morning.

The meeting broke up, and Tom and I exited the conference room feeling considerably better than when we had arrived. Mom's safety was strongly being addressed and the staff was genuinely concerned, but I could not shake my belief that Mom would be safer if all staff members were informed.

On the way out, Andrea turned and said, "Jackie, I almost forgot. I was going to call you this afternoon before all this happened and tell you that Julie and I dressed your mother this morning. I checked out her wardrobe and wanted to see how much pain she experiences when she is being dressed."

"And?" I looked at her expectantly.

"Actually, we didn't see any pain. In fact, she was chatty and enjoyable to work with. The elbow on her right arm offers the greatest challenges to dressing, but overall, it went well."

I thanked Andrea, who most likely did not fathom the degree of comfort her message delivered. Mom's doctor and now Andrea both confirmed what I had known all along: having Mom dressed in her own clothes did not cause her pain when she was handled gently. Thankfully, Andrea and Julie both had firsthand knowledge of that reality. Although reassuring, this fact did not eliminate another: someone in this building wanted our family gone. Tom and I returned to third floor and spotted Mom, oblivious to the commotion of the afternoon. A male aide was feeding both her and Esther. Exhausted, we slipped out before she noticed our presence.

...

"AREN'T YOU COMING TO BED?" asked Tom around 10:30 p.m.

"Soon," I answered and then returned my attention to the computer to enter the happenings of the day into my journal: *Pens can be extensions of the mind, just like Jim believed. But, they also can be used by petty, cowardly people as vicious weapons . . .*

...

STANDING OUTSIDE MY CLASSROOM DOOR at Irondale High School, I attempted to push the incidents of the previous day to some dark recess in my brain and focus on the students who streamed down the corridor. They entered the school as wide-eyed freshmen, expectant yet insecure, and they graduated four years later, older, wiser, and headed for unique futures. I never tired of witnessing the transitions. And, it was my job at Irondale that grounded me and helped me maintain my sanity as I dealt with the ludicrousness of a poison pen letter sent through a batch of dirty laundry.

Two classes and a prep period later, I stuffed my lesson plan book and a folder filled with student homework into my briefcase and headed over to North for the latest update.

On the short drive I mulled over the part of the note that had me most confounded: "YOU HAD TROUBLE AT SOUTH." What did that mean? When people at Mom's facility talked about South they were talking about the sister nursing home a few miles away, namely Riverside South. Since Riverside North, Mom's location, was the only one of these two facilities that accepted Medicaid, many residents moved from South to North when their money ran out. However, this wasn't the case for Mom. She had never resided "at South," nor was she on Medicaid. In fact, Mom was a private-pay resident, and she was paying dearly for her care: currently $171.95 per day, a price tag that should guarantee her the simple decency of being dressed appropriately and positioned correctly.

"Okay," I said talking to myself as I exited the car in the nursing home parking lot, "stop trying to analyze the demented thought processes of a poison pen scribbler."

The whole note-writing episode seemed so juvenile, like a middle-schooler's cowardly attempt to emotionally injure someone. Yet, the act invoked a disconcerting level of fear.

Expecting to speak with Audrey Jorgenson, I continued down the hallways to her office. No one had seen her, so I left a message that I could be found with my mother in the third floor dining room. As residents filled the tables, I scrutinized every staff member's face wondering who might be the creator of the message that had thrown our family and the administration into a tizzy. Mildred was the logical one, but an anonymous note did not seem to be her style.

Kate stopped by the table and chatted about the upcoming Ladies Tea. Her demeanor clearly indicated that she was unaware of what was going on. *Kate was a member of Mom's care team. Why hadn't she been informed?* But, Tom and I had been sworn to secrecy, so asking Kate anything about the investigation was out of the question. I felt like I was in the middle of a poorly written soap opera until I looked at Mom and wondered, if a person was crazy enough to write the note, an action that could result in job termination, what else might she or he do? I kept the chilling question to myself, but after Mom settled in for an afternoon nap, I sought out Andrea and Julie.

They had information to tell me, but little in the way of identifying the note writer. Interviews with staff had begun, and they reported that all spoke very fondly of my mother. I wondered what questions they asked during the interviews, since they refused to speak about the note. The thirty-six-hour video camera was running in Mom's room. Handwriting comparisons were also being done but nothing had materialized. I was informed that the nurses on the floor were the only people in the loop, since they were responsible for making sure that Mom had two aides working with her at all times for her protection.

With Andrea and Julie, I shared my doubts that Mildred was the author of the note. However, I also explained that I would not be surprised to learn that she was somehow instrumental in the whole affair. I suspected that she broadly expressed her disgruntlement over my advocacy for Mom, since her disparaging remarks about my mother's wardrobe had been relayed to me through Pearl. At the very least, Mildred's comments to one resident about another were unprofessional breaches of confidentiality. I could only imagine what she said in the break room to the other aides. Had another staff person decided to take matters into his or her hands and to rid the building of the sweet little lady with the demanding daughter?

When I left, I passed Mildred in the hall. She refused to make eye contact. Yes, the cold shoulder was more her style. I felt the hostility, but it just didn't make sense that she would jeopardize her job by attacking the family through a poison pen note. Strangely, as angry as I was, I was beginning to feel sorry for her.

Then my mind veered in another direction. Perhaps Mildred was the target of this whole mess. Could it be that someone was intentionally setting her up to be the likely suspect? An earlier incident fueled my speculation.

One afternoon Mom and I had been enjoying the view of fall foliage through the windows in the dining room. Once again Mom had slid sideways in her wheelchair because her hips were not squarely centered underneath her. The first staff person I saw was Mildred, so I asked if she would help me reposition Mom. I stood up to assist, but Mildred had other plans.

"I'll just take your mother and lie her down," she said, grabbing the wheelchair and pushing it down the hall. I'm not sure who was more startled: me, because my simple request had ended a pleasant visit with my mother, or Mom, who registered alarm when her wheelchair unexpectedly lurched backwards by a force she couldn't see and hadn't expected. Stunned, I remained in the dining room as Mom, her upper body listing over the right side of her wheelchair, disappeared down the hall at rapid speed.

Any other aide would have simply helped me adjust Mom's position and allowed us to continue our visit. At the time I chalked the incident up as an overworked aide's attempt to finish up required duties before the end of her shift, even though the shift change was over an hour away. Or, perhaps Mildred was just insensitive to the fact that her solution had interrupted our visit. Either way, I dismissed the occurrence as one more example of her abrupt style.

Now, a third scenario crept into my mind. What if Mildred had taken Mom away that afternoon, not because she didn't want to help me reposition her, but because she couldn't? Considerably older than the other aides, was she unable to do the lifting required? Perhaps inability had been the issue all along, and residents with physically demanding cares were too challenging. If so, other staff members would be forced to take up the slack—causing resentment—creating an atmosphere ripe for attempts to discredit her—setting her up to take the fall as the person who openly complained about the family whose laundry eventually became a mailbox.

I sat by Mom's bedside as she relaxed for an afternoon nap. Fearing that she sensed my tension, I dug into my bag for the *Star Tribune* newspaper, opened it and began to share the headlines of the day. I doubted that she cared much for the latest crime statistics, so I related the weather forecast and read a review of the opening of the newest play at the Guthrie

Theater. She listened intently. Did she remember opening nights with the other Hamline thespians? Back stage jitters? Applause? If not, where did those memories go?

Late in the afternoon, disappointed that I had not heard from Audrey Jorgenson, I walked along the asphalt path between the pond and the parking lot. She was probably ready to jump a plane and take a break from this place. Lucky her, I thought as I climbed into my car.

An evening at home soothed my soul. Tom reminded me that I was not losing my mind. He helped me sort through events of the last few days and succinctly summarized our discussion: "We don't know the truth behind the note, but we do know that the veil of secrecy shrouding this whole event has become increasingly troubling."

Vows of Secrecy

ALMOST EVERYONE, TEACHERS AND STUDENTS ALIKE, enjoyed the relaxed atmosphere that Fridays brought to Irondale High School. Teachers exchanged dressier clothes for casual sweatshirts and denim shirts with Irondale logos, while students radiated a subtle energy as they anticipated weekend plans. For three hours I submerged myself in second-semester teaching tasks, first leading a discussion in a family relationships class and then moving next door to supervise organized chaos in the foods lab where students cooked, evaluated and devoured a huge pot of vegetarian chili. Student involvement, I loved it, and I left the building at the end of the morning energized. I would have relished jumping in my car and doing something fun, like checking out a yarn shop or meeting a friend for lunch.

Instead, I headed over to the nursing home and fed Mom as usual. And as usual, she smiled when she saw me. Somewhere deep inside I believed that she knew that I was her daughter and not just some nice lady who dropped in at noon. Praying for the spark of lucidity that recognized me as her daughter Jackie, I returned daily. Yet, I selfishly wished to be anywhere but on third floor, especially considering the secret investigation that was being carried out in an attempt to put a signature on an anonymous note.

I couldn't even make the day's visit a short one, because later in the afternoon residents and their families had been invited to the Ladies Tea. The residents were abuzz in anticipation of the event that was held each year around Mother's Day. So as much as I would have liked to escape, I planned to feed Mom and then spend time with her in her room until the tea began.

Before Mom finished her salad, an angel arrived in the form of Zippy. Just like she had done so often these past few months, she pulled a vacant chair up to Mom's dining table, greeted everyone and struck up conversations with Mary and Pearl. Her presence was not only a comfort, but a diversion as well. Worthless with small talk, I feared that Mary or her daughter Luann would start asking questions about my strange demeanor. While Zippy helped Mom with her meal, I assisted Esther. As she quietly polished off her dinner, I found myself studying staff again, knowing the culprit with the poison pen might very well be in the dining room, serving a meal or feeding a resident. My vow of secrecy meant that I could not tell Zippy about our family's latest struggle. And, I hated it.

After lunch Mildred and a young aide named Stacy, who were now working together with Mom, laid her down, not for a nap but to exchange her incontinence pad for a fresh one in preparation for the afternoon tea. While they were busy with this task, I walked Zippy down to the front door and gave her a hug.

"You are much more than a friend, Zippy." I tried in a feeble attempt to thank this young woman whose concern for my mother had touched me deeply. "Mom lights up when you visit. She responds to your voice. She loves you."

"She's like a grandmother to me," Zippy responded with a wide smile. A faint blush radiated from her ebony cheeks.

I waited until she walked out of earshot before muttering to myself, *I can't believe that I can't tell you about the poison pen message.*

Upon return to third floor I found Mom back in her wheelchair, sitting upright but with knit pants so twisted that one side seam ran across her knee and down the inside of her leg. I set about adjusting it, not a difficult task, just a couple of additional pulls to unravel the twist. I shook my head. What simple efforts would have been required to provide this little bit of comfort and dignity! I cringed at the thought that this lack of attention to a resident's care was the standard being passed down from an older, supposedly wiser staff person to a new, younger aide.

An hour later, residents began making their way back to the dining room for the Ladies Tea. I searched Mom's drawers for two special touches. I applied lipstick to her lips and opened a small box that contains three pairs of earrings, the clip-on variety now that the holes in Mom's pierced ears had closed. I asked her which pair she preferred to wear to the tea, but she just smiled, so I picked a gold pair with a faux pearl in each center and clipped them on, then ran a comb through her hair. Ready to go, we headed down to the dining room, brightly decorated in springtime greens, yellows and pinks.

Delicate finger foods lined a buffet table from which staff and family members filled plates of goodies for the residents. Tea, of course, and punch were served at each table. Laughing and talking drowned out the soft music playing in the background. The Ladies Tea was a big hit with the residents, and I found myself resenting the fact that I was allowing some crazy person with a pen to cast shadows on what should be a very pleasurable afternoon with my mother. So, with intent, I focused on her enjoyment of the special occasion.

At the end of the tea I returned a very sleepy mother to the care of her afternoon aides. On my way out, a "Do Not Disturb" sign on Andrea's door stopped me from inquiring about the investigation, so I resigned myself to no new information until Monday. Mentally I decided to leave all the baggage of the week's events within the walls of Riverside North and enjoy my weekend.

However, one revelation changed everything. It becomes apparent that Riverside North was similar to a small town in some regards, especially in the speed at which gossip spread among the staff and eventually to me. The gossip that reached my ears was not about the poison pen note. No one was aware that for Mom's safety two aides had been assigned to work with her. Rather, I was informed via the gossip grapevine that Mildred was complaining about our family—how we had insisted that two people take care of Mom and how our family was leaving demanding notes for her.

Livid about the half-truths and disheartened that the relationship with Mom's aide had disintegrated to this level, I equated my silence with self-induced powerlessness. First, I had agreed to uphold a vow of secrecy regarding the note as the administration requested. Second, concerned about her possible dismissal for sharing information with family members, my source for Mildred's rants had asked me not to report the latest gossip to the administration. I was gagged on two fronts by vows of secrecy.

When Tom arrived home from work, he found me seething at the latest development, especially since I could not respond to Mildred's allegations. We decided the best way to squelch the rumors was to push for the telling of the truth. If the third-floor staff was informed about the note, hopefully they would understand the need for safety measures. Tom left a message on Andrea's phone, but since it was 6:30 p.m. on a Friday, we did not expect to hear from her until she checked her messages, probably on Monday morning at the earliest. And, that seemed a long way away.

Instead of simply a place to record the details of Mom's care, my journal was morphing into a therapeutic sounding board.

Saturday, May 10, 2003

I'm beginning to feel like the messenger that gets shot.

Demanding messages???? "Please close the window" equates to a demanding message?! I am furious. And the reason I wrote that note to Mildred in the first place was because I was unable to locate a crank to close it myself.

I hear from Mom's care team that she is at North because this is the best fit for her care needs. I hear that advocating for her is not just okay, but important. I hear that my concerns are not out of line or unnecessarily demanding.

But harassment, via a poison pen and the gossip mill, sends a different message. Fallout and backlash—what next? Is Mom safe?

Riverside North can either deal with this completely and live up to its positive reputation, or this institution can cover up the situation and allow harassment to win out. Which will it be?

Sunday, May 11, 2003, Mother's Day

Visited Mom at 11:30 a.m. Took her off the floor and downstairs for pizza, cake and lemonade supplied by Tom and Krista. Happy Mother's Day, Mom! I am so sorry that you are here.

Monday, May 12, 2003

Visited Mom at noon. No return call from Andrea. Happy Birthday, Dad!

Tuesday, May 13, 2003

Tom called and got an update from Andrea this morning. The investigation continues and interviews are now being done by HR, but there is no headway in determining the author of the note. She also informed him that the tapes reveal that Mom's aides are "handling her cares nicely." Tom stated our desire that we would like to see full disclosure of the situation to the staff as soon as possible. She responded positively.

I visited Mom at 3:30 p.m. and gently reminded Eleanor that she had agreed to put a sign in Mom's room requesting that the staff leave the window closed. She typed up an official looking one but on the bottom wrote "per family's request." I cringed when I saw it, because I want the sign to be seen as a joint decision of the care team and not just the "daughter" making "trouble" again. I explained my concern and she adjusted the sign, but I'm not sure she got my point. I wish I could tell her about Mildred's gossipy remarks. Such petty little things are now taking on such importance, when all I want is simply good care for Mom. Eleanor also has received the order of stretchy undershirts. They fit, so we are ordering more.

Wednesday, May 14, 2003

Visited Mom at noon. No news on investigation.

Thursday, May 15, 2003

Eight days since the poison pen note was reported. Today Kari Henrikson, another administrator at North asked to speak with me. In Audrey Jorgenson's absence she has been asked to work on the poison pen situation. We shared information during our long conversation. Kari informed me that the investigation had netted no revelation about the note writer. She will be meeting with "corporate" on Tuesday and will share with me whatever she learns.

There's that elusive entity again! Corporate. The powerhouse that communicates to me through administrators, first directing Mom's relocation to the nursing home and now dealing with poison pen messages. *Corporate. Faceless, formless, yet so powerful it earns a capital C. I hope you will become a superhero for Mom. A benevolent wizard behind the curtain in this world of Oz.*

Kari shared her feeling that the note writer was probably doing the "worst" thing that he/she could think of, and she doubted that the note indicated "anything dire happening." She looked at the situation from the perspective of the note writer—that he/she must be so frustrated—and the staff needs to attend to this kind of frustration before it blossoms into what our family experienced. She assured me that it was okay to advocate for my mother.

I responded that I wish I were as confident as she that nothing else dire would happen, but she offered no rationale for her optimism. What does she know that I don't know?

I explained my timeline for the week before the discovery of the note including the confrontation with Mildred. I offered to give her a copy of my journal's documentation of the days surrounding the event.

We are now into our second week of this mess, and it will extend until at least next Tuesday after Kari meets with Corporate, the anonymous player in this anonymous letter writing drama. (How ironic is that?) I can't believe all the time this issue is taking away from other residents. And I am beginning to feel blamed for that too. Whistleblowers are unpopular people, and I have blown the whistle, loud and strong.

Since Mom arrived at North there has been such a discrepancy between the quality of care that she received on her last day at the Gardens and almost every day at North. It has been a conundrum to witness. And, this is reputed to be one of the best nursing homes around. Frightening! Tom and I talk about moving Mom—but where? Nursing home horror stories abound. I fear most problems are systemic, universal. Is there a safe place?

Thanks to a note writer Mom has two staff people attending to her. Plus, nurses are on high alert. For those reasons, she will stay—at least for now.

Throwing Andrea Under the Bus

As I waited for Kari Henrikson's call regarding Corporate's discussion of the poison pen situation, I formulated questions in my journal:

Has Kari read my journal entries? Did she share them with Corporate? What would decision-makers say if they knew that I arrived yesterday to find Mom's pants hiked into her crotch and cutting off circulation in one leg? (Now, two staff people are unwilling to take the ten extra seconds it takes to pull her pant legs down.) Isn't it enough to lose a parent to this merciless disease? Must I also fight for every ounce of comfort for her?

I am struck by an enigma. How could a fastidious woman like Mildred, whose uniform is always immaculate and her hair neatly styled, ignore the discombobulated results after she dresses and positions my mother in her wheelchair? What causes this kind of blindness? Is she pointedly making my mother miserable in an attempt to discredit her wardrobe? Is she retaliating for my insistence that my mother be allowed to wear her own clothes? Or, is she simply too overworked, too burned out, or too weak to perform at the necessary standard?

The phone rang, interrupting my perplexing thoughts. Kari's first words were encouraging. She informed me that during a gathering of third-floor staff, Andrea revealed the saga of the anonymous note. Relief! The secret had been shared.

"I was very proud of Andrea," said Kari. "She started out the meeting by saying, 'I'm afraid I have let you down . . .' and then she explained that someone had become so frustrated that they had written your family an anonymous note." Then Kari described the limited details that were shared, plus the reaction of the staff—gasps, shock, anger, verbal support for the family.

Although Tom and I were now free to openly discuss the poison pen note with others, a sickening wave rose from the pit of my stomach when I realized that Andrea had taken full responsibility for the note writer's actions. How could this young woman, newer to third floor than my mother, be totally responsible for a work environment so frustrating that it encouraged a staff member to yield a poison pen?

Andrea appeared to stand alone, even though our family's experience with unexecuted care conference decisions originated well before her arrival as third-floor clinical coordinator. I realized that a supervisor was responsible for what happened under his or her watch, but what about Andrea's supervisors? How far up the ladder should this responsibility go? As I hung up the phone, I imagined Andrea's selfless act, claiming responsibility by throwing herself under the bus with Kari cheering her on. I guess I was supposed to be heartened by this development, but all I saw was one more victim of the person who wielded a poison pen.

A lengthy telephone conversation with Andrea the following day revealed more about the staff meeting. Her directives to those in attendance were:

- The highest quality of care is essential for all residents.
- There must be different levels of care because people have different care needs and sometimes because of health setbacks a person's needs might change. For these reasons the job of the staff/caregivers is critical.
- Anonymous note writing is unacceptable.
- If a person is struggling with his/her job, he/she should come forward because there are other jobs at Riverside North that might be a better fit.
- Don't forget about the needs of residents who have no family advocates.

Hearing nothing new, I simply asked, "Where do we go from here? Is Mom safe?"

"The hidden camera will continue to record for the time-being," she assured me. "So far the tapes reveal that your mother is being well cared for. We are also getting an opportunity to see that no one is excessively struggling to dress her, which is a good thing."

I appreciated the confirmation, but returned to the issue of safety to which she replied, "Everyone is on alert. We are watching your mother carefully."

I expressed my concerns that Andrea had taken the fall for someone's hostile behavior, and we discussed the difficult position of being a supervisor. Finally, at the end of the conversation she asked the family to allow Mildred to remain as Mom's aide. "With monitoring," she emphasized.

Incredulous, I hesitated. Andrea assured me that goals for Mildred's improvement had been set and evaluation would be ongoing. Reluctantly, I agreed, primarily because a switch would cause another resident to lose his or her designated aide. "I reserve the right to change my mind" was my feeble disclaimer.

The best news was that the secret had been revealed. Third-floor staff was informed, and Tom and I were free to tell friends and family about our bizarre experience and to ask them to tune in their radar when they visited Mom. The shift in momentum stirred hope that improvements in her care were forthcoming, even though the authorship of the poison pen note was yet to be established.

Although I gritted my teeth during nursing home visits each afternoon, many aides and nurses expressed support. Nevertheless, my eyes traveled from one staff person to the next as I searched for tiny clues, hints of discomfort, embarrassment, or animosity, as I sleuthed for the originator of the hate-filled message.

With me, Mildred remained silent and distant. I followed her lead and cowardly chose avoidance over attempts at reconciliation. Mom, thankfully, was oblivious to the hubbub surrounding the threats against her family. Instead, as a result of the poison-pen-induced security breach she unknowingly became the beneficiary of extra supervision. This unexpected bonus quelled my thoughts of uprooting her and moving her away from her friends, Pearl, Mary and Esther.

Finally, Audrey Jorgenson returned from Europe and telephoned with a request. Without referring to our inability to connect the day after the anonymous note was discovered, she asked permission to share the copy of my journal that had been passed on to her through Kari Henrikson.

"I would like to show it to Andrea. Perhaps it will be insightful."

Hesitant to share my personal thoughts with an even wider audience, I granted permission once I heard that I would be included in the communication loop.

"I'll get back to you after that happens" was her promise before a cordial goodbye.

Days passed, then weeks. No identification of the poison pen author. No resolution of any kind. No contact from Audrey Jorgenson, as promised. No further information from any staff member.

My optimism faded as reality set in. Either communication about the incident bypassed the family, or the facility had chosen to quietly close the file on an incident that has created an ugly smudge on its good name. Obviously, administration had moved on.

Finally, weeks after our last conversation and well into the summer I spotted Audrey Jorgenson sitting behind the reception desk as I signed out. I reintroduced myself and reminded her of her intention to contact me after she shared my journal with Andrea. She responded with an apology and offered an excuse that "things moved so slowly" that she just did not get back to me.

Her simple statement spoke volumes and allowed me to finally name one of the most troubling realities that confirmed the fact that Mom's care would never measure up to what she experienced at the Gardens: good intentions set adrift with insufficient follow-through, otherwise know as lip service. I had discovered a fault line that ran from within my mother's single room right through the care conference table to the office of the building's administrator. Failure to follow care plans, failure to close communication circles. Details disregarded or simply forgotten. One disappointment followed by another, and another, all recorded in my journal. Each chiseling away at the façade of my mother's home.

•••

ARE EMPTY PROMISES A SURVIVAL TACTIC for all nursing homes? *Unlike other businesses if a nursing home waits long enough, residents' problems and concerns disappear into waiting hearses. But, Mom has a healthy heart and so she stays, and I renew my vow to pay close attention and to educate myself on the business of taking care of the elderly.*

Two Lives

I WAS LIVING TWO PARALLEL LIVES.

My simple life was detailed in a slim calendar tucked carefully in my black handbag. Small, neatly printed entries filled the monthly grids. Reminders of birthdays, dental appointments, haircuts, meetings, and book group gatherings meshed with details of the school year calendar. Notations of parent-teacher conferences, grade reporting deadlines, and holidays speckled the pages from September through June. Comings and goings—hectic at times yet comfortably predictable.

My life as Mom's caregiver, with attempts to advocate for her dignity and health, ran in parallel existence to my simple life. I had envisioned that once Mom had transitioned into her final home, the execution of her care plan would be forthcoming, the promise of high quality care would be realized, and I would return to my simple life. The opposite seemed to be the case. Although Mom had been placed in this environment because "this is where her needs can best be met," the truth remained that Mom's care had not lived up to the pledge.

My visits to North had become embedded into my daily life, so I no longer bothered to note them in my trusty calendar. My engrained habit was to plan nothing extraneous around lunchtime. Instead, feeding Mom her noontime meal was the routine rather than the exception, so no calendar notation was necessary.

Each night I journaled my second life as I sat before the computer. In addition to factual updates, my entries recorded the tough lessons I was learning:

> Mom's care continues to be "spotty" at best, reflective of the time, strength and commitment given to her by the aide-of-the-day. Some aides, skilled and compassionate, shine like beacons, while others,

Mildred unfortunately included, continue to need prodding from monitors, supervisors assigned to periodically oversee and instruct. Unfortunately, improvements lack permanency . . .

Slowly, and perhaps naively, I have begun to believe that the poison pen note was a cowardly, sideways act from an immature, frustrated employee with no intention to physically harm Mom in any overt way. The hidden camera has been discontinued, but it revealed a truth: when Mom is handled gently, she relaxes, easing caregiving tasks and improving the day for both her and her aides. Care can be good here . . .

A simple glance at the position of Mom's right foot upon the footrest tells me whether she is in for a calm or stormy day, care-wise. That foot position becomes an accurate barometer, because it indicates whether Mom has or has not been positioned correctly in her chair. The occupational therapist has equipped the chair with footrests properly adjusted to fit the length of Mom's legs. The right footrest is permanently raised 45 degrees to support a leg frozen by stroke and inactivity. When Mom is seated properly, her right foot nestles comfortably into the upturned end of the apparatus. In comparison, when she is improperly seated, she ends up in a slouched position with her weight on her tailbone and her foot extended beyond the length of the footrest. In this position not only is the footrest useless, but Mom's right ankle ends up perched on a thin metal edge. In this position both tailbone and ankle are ripe for pressure sores. So basically, on days when I find Mom's foot in the footrest where it should be, her other care needs seem to be conscientiously attended to as well. Unfortunately, the inverse is also true...

I have learned to check the staff assignment sheets that are posted on the bulletin board by the elevator. Now that I am paying attention, I notice patterns. Heroes have emerged—heroes who routinely position Mom correctly in her wheelchair, who notice discomforts and try to rectify them, and who patiently feed residents who always chew thoroughly (Mom) . . .

What if parents sat next to their teenagers in my classroom and daily observed my teaching methods? Would they be critical of my attempts to meet their children's individual needs? The question grounds me—a reminder to look at Mom's care issues from all angles, to be respectful with my requests, to be mindful of their effects on others, to be empathetic to the challenges of the staff . . .

On quiet days when I am the only daughter sitting at my mother's table, I glance around the dining room and ponder the staff's diversity. Why do I sometimes sense hierarchical or racial tension among staff people? What brings each person here? What level of commitment to the elderly accompanies each to his or her job? Why do some "see," and others wear blinders?

Follow the protocol, attend care conferences, insist on a care plan that will meet Mom's needs, expect follow-through.

Pick your battles.

Ignore the fact that an aide is dozing rather than encouraging a reluctant resident to continue with her dinner (BECAUSE THAT RESIDENT IS NOT YOUR MOTHER, EVEN THOUGH AT A DIFFERENT MEAL WHEN YOU ARE NOT THERE, SHE MIGHT JUST BE THAT RESIDENT.)

Ignore the fact that the call light of your mother's neighbor has been blinking for what seems like forever (BECAUSE YOUR JOB IS TO ADVOCATE FOR YOUR OWN MOM, AND NOT TO INTRUDE ON THE CARE OF OTHER RESIDENTS, JUST LIKE SOME STAFF WHO IGNORE YOUR MOM'S NEEDS BECAUSE SHE IS NOT ONE OF THEIR AS-SIGNEES)

Put on the blinders. (BECOME WHAT YOU HATE!) Or not.

The Wedding

THANK HEAVEN FOR CELEBRATIONS. Clay's wedding to Becky Lietzau on July 26, 2003, proved to be a monumental event. Her addition wove a beautiful thread into the fabric of our family.

"She reminds me so much of Grandma," Clay said, describing Becky to me over the phone shortly before he proposed. "She is just so kind, so good," he added, conveying her inner beauty without mentioning her tall, blond, striking appearance. All of that plus her pleasant, upbeat attitude, her commitment to Clay, and her comfortable demeanor confirmed to our family that Clay had found a jewel. Employed by the Apple Valley School System, Becky shared her enthusiastic spirit with classes of excited kindergartners. Mom, if she could have spoken, would have enthusiastically voiced her approval.

On a hot, sultry weekend in July, Becky married Clay. Mom's presence at the event was more than symbolic. She and Dad had always adored Clay, their first grandchild and only grandson. In Jim's absence they had stepped up. Not just grandparents they became surrogates for Jim, honoring Clay at each juncture of his life. Now only Grandma remained. The animated, affectionate, adoring grandma who has been ever present at everything from cross-country meets to graduations was now trapped behind a placid façade. Even so, no one in the family was about to allow dementia to steal her presence from her grandson's wedding.

Because Mom's rigid right leg complicated travel in a regular automobile, I hired a transportation company that could transport Mom in her wheelchair across the Twin Cities to the wedding site in Eden Prairie. On the wedding day I rode along in the passenger seat and chatted with the driver/owner of the handicap-accessible van. Mom, somewhat confused, sat quietly in the space behind, her eyes darting cautiously as we proceeded through the Twin Cities. The driver, a young immigrant, described dreams for his relatively new transportation business and his willingness to work extended hours and weekends. By the time we arrived at the Olympic Hills Golf Club, I had tentatively enlisted him to deliver Mom home to New Brighton for future Thanksgivings and Christmases.

Mom, bedecked in flowing black pants, a black knit jacket with shimmering silver flecks and satin ballet slippers, joined the rest of the family and other wedding guests on the patio for the formal outdoor ceremony. Quiet but observant, she sat unflinchingly until Becky, the epitome of the glowing bride, and Clay, tall and handsome, shared their first kiss as husband and wife and led the procession back into the air-conditioned banquet hall for a candlelit dinner. As they passed, a glowing smile briefly warmed Mom's face. A lucid moment, perhaps? Then she retreated again.

Teen with Becky and Clay on their wedding day.

Not surprisingly, Mom enjoyed every morsel of her dinner and slice of wedding cake, thanks to the assistance of Krista and Angie. After dinner relatives pulled up chairs beside her and carried on monologues with the hope that a favorite memory would clear away the fog. Finally, as Mom's eyes drooped, the van returned to transport her back to Riverside North. The driver pushed her up the ramp and into the van, and before her wheelchair was firmly belted into the safety straps, her eyes closed, an assurance that she would not be anxious about riding across the Twin Cities unaccompanied by family. I rejoined the wedding guests who were about to start dancing. Relief! Mom's eventful day had ended.

The following day and the next and the next I reminded her of each detail of her grandson's wedding and showed her photographs that documented the event. She was there, I reminded her. The pictures proved it. Sometimes she smiled.

Missing from that memorable day were two people who loved Clay beyond measure, his dad and his grandfather. Both would have celebrated in their own unique ways. I pictured Jim, with a ready joke to cover his sentimentality, and Dad, making himself available to offer assistance with last-minute details. Both smiling proudly. Both happy for Clay. Both welcoming Becky.

With the addition of Becky, our shrinking family had expanded for the time being, a fact worthy of celebration.

Bang for the Buck

IT WAS THE FIRST WEEK OF THE MONTH and the dreaded nursing home bill, which escalated each year, had arrived. This month's "amount due" was a pleasant surprise, $33.83 short of the $6,000 mark. Rarely did it drop this low, but then I realized: we were paying for February, the shortest month of the year.

Mom's monthly bill was calculated quite matter-of-factly. According to the 2004 cost table, she was being charged $177.73 per day plus $28 per day for her private room. To that was added her beauty shop bill, the best deal around at fifteen dollars for a shampoo and set. The annual cost totaled around $75,000 annually. I took inventory of what my father used to call "bang for the buck" and the results chilled me.

How would Dad have evaluated this nursing home investment? He and Mom had grown up during the 1930s, so the lessons of the Great Depression greatly affected all of his financial decisions. One of Mom's mementos, tucked safely away in her important papers, was her 1939-1940 teaching contract from the little Minnesota town of Milroy, where she taught two years before they wed. Her gross pay, $100 per month, was earned by teaching English, directing the school plays, and opening the school library to city residents on Saturday mornings. Once wed, she seldom worked outside the home with two exceptions. She taught in Ivanhoe, Minnesota, for one year while her new husband served in the Navy during World War II, and years later, she occasionally substituted for teachers in Crookston. Basically, before Jim graduated from high school, our family modestly lived on my father's teaching and coaching salary or later his paycheck from the State of Minnesota for work in the Department of Corrections. Then while Jim and I attended college, Mom became certified as a reading specialist and returned to full-time teaching, this time in White Bear Lake.

Growing up, I witnessed Mom and Dad's frugality on a daily basis. They saved their dollars and produced cash for every purchase, whether it was a half-gallon of milk or a new Chevrolet. It was from their retirement pensions, investments and savings that I wrote the checks that financed Mom's stay in the nursing home.

The Minnesota Department of Health set the standard for nursing home rates. This was built on the case mix classification assigned to the resident based on an assessment by the facility staff. Each classification was assigned a daily rate that was billed at the end of the month. Notification of Mom's care mix classification was accompanied by a "Request for Consideration thirty-day option" if I had wished to dispute it. However, I chose to accept her CC1 designation, the ninth most expensive out of the thirty-six categories.

Bang for the buck? For Dad, the price tag for Mom's care would never have been the issue. He saved for the eventuality that she would outlive him and that she might experience the same dementia that challenged her own mother and require long-term care. I heard his message: Pay the cost, whatever it takes to provide the best possible care.

So in his absence, instead of grieving the shrinking savings account I focused my energy on ensuring that Mom got the care that she required and for which she dearly paid. Some days I witnessed bursts of compassionate care from skilled staff members who conscientiously followed Mom's care plan. Sadly, other days fizzled, even backfired, for a variety of reasons, some avoidable, some not. It was no longer just a matter of money.

The year 2004 started out with positive changes in Mom's care. After being told by Andrea that "unpopular" decisions were being made in the best interests of the residents, I saw changes. One was obvious. Mildred no longer provided direct care to residents. She had been reassigned to another job within the building. I heard about this permanent change through the grapevine.

Nicole, the third person to tackle the job of third-floor clinical coordinator since Mom's arrival, was up to the plate. Her presence was my only indication that Andrea had left, since I had seen no formal communication about her departure. Sadly, I lost the opportunity to thank Andrea for her strength and persistence under negative conditions. Was she the sacrificial lamb—the one who came in, made the tough decisions, forced change on an entrenched culture, became unpopular, and was forced to leave? Or, had she grasped a job opportunity that allowed her to go to work elsewhere with a smile on her face? Either way, one thing was certain: thanks to Andrea, changes had occurred, and Mom's care had improved.

So, was Dad getting bang for his buck? On days when Mom was well cared for, I wrote the check to Riverside Homes with no remorse. Those days were stacking up one on top of another thanks to my mother's new designated aide, Anna, who worked each morning with skilled hands and a compassionate heart. Mom's relaxed demeanor around Anna was refreshing to witness. Locking her gray-green eyes on the face of this strong, compassionate Black woman, Mom relaxed, and so did I.

March 1, 2004

The dressing issues, the uncomfortable positioning of Mom's petite body, and the lack of oversight and follow-through by the nursing staff to correct these concerns have yielded disappointments and a loss of respect for North. Would I have felt differently if Mom had been assigned a different a.m. aide on day one? I guess I'll never know. But, clearly things are consistently better for Mom now. And, I arrive at North each day with a purposeful, conciliatory attitude.

Nonetheless, on many days, I am overwhelmed by sadness as I discover so many residents like Mom, people with dementia with no voice to advocate for themselves. Third floor for them has become "a place to die." What systemic changes in this nursing home will have to take place before it becomes their final "place to live"? Are these changes even possible under the facility's current configuration as a mini-hospital with long corridors and sixty residents per floor?

Bang for your buck, Dad? I don't know.

April Bruises, 2004

APRIL ARRIVED ACCOMPANIED BY UNEXPLAINABLE bruises on Mom's body. One then several appeared like the first raindrops that precede a major storm, and, after a weeklong gale subsided, severe erosion of Mom's quality-of-life, her spirit, and my newly regained trust in Riverside North had taken place.

On April 18, I contacted my friend Cindy, a nurse practitioner, and asked, as I have done so many times during the last twenty months, for her medical input. First, I retraced events of the previous week.

. . .

THE ONSET OF THE STORM ANNOUNCED ITSELF Monday, April 12, when Delores, the nurse from the morning shift, called to inform me that Mom had a bruise about the size of a quarter on the inner side of her upper left arm (her good arm). No explanation could be given for its origin.

On Tuesday, I checked out the bruise and found it clearly apparent but not bothering Mom in any detectable fashion. That evening I received another call informing me of more bruises on her arm. The latest injury consisted of a large bluish mark surrounded by dime-size spots. Again, the cause was undetermined. I informed the nurse that I had checked Mom's arms only hours earlier and had seen no bruises other than the one identified the day before. Surely, that information could be used to establish the timing of the new bruises and to provide clues to the identification of the person inflicting them, I offered. Could supervisors intervene, I asked? The situation will be investigated, I heard.

Wednesday I checked out the latest black and blue marks, a handprint of sorts, four dots of blue in varying sizes. They looked disturbing, but Mom did not flinch while I examined them.

Thursday, another call.

"Jackie," the nurse began. "I hate to call again. I'm not sure what's happening but your mom has another bruise, this time on her bad arm near the wrist. Nicole has suggested that we put cloth arm protectors on her," she added, "to offer a little protection."

"Cloth arm protectors?" I asked, wanting clarity.

"The lightweight ones usually used to protect residents from skin tears?"

Skin tears I was familiar with. The skin on Dad's forearms had become paper thin during the final months of his life. A simple brush against a firm object resulted in skin peeling away and bruising. Often he noticed bleeding before pain. However, unlike Dad's skin, Mom's was strong and supple and not easily torn or bruised. So what was happening?

"This is a reoccurring problem," I said. "Is anything being done to figure out what's happening?"

"We're trying, but we haven't been able to pinpoint the cause of the bruising," she answered.

The nurse and I ended our conversation, and I headed over to check on Mom. I found her, sitting in her wheelchair in her room, wearing a short-sleeved yellow knit top. Both forearms (and her identification bracelet) were hidden behind gauzy, beige fabric. She sat with her newly injured wrist cradled in her opposite hand. Before I began to examine her skin, I knelt down in front of her to make eye contact.

"Mom, I hear that you have a bruise on your wrist. I'm so sorry. May I look at it?"

Then an amazing thing happened. Uncharacteristic of the last two years Mom peered back into my eyes and with an unusual determination to communicate she uttered, "Shouldn't—shouldn't—shouldn't—" as she shook her head with more anger and frustration than I had seen in years.

Something had happened; something bad had happened!

I peeled down the skin protectors and revealed a very large, ugly swelling on the bone of her right wrist with bruising extending in both directions, up her forearm and down into her hand. The swollen appearance alarmed me, and I summoned Delores, the nurse who had telephoned earlier.

"This looks ugly. Are you sure there is nothing broken?" I asked.

Instead of a direct answer she attempted range-of-motion movements with Mom's wrist and forearm but stopped when the slightest movement elicited cries of pain.

"We can have it X-rayed," she concluded, and left to contact the nurse practitioner for orders.

Flabbergasted that two nurses had examined this injury without ordering X-rays, I seethed. Instead, they had covered the injury with gauzy fabric and continued on with their day's business.

I stared at the flimsy arm protectors and threw them aside. They offered no protection, no cushion. All they did was hide the injury, making her all the more vulnerable to re-injury and harm by non-alerted caregivers. In addition, I wanted her identification bracelet clearly visible. My renewed trust in the system, shaky at best, began to erode again.

"Let's go down to the dining room," I said, hoping that the sight of her tablemates would offer a distraction from the pain.

During lunch I listened to Mary as she remarked about seeing Mom's ugly bruise at the breakfast table before the arm protectors were added.

"We've got enough pain," she commented directly to her friend Pearl across the table. "We don't need the aides causing more."

"We have to stick together around here," Pearl replied as she continued to devour her plateful of mechanically softened foods.

Mom's injury evoked renewed empathy for Mary and other residents whose diseases and conditions produced constant pain. Until now, pain had not been one of Mom's issues, and I had not fully appreciated that blessing.

"Did I tell you about the time I called 911 when no one would answer my call light?" Mary said, lightening the conversation. "I just dialed them right up from my phone in my room. Then I got some service," she added with an emphasis on then.

The resulting laughter from those around the table reached out and snared Mom from some faraway place. A tiny smile turned up the corner of her lips, the first I had seen all day.

At home after my visit, I picked up the phone when it rang around 4 p.m. Nicole, the clinical coordinator, reported that X-rays had been taken, but results were pending. The cause of Mom's latest bruising, however, had been identified. A trained medication aide filling in for Mom's nursing assistant on the evening shift had forced Mom's bent wrist into a long-sleeved nightgown.

Two hours later I received another call, this time an update from Grace, the nurse on the evening shift. X-ray results had arrived. She described a non-displaced hairline fracture and explained that the X-rays would be sent to an orthopedic doctor at Regions Hospital for further evaluation. In the meantime, she assured me that Mom's wrist would be immobilized with a splint.

Friday I headed over to check on Mom. I found her in the dayroom without her glasses, so I took her back to her room. Paulette, a nurse whom I had never seen before, introduced herself to me. She informed me that she had assisted the morning aide, a young man newly assigned to dress and care for my mother, and that Mom had seemed quite comfortable with him. She also shared that she had given him suggestions regarding how to lift a limb ("not to grab, but to raise by cupping under the elbow") so as not to create injury. *Aren't aides routinely taught this?* I asked myself. Paulette improved my spirits, and I was comforted by the knowledge that she was keeping an eye on Mom. I had no way of knowing that this would be the last time I would ever see Paulette.

That evening Kelly, another nurse, called to report that the X-rays had not been picked up and delivered to the hospital as expected. The delivery service was to blame, according to Kelly. As a result no further information would be available until at least Monday, she related, because we were entering the weekend. Until then, she assured, protocol for Mom's injury would be strictly followed: the wrist would be immobilized by a splint; staff would be icing Mom's bruise; Tylenol 3 would be given for pain. She added, to prevent re-injury a nurse would always be present when Mom was repositioned.

Okay, storm over. Damage evaluated and corrective measures taken. Mistakes happen. Repeated injury no longer likely. Protocol clear. Trust regained—well, not totally, but a turn around within a week. Okay.

Saturday, I visited Mom in the late afternoon. I found her in the dining room, sitting in her wheelchair, peering vacantly out the window. An ice pack covered her splinted wrist, which was comfortably positioned on a pillow in her lap. She smiled as I pulled a chair up next to her, planted a kiss on her forehead and offered her some juice. Seeing Mom so comfortably arranged with splint, ice, and pillow quelled my nerves. Obviously, protocol was spelled out somewhere, because it had been followed to the letter. As if on cue, Jeanine, Mom's skilled and conscientious designated evening aide entered the dining room, greeted me and expressed sadness over Mom's latest misfortune. After supper I returned home, secure that Mom was in good hands. A stormy week was over.

On Sunday, it did not take long to realize that although a new week had started, the storm was hardly over. Saturday's calm had seduced me into a false sense of tranquility, but the peace dissolved when I spotted Mom in the dayroom when I arrived about an hour earlier than usual. She resembled a storm survivor who had wandered out during the eye of a hurricane thinking that the worst was past only to get blasted again. She was asleep with her head propped against a metal bar that should have been holding her wheelchair's padded headrest. Her left ear, reddened by prolonged contact with metal, became my first clue that she had sat in that position for quite some time. She looked uncomfortably twisted in her chair with her weight unevenly shifted onto her left hip. No headrest was present, but more importantly, no splint, no ice, and no pillow for support were anywhere within the vicinity. Even worse, her injured arm was wedged between the side of her body and the edge of the wheelchair. I gently removed it, before pushing Mom out of the dayroom in search of her splint and some answers.

Val, the only staff person in the hallway, was the nurse on duty, and I angrily reported the breach in protocol. Together we returned Mom to her room and located the splint lying in clear sight on the bedside table. Val's first words conveyed excuses, justifications, coverups . . . Mom's splint had been removed for "skin cares" . . . she had been without it for "a very short time" . . . the intention was to replace it "very soon."

Internally, I screamed: *Do you really expect me to buy that? I arrive an hour earlier than usual, and this is how I find her! Intentional, unintentional— does it matter? Look at her! Really look at her and then tell me again about skin cares!* Out loud, I stuck with the facts: the reality that Mom was sitting in the dayroom while her splint had been left behind in her room. The fact that I had found her sore arm wedged against the side of the wheelchair! The fact that her reddened ear indicated that she had been in her current position more than a very short time. The fact that there was no ice on her wrist. The facts.

Val deflected my concerns by turning the conversation another direction. "Your mom was very hard to dress this morning. She kept recoiling," she said as she placed the splint on Mom's arm.

Should I be surprised? Wouldn't you recoil if staff had broken your arm and you were in pain? "Judging by her injury, I'm not surprised!" was what I actually said.

I changed the subject by pointing out Mom's poor positioning as I retrieved the headrest lying on the chair next to the bed and inserted it into the metal receptacles on her wheelchair. Val pushed Mom out to the dining room and sought out another staff person to help her. She flagged William, and together they gently lifted Mom up and settled her squarely back into her chair. For the first time since I had arrived, a smile crossed my mother's face. It was intended for William, I suspected, one of the few morning staffers who without prompting routinely noticed and rectified Mom's need for repositioning. Mom trusted him. Yes, the smile was for him. I was sure of it.

Krista, concerned about her grandmother's injury, arrived to feed her Sunday dinner. Krista's presence was a glorious distraction for both Mom and me. She managed to cover her shock at the sight of the bruises, and the two of us carried on a light banter as Mom chewed a few bites.

Down in the parking lot, Krista expressed contempt for the care that produced her grandmother's injuries and pain. We parted, and I headed home to phone Mom's nurse practitioner to discuss the morning's incident. I talked instead with an on-call staff person and left my phone number.

• • •

AFTER LISTENING TO THE WEEK'S SAGA, MY FRIEND Cindy proposed suggestions. She recommended that I request a blood test to rule out medical reasons for my mother's bruising. She reminded me that along with the doctor and nurse practitioner, I was responsible for a vulnerable adult like my mother, and that included reporting injuries such as Mom's. Very important, she emphasized, was placing everything in writing.

So I returned to the computer. After the facts I added paragraphs of emotion, the sadness, anger, indignation, and despair over the injustices suffered by a helpless woman and my inability to protect her.

> *Again the care instructions and the care don't jive. The protocol guaranteed by nurse Kelly has become one more victim of weekend understaffing. No matter how vigilant I am, I fear I cannot prevent Mom from falling through the cracks again and again. But, I can document it all. And I do. I can report. And I will. But to whom?*

Evidence for All to See

On Monday, April 19, 2004, Tom checked Mom's bruises on his way to work and called to say that he had found her in the dayroom. Two and one-half hours later I arrived and located her in the same place. Thankfully, she had a splint in place and an icepack over her wrist. Hopefully she had been repositioned between our visits, but doubt crept into my psyche. I pushed her into the dining room and attempted to feed her lunch, but in an uncommon fashion she continuously pushed my hand, glass, and fork away. She accepted only her strawberry sauce and a few bites of bread, while her face expressed both pain and anxiousness. Mary's daughter Luann inquired about Mom's bruises, and loudly enough for the residents and staff at several tables to hear, she said, "I'd go right to the state!"

I wished I could find within me Luann's directness and mental strength. What was governing me? My distaste for confrontation or my belief that diplomacy trumps force? How could I best use my mental anguish to turn heads, put people on alert and demand accountability for my mother's care? Wasn't it better to start right here with the powers that be, rather than skirt them entirely and report to the state? Staring down at the black and blue marks, the earliest ones starting to turn a greenish yellow around the edges, I gathered strength.

With resolve I returned Mom to her room for her afternoon nap and set out to find Nicole and report the weekend breaches. Her office was empty, and I realized that I had not seen her on the floor since I had arrived. Mondays had to be terrible for her. How many "problems" arose over the weekends, when staffing was at its lowest, then landed on her desk to be dealt with on Monday morning?

How many nursing home deaths occur during the weekends? The question haunted me as I sadly recalled that my father died during a Saturday night shift in a nursing home just down the road. "There are no end signs," the nurse had said, but her shift ended, and he died less than three hours later. I never asked for more information. I trusted that he had just decided to leave us. *Why hadn't I asked for details? Had someone been monitoring him? Who found him? Did he depress a call button for help? Did anyone come? Why didn't I demand to know it all? Because I trusted. I don't anymore. How many nursing home deaths occur between Friday night and Monday morning? Has anyone studied this? Will Mom die on a weekend? I am so sorry, Dad.*

The questions swirled in a vortex of emotion as the elevator delivered me down to the basement, to the laundry room where I unsuccessfully searched through unclaimed items for a missing pink nightgown that had disappeared from Mom's closet. When I returned to first floor, the door opened and standing on the other side was third-floor clinical coordinator Nicole along with Kate, another member of Mom's care team. IT WAS TIME TO REPORT, so I requested a few moments of their time. When Nicole asked how things were going, I shook my head. Quickly, she cornered social worker Eleanor and together the four of us sought out an empty room for a makeshift conference.

With newfound conviction I spilled it all by reminding them of the facts: that a week earlier I had received three separate phone calls each announcing new bruises, yet saw no effort to pinpoint and correct the caregiver responsible until a broken bone occurred; that I had to be the one to insist the arm be X-rayed even though two nurses had looked at the bruised and swollen injury and decided to cover it with gauze. I summarized the disaster of waiting three days for the X-ray to be read, and the lack of follow-through with the protocol, causing pain and possible re-injury.

I asked them if they would be comfortable with this standard of care for someone that they loved. I poured out tear-laced anger at a system that failed at so many junctures. I pleaded with them to help me protect my mother, to be the ones to spot the deficiencies before I needed to report. I explained how I hated to be put in that position over and over, since it had been my experience that whistleblowers were not treated very nicely at North.

Then I listened. Nicole emotionally apologized for lack of follow-through from the staff and assured me that staff members responsible for

Sunday's failure to follow doctor's orders would be written up. She was clearly upset at the breach. She would place a call for a new X-ray and communicate the results. She offered to ask weekend supervisors to check in on Mom in the future. Eleanor encouraged me, for the sake of all the residents, to continue to report problems. Kate followed me out of the meeting and offered me words of encouragement.

Again, I heard all the right things. But, to write up staff member was one thing; to change behaviors was something quite different. Yet, Nicole, who was ultimately responsible for the care received by the residents of third floor, impressed me. The bar she set for quality care was high, and she took the staff delinquencies personally. Monday had been a stressful day for both of us, and for Nicole it was not over. True to her word she checked on the X-rays and called at 6:30 p.m. and reported to Tom the findings of two doctors at Regions Hospital: no acute fracture; evidence of hairline fracture; will treat as sprain or trauma and continue with splint, icing and Tylenol. We moved forward.

I called Zippy with the update. She related her conversation earlier in the day with an aide on Mom's floor. The aide had heard that the family was upset. Zippy responded, "It is not the family who should have to complain; the handprints are there as evidence for all to see."

Again I left a message for Mom's nurse practitioner, who returned my call a little over an hour later. She informed me that she had seen only the first and smallest bruise but that she had been informed of them all, including the last and most severe. Then I heard a curious and unsettling remark: "Some aides just don't realize how fragile the elderly can be."

The nurse practitioner had been informed about the lapse in protocol regarding the splint, and she agreed to order a blood test to rule out other possible causes for bleeding/bruising. She explained that anxiety might now be part of the disease process and suggested that Mom receive Ativan. The side effects would be drowsiness, she explained.

Mom was exhibiting anxiety, but I questioned the source. Did it stem from the disease process or, more likely, her most recent care-related injury? Either way, medication was prescribed, and I lobbied for the smallest dosage possible and for monitoring to see if it worked and was necessary.

The conversation concluded. I hung up the phone. Once more tears flowed. Not in anger and frustration this time, but in gut wrenching sorrow. Mom's disease had stolen her voice, and now reckless care providers had stolen her smile.

Autumn 2004

We passed the two-year anniversary of Mom's arrival at Riverside North. Many nursing home residents expire by the end of their second year, if not their first, but Mom was hanging in. We were three years beyond a doctor's declaration of "end stage" Alzheimer's/dementia to describe Mom's position on the continuum of this disease. In 2001, I gasped at the "end stage" description and feared that Mom would be leaving us at any moment. But, that was thirty-six months ago, and all things considered, she seemed quite stable to me. Angie was my barometer. Since she saw her grandmother intermittently when she returned to Minnesota for an occasional holiday, she was more aware of the subtle changes that went undetected by me during my daily visits. Her latest evaluation was hopeful: Grandma appeared comfortable with her circumstances.

We were enjoying a plateau, of sorts.

Sadly, Nicole, the most effective third-floor clinical coordinator to date, left. Over the summer I had watched her direct third floor with the best of intentions and genuine compassion. Unfortunately, she would not be returning. Val, Nicole's replacement, was the nurse who had been responsible for Mom's care on the Sunday morning when correct protocol had not been followed for her injured wrist. She became the fifth nurse in this role.

September 10, 2004

Moving forward.

I can forgive the TMA for forcing Mom's arm into her nightgown in such a manner as to create injury. I have not arrived at a place where I can forgive her for not reporting the injury once it happened (so immediate steps could be taken to reduce the swelling and pain).

I can forgive the third-floor staff for the breach in protocol on an understaffed Sunday morning when they tended to other residents and forgot about Mom. I am not able to forgive a system that considers weekend staff reduction acceptable and humane. The needs of sixty residents do not shrink on weekends. Who really believes that weekend staff/resident ratios are adequate? The nursing home administrators? The state? The federal government?

...

MOM'S CARE HAD IMPROVED. Our good fortune could be summed up in one person: James. James, a strong, friendly, competent young man from Liberia, had been assigned to work with Mom as her designated morning aide. Perhaps having him assigned to her was grease for the squeaky wheel, because James was wonderful. I definitely believed that Mom was blessed to have his assistance five days a week during the a.m. shift. He was the one who readied Mom every morning, who dressed her, changed her and monitored her needs both inside and outside of her room. He approached her with a smile, and she lit up in response to his friendly, non-patronizing style. Most importantly, he knew her. He knew she did not suffer from any degree of hearing loss so spoke to her accordingly. He knew how to use his strength gently while dressing her, and as a result she relaxed in his care. He recognized subtle clues to her daily condition. He advocated for her with the staff. My entire family grew to love and appreciate him. And, he was the reason, along with Jeanine, Mom's p.m. aide, that I did not seek out another nursing home for my mother.

Zippy graduated from nursing training, and I joyously attended both her pinning ceremony and graduation. For Zippy her licensed practical nursing status was a steppingstone, and she immediately enrolled in a nursing program at Century College that ultimately, once boards were passed, would certify her as a registered nurse. Although she juggled a nursing job with classes and schoolwork, she did not forget Mom, her friend, and often popped in to assist with a meal or to simply enrich the day with a laughter-filled visit.

Yet, often Zippy was not treated with the respect that other visitors received. One afternoon while she and I were visiting with Mom in her room, a staff member barged in and summoned Zippy.

"You're needed down the hall," the woman said.

"Zippy doesn't work here," I responded.

Stunned, the woman offered a quick apology and left.

"It's okay, Jackie," Zippy said, responding to my groan of disappointment.

"No, it is not okay," I replied.

"Please consider Zippy a member of the family," I explained to my mother's care team during a care conference, but the message was never relayed. After the director of nursing ordered Zippy to feed a second resident while she was visiting my mother, my daily journal entry included: *Can't my mother have a young, Black friend without staff members making racial assumptions that she must be either one of the nursing assistants or a care attendant hired by the family?*

Fall semester began, and I returned to a schedule of visiting Mom directly after the conclusion of my morning teaching responsibilities at Irondale High School. I knew I should vary the time of day that I checked in on Mom, but the noontime schedule allowed me to feed her dinner, the largest meal of the day.

Often Luann arrived to assist her mother, Mary, and at least once a week Brenda, Esther's daughter, arrived with a special takeout meal for the entire table. Sometimes it was Kentucky Fried Chicken or burritos from Taco John's or spaghetti and meatballs from a nearby restaurant. Each week a different tablemate chose the meal, and when it was Mom's turn, Brenda arrived with Mom's favorites, cheeseburgers and chocolate shakes. I had learned that survival (mental and physical of both resident and family) required sticking together. On the days when Brenda did not visit, I positioned my chair between Mom and Esther and fed them both. When responsibilities at school altered my schedule, Brenda often returned the favor.

Occasionally, I varied my routine and arrived at suppertime. In many ways dusk at North brought a peaceful ambiance. The remaining staff members appeared relaxed and jovial, but their reduction in number also raised my antenna. I asked Pearl and Mary about my mother's food intake at suppertime, and their answer was disconcerting. Mom's ingestion correlated with the conscientiousness of the staff person feeding her. Sometimes she ate well; sometimes only feeble attempts at feeding were made before her meal was concluded. In addition, because of staff shortages, weekends were still high-alert times, especially when James or Jeanine were not scheduled.

No matter what time of day I stepped off the elevator onto third floor, my arrival set off a predictable reaction from staff. Many staff members had become trusted friends, especially those who worked most closely with Mom. They greeted me cordially and continued on with their tasks. Others, judging by their abrupt changes in behavior once they spotted me, aroused my suspicion that the staff grapevine has labeled me *whistleblower*, someone out to catch them slacking. Others ignored me completely and gossiped within my hearing, unaware that their complaints about residents and other staff members demolished the trust level that I was wishing to rebuild.

I hated that my presence in the dayroom abruptly prompted nearby staff to notice for the first time that Mom was slumped over the side of her chair. Many days all it took for her to get repositioned was for me to step off the elevator and turn the corner. Eyes spotted me and then searched for Mom, and if she was lopsided, staff ran to assist her. I was willing to live with whatever label was circulated by uncomfortable staff if it improved my mother's care, but I often wondered how long Mom would have waited if I hadn't made an appearance. Furthermore, I had serious concerns regarding residents who had no visitors at all.

Hearing a nurse direct a staff member to "find [so-and-so's] hearing aides" because "her son is visiting soon" was disconcerting to say the least, along with comments that led me to believe that attempting to feed reluctant residents was important for the simple reason that documentation of said attempt was required for reimbursement. Where did concern for the resident's wellbeing rank? I tried to close my ears and focus on Mom's care, while I reminded myself that I had no business with the care of other residents. Turning a deaf ear and a blind eye, characteristics I loathed in the least impressive staffers, were now required of me. So, I chose my battles carefully until an unanswered alarm got the best of me, and I headed down the hall looking for assistance for one of Mom's neighbors.

I summed up fall 2004 in my journal:

> . . . a stable time, a time for reflection, a time free from crisis, a time to be grateful for the good things that North offers. I am thankful for James, Jeanine and many other aides whose pay checks hardly reflect their worth; the occupation therapist who continually adapts Mom's wheelchair so she can sit as comfortably as possible; the kitchen staff that prepare comfort food from recipes popular with the elderly (and the best potato salad I have ever tasted); a music therapist who looks directly into Mom's eyes when she sings to her; a custodian who wears with pride the native garb of his African homeland as he scours out toilets and mops the floors; a recreational therapist whose one-on-one interaction with residents and families builds bridges of understanding; a receptionist who spends endless hours of her free time changing the décor from season to season because she understands the importance of bringing a feeling of "home" to an institution.
>
> Mom continues on her journey. I enjoy the evenness of Mom's latest plateau. One day at a time—for her and for those that love her.

Christmas 2004

WHEN CRISES ARRIVE, SURVIVAL MODE KICKS IN, and one becomes totally immersed in the situation at hand. When crises are replaced with quiet, peaceful times, one's mind often resurrects thoughts that have been temporarily submerged by more pressing demands.

During the relatively tranquil fall of 2004, one such reflection bubbled to the surface. No longer was I able to ignore the simple fact that I had become the sole inheritor of Mom and Dad's life story. Thanks to my woefully incomplete memory bank, their tale could not be accurately passed on without considerable research. Where did all those towns fit in the chronology of Mom's life? All those "M's": Murdo, Milroy, Madison, Montevideo, Milbank. She had explained her family's relocations from one small South Dakota or Minnesota town to another numerous times, but now they melded together in pockets of my inattentive mind. Dad's physical locations were easier to reconstruct, yet the details of his life's work as teacher and coach and his subsequent positions with the Department of Corrections remained hazy.

With Dad gone and Mom's stories locked behind a wall of dementia, I headed to the basement in search of information. Within dusty boxes of memorabilia, documentation of their lives was scattered like odd-shaped pieces of a jigsaw puzzle. One thing became certain the moment I hauled the boxes upstairs and began culling through them: the pieces were here in various forms—newspaper clippings, photographs, business cards, yearbooks, scripts and playbills, obituaries, Naval papers, real estate deeds. My task would be fitting them together, completing the puzzle without the benefit of a box top photo.

Thankfully, I had at my disposal one priceless addition, a tape recorded in 1997. One evening in a hotel room in Rochester, during one of Dad's three-day evaluations at the Mayo Clinic, I gathered my parents around a small table and pushed the record button on my mini-tape recorder. I asked questions about their lives, bits and pieces, hit and miss. Dad's responses were slow, deliberate, articulate and punctuated with wry humor. Mom's, on the other hand, provided sad clues that memory retrieval was already affected by the early onset of a disease we were trying so hard to deny.

"Help me, Warren! What is the name of that town? I know it as well as my own name," she said, when I asked her which "M" town was the home of her birth.

"Murdo," he replied.

"Of course, Murdo," she repeated and then gave a few passing comments about this little town in South Dakota, before trying and failing to give me an accurate chronology of her early moves throughout that state and into Minnesota.

As the tape continued, Mom's brain warmed up. She never initiated a story, but she jumped in to contradict her husband, or to add a retort as he told one story after another.

I prompted him to tell a story I was very familiar with, just to hear him tell it. We laughed as he related the time as teenagers he and his brother Wayne unloaded watermelons from a train.

"I'd pick a rotten one, a real juicy, heavy one, and heave it off to Wayne. He'd stick his arms up to catch it, and his fist would go right through it, bathing him in watermelon juice."

"That's terrible," replied Mom, with a laugh that contradicted her comment.

Listening to the tape dissolved me emotionally. Hearing their voices. Missing their banter with each other. Missing them, period.

Like a sleuth I investigated the intriguing contents of the boxes of memorabilia. I read each written word, trimmed photographs, photocopied everything and filed each piece into file folders organized into each stage of my parents' lives.

I discarded the idea of making scrapbooks with permanent pages and instead bought four easily expandable three-ring notebooks, one for each of the grandchildren and one for myself. Systematically in chronological order I retrieved a file folder, reviewed its contents, wrote a narrative about that period of Mom's or Dad's life and followed the written piece with photocopies of pictures, clippings or whatever tidbits I could find that related to that period. The process soothed my soul.

The story began simply:

> In 1917, President Woodrow Wilson signed into law the Selective Draft Act, Chicago captured the World Series, a gallon of gas cost $.08 and the average new home was valued at $5,520. But most importantly, two very special people, Warren Thomas Johnson and Ernestine Ellen Young, were born. And they were destined to meet, fall in love, marry, raise a family and welcome grandchildren.

Their childhoods, the story of their first meeting in a sweet shop on a Friday night, their college years together, their wedding and married life, World War II separation, movements from town to town and job to job, children, grandchildren—in each three-ring notebook I included all I had learned and tucked away each page into an archival-quality plastic sleeve. The time-consuming process was strangely energizing as the puzzle took shape. Finally, I concluded each book with the tributes that Tom, each grandchild and I delivered at Dad's memorial service.

Finally, my parents' story was as complete as I could make it. With relief and excited anticipation I placed my book in the living room bookcase right next to the family Bible and family photo albums and wrapped the other three and placed them under the Christmas tree.

On Christmas Eve, with Mom in attendance, our small family gathered. Clay and Becky, Krista and Steve (now an engaged couple), Angie, Tom and I enjoyed an early evening celebration. After a traditional dinner of oyster stew and egg drop soup, Swedish meatballs and sausage, riced potatoes, scalloped corn and other accompaniments, we moved from the dining room to the four-season porch to exchange gifts. Last to be opened were the books for Clay, Krista and Angie. After a few quiet moments while the inscriptions were read and the reality of what they were holding sank in, the contents came to life as the pages were turned.

"Grandpa and Uncle Wayne played basketball together in the state tournament," Clay commented with surprise when he discovered their newspaper photos among the sibling groups who played in the 1933 Minnesota State Basketball Tourney. He read aloud bits of the coverage of Montevideo High School's first round victory over Rochester and their later elimination by the North High School Polars.

"Listen to this," he added as he focused on a headline from an opponent's home town newspaper dated 1935. "'Too Much Warren Johnson Is Story at Montevideo: Bob Wasgatt's Lanky Center Controls the Whole Show . . . A towering string bean,'" he read with a flourish, "'from the home of mighty athletic heroes was a little too much for Willmar's classy Cardinals in the Montevideo armory last night . . .'" His melodramatic flair of the article's text brought to life a game that had occurred seventy years earlier.

Paging through her book Krista read about the exploits of her grandmother during her college years. Programs, reviews, and photos gave evidence to her involvement in the Hamline Players. She looked over at her grandmother. "Hey, Grandma, you were quite the star," she commented, as she perused a program and discovered that her grandmother had played the title role of Miss Lulu Bett. Grandma smiled. "You did radio skits, too, on KSTP, no less." More smiles.

The books in the grandchildren's laps told complete life stories of both of their grandparents, minus one final, yet-to-be-scripted chapter for Mom. I

1938 - Teen on opening night at Hamline.

relaxed, relieved that the puzzle had been completed, the story had been told and the heritage passed on.

Shortly after Mom was collected for her return trip to the nursing home, Angie spotted probably the shortest newspaper clipping in the entire history. The Murdo paper reported on the success of one of its townspeople, her grandmother, who had recently moved to Milbank and had won first place in the humorous division of a declamation contest. Enjoying the homey style of small-town journalism, Angie read the last sentence of the piece: "'She is a mighty fine little reader and has delighted many audiences in Murdo with her readings and we are not surprised to note that she is in demand on programs at Milbank.'"

Her grandma had loved humorous recitation, acting on the stage and performing on the radio. No wonder her bedtime stories were memorable. Sadly, dementia had replaced that expressive voice with silence.

And, for her family that silence was deafening.

Falling Off Yet Another Plateau

Mid-January brought not only closure of first semester, but also, under my present teaching contract, the conclusion of my teaching responsibilities for the school year. Increased free time and the anticipation of an upcoming family vacation should have brightened my spirit, but a change in Mom's condition dampened my enthusiasm.

Clearly, Mom had slipped off her plateau and had dropped a notch or more in her disease process. Reoccurring urinary tract infections had plagued her since October. First indications were lethargy and my sense that "something just wasn't right." Since both Mom and Dad had been treated for this insidious ailment during their stay in assisted living, I was already aware of the peculiar effects of UTI's on the elderly. Before then I had no understanding of the strange power that such an infection had on mental functioning and general health. So, when Mom's nurse suggested that she be tested for a UTI, I quickly agreed. A urine sample was taken, and sure enough, it tested positive. A course of antibiotics followed. A month later Mom's lethargy and discomfort continued, and I requested another test. The nurse on duty assured me that Mom had already been treated for the infection.

"What your Mom is exhibiting," she explained, "I often see in residents right before their monthly B-12 shots. She is scheduled for her shot in a few days, and I'm sure once she gets it, she'll perk up."

"I'd like another urinalysis just to make sure that the infection has cleared," I pressed.

"To do that we have to catheterize your mother, you know, and we don't like to put her through that unnecessarily."

"I realize that," I responded, "but she appears so uncomfortable."

I wanted the nurse to be right. Plus, I hated to subject my mother to catheterization. However, Mom's demeanor nudged me past the point of feeling guilty for the request. The conversation ended with the decision to repeat the urinalysis.

I received a call the following day from another nurse, who obviously hadn't talked to the preceding one, because she started the conversation with, "Jackie, you won't believe this, but your mom has another UTI."

Thus began a sickening repetition.

Another course of antibiotics.

Another month. No change.

Another request by me for a urinalysis. More hesitation.

Another UTI confirmation.

"Duh!" I wanted to say in the vernacular of my high school students when I received the call from still another nurse who acted surprised.

I asked questions. I researched and found two common causes for urinary tract infections: a hygiene problem caused by inattention to perineal care and a lack of fluid intake necessary to flush bacteria out of the body. Staff ruled out a hygiene problem after observing my mother's cares. "Push fluids" was added to her care plan. Still more antibiotics were ordered.

It was mid-January, and the problem still persisted. Tom and I were scheduled to leave on vacation, and Mom continued to appear lethargic and uncomfortable. Additionally, Mary and Esther had deteriorated, and both had been placed on *comfort care*. The reality of this term failed to fully register.

I spoke with Val, the third-floor clinical coordinator, who assured me that Mom would be monitored closely while I was gone. Julie, the community coordinator, shared her email address, so we could keep in touch via email. Kate, the recreational therapist, was scheduled to feed Mom her weekday noon meal in my absence. Krista and Zippy promised to be regular visitors. Everything was in place. We packed our bags, and Tom and I with friends Lyn and Warren flew off to sunny Maui to spend some relaxing time in the same condo in Kihei that had often housed my parents during their holidays.

Shortly into the vacation the phone rang. On the other end of the line a nurse at Riverside North informed me that the pharmacy refused to send over the latest antibiotics until the pharmacist personally received assurance from me that the family intended to pay the $1,702.41 bill for twenty-eight Zyvox/Linezolid tablets that were not covered by my mother's insurance. I was sticker shocked. This was the first expensive medication that Mom had ever required. I asked questions and discovered that she had become antibiotic resistant from attempts to treat her with antibiotics that were not good matches for the bacteria that she was fighting. Immediately my mind rewound to the year 2000 to a hospital in Baltimore. I watched as doctors adjusted medications until a good match was found to quell Angie's blood infection. Then, a crisis had been averted within a week. Mom's situation had dragged on for months. I called the pharmacist and assured him that the family would pay for the medication, and I pleaded with him to send it over to the nursing home as quickly as possible.

The medicine proved powerful. Emails with Julie and Krista confirmed that it had wiped out good as well as bad bacteria, and Mom now suffered from a case of thrush that filled her mouth with sores. Adding yogurt to each meal to help restore the positive bacteria was added to Mom's care plan. I relaxed knowing that when Kate, Krista, and Zippy fed Mom, her menu would be supplemented with yogurt, cooling ice cream, and plenty of fluids. But, would aides unfamiliar with Mom and her condition understand the importance of yogurt? If she balked when spices and textures lodged in the cankers in her mouth would they substitute soothing foods and encourage her to eat? Would they be patient enough to give her the time she needed to down glasses of water and cranberry juice?

Long-distance worrying was nonproductive, yet I found it almost impossible to unwind in a carefree way. Relaxing vacations were now fitfully elusive, even in the most beautiful, tropical settings.

Perhaps after years of advocating for Mom I know too much about the realities of nursing home care. Living in a state of denial of these realities was tempting, a mental luxury, of sorts. Perhaps that explained why so many families were able to deposit their loved ones in nursing homes and simply walk away.

The State Visit

PERHAPS MY ANXIETY OVER LEAVING MOM would have been alleviated a bit if I had been aware that on January 25, the same morning that Tom and I boarded a plane and left Riverside North behind, surveyors from the Minnesota Department of Health arrived on its doorstep for a recertification evaluation. Had I known about their visit, I might have relaxed in the knowledge that during the days of the survey there was a greater likelihood that Mom would be fed conscientiously and her care plan would be followed to the letter. How had I arrived at this understanding? Because, it was not hard for a regular visitor to the nursing home to detect the increased activity in the building once the surveyors arrived with pens and clipboards.

I recalled my initial reaction two years earlier. I arrived at noon to find Mom at her dining table, but before I could sit down next to her, I needed to drag a chair from the dayroom. Where were all the vacant chairs that usually inhabited the dining room? Then I looked around and formulated a more pertinent question: Who were all these additional people sitting around the tables assisting residents with their noon meal?

"The state is here," Luann whispered as she doctored her mother's baked potato.

I looked around. Had an alarm sounded, coaxing administrators and other personnel out of their offices and up to third floor to assist with feeding? People I rarely, if ever, saw during my daily visits at noontime were conscientiously aiding uncharacteristically happy residents, who like Mom had lost their ability or inclination to raise a forkful of meatloaf from plate to mouth. The dining room was alive with chatter and chewing. One huge family.

"Wow, wouldn't be great if all these people showed up everyday?" I asked enjoying the new ambiance.

"Especially on weekends," added Mary, with a wry smile.

"Doesn't this facility have to carry on 'as usual' for the state?" I asked.

The answer flashed non-verbally, from faces around the table whose rolling eyes and skewered smiles communicated simple messages: "Are you kidding?" and "How naïve are you?"

The sad reality was that Riverside North was opting for appearance over an ethical representation of everyday life. *I guess one always puts on one's best face for company.*

I looked at Mom, totally oblivious to the flurry of activity around her, and remembered an exchange between us when I was about ten.

"Mom, why do you have to clean the house every Friday?" I asked after I arrived home from school to find our small house spotless and the living room furniture rearranged.

"Because it needs it," she replied simply. "And if I clean a different room really well each week and do a spiff on the others, cleaning isn't a chore. Besides, I like to clean. And I love a clean house."

"I don't like to clean much," I replied and then added in simplistic fashion, "when I have my own house, I'm only cleaning for company."

"I want our home to be clean for the most important people," she said, with emphasis on the word *most*.

"Who?" I asked.

"You," she said with a wink. "And your dad and brother, too."

As I sat next to Mom in the crowded dining room, I wished that North considered the residents the most important people.

...

WE RETURNED FROM OUR HAWAII TRIP, but I couldn't ask Mary to tell me about the state's January visit. Both she and Esther had passed away while Tom and I vacationed. Now two new residents occupied their places around Mom's table. With each death, life in the nursing home continued, as new residents filled vacated rooms and dining room spaces.

The absence of these dear friends staggered me. Did Mom understand this finality? Pearl, Mom's other surviving tablemate, definitely did. Mary, her dearest friend and confidante, was gone. For years Mary and Pearl had been soldiers on the same side, sharing each other's hardships and advocating as best they could for their other tablemates, Esther and Mom. I missed Mary's entertaining, often irreverent mealtime repartee. And Esther, the quiet and sleepy one, no longer needed my assistance at mealtime. Besides Mary and Esther I missed Luann and Brenda who had become my compatriots in the mother-advocacy business. Four missing faces around Mom's dining table. Two silenced voices. Death. Sadness. Loss.

Every three months or so, a service was held to memorialize those on the floor who had passed, and I attended the one that honored Mary and Esther along with other deceased third-floor residents. Although there was a beautiful chapel connected by hallways to the facility, the memorial service was held on third floor in the cluttered dayroom with people meandering in and out. During the service a candle was lit for each deceased resident as he or she was memorialized, but sadly, the chaplain referred to Esther as "Emma" throughout a short eulogy in her honor. That evening I added reflections conjured by the day's event into my journal:

> When will Mom's third-floor service be held? Will her name be remembered? For the first time I am seriously contemplating the minutes and days after Mom's heart stops beating. I have been so focused on advocating for her day-to-day needs that I haven't looked beyond. But today, after the finality of Esther and Mary's departure, the future occupies my thoughts. Mom is dying—slowly. And when that last breath is taken, her family will reclaim all that her disease has taken away from her. I don't know the details of her memorial, but I do know that her service at Peace United Methodist Church will be a celebration of the wonderfully witty and wise woman, so loved by so many.
>
> And, our family's attendance at the inevitable third-floor memorial service will be only a formality.

Focus and Priorities

"FOCUS AND PRIORITIES." Tom's ability to succinctly reduce my nebulous, circular thought pattern to two key words was both exasperating and helpful. Exasperating, because I wished that I had that skill. Helpful, because I didn't.

As a result, Tom, for me, was the go-to guy when my thinking spun faster and faster and further and further down a grief-filled vortex of despair. Like an anchor he stabilized me during the stormy times, and with calmness and clarity he helped me make sense of the scattered debris left behind.

The evening's discussion with Tom centered on different aspects of the state's inspection of my mother's building: the necessity of the State Department of Health's oversight, the timing of the surveys, the procedures, and the availability and dissemination of the survey results. Definitely we had more questions than answers.

The appearance of additional staff in the dining room during the survey awakened emotions that prompted rhetorical questions: *Would "business as usual" on third floor really satisfy the state surveyors? I understood teamwork among staff, but didn't temporarily bumping up staffing during mealtimes cross an ethical line? Didn't this practice actually prove that normal staffing was inadequate at mealtimes? What would happen if the state arrived on a weekend to begin its inspection? Were Mom and the many other feeders on third floor receiving adequate help with their meals when the state was not around? Wasn't the label "feeder" dehumanizing in the first place? Did Mom drink enough fluids during night and weekend shifts when even fewer staff were available to assist? Will UTIs continue to haunt her if she doesn't? Will the next one kill her? Does no one else ask these questions? Am I insane?*

"Focus and priorities," Tom repeated, in succinct clarity honed by years in the business world. "It is all about the focus and priorities of those in charge. Is the focus on the residents and their best interest, first and above all? If staff's appearance at the dining room is an occasional occurrence that coincides with the state's inspection, then their first priority is appearance, not the feeding of residents. Running a nursing home is a business; reputation and financial repercussions, in this case, rank above honest portrayal of resident care."

"How can a corporation expand, build new facilities in other suburbs, and not adequately staff the ones they have?" I asked.

"They will say they adequately staff because they meet or surpass state guidelines even if their residents' needs are not being met. Plus, benefactors are interested in building new, not maintaining old."

"But they can't possibly feed everyone on third floor with the present weekend staffing."

"True, but it's a matter of focus and priorities. Theirs just don't match ours."

"They? Who are 'they'?" I spit out, and then realized for the first time I was using the term *they* in a derogatory, accusatory way, the adversary to *us*.

Exactly who were "they"? Not James or Jeanine, scores of other hardworking, underpaid nursing assistants with only two hands to care for Mom and all the others under their care. Not the many nurses who brought to their workplace a desire to do their best and work tirelessly toward that end. Not the third-floor staffers who tackled the job of being on the frontline with each resident, all sixty of them! Not even the less conscientious nursing assistants and nurses who exhibited mild to serious degrees of burnout that at times frustratingly manifested itself in blindness and insensitivity. As a classroom teacher in public education with growing class sizes and shrinking educational funding, I empathized with those in the trenches.

No, "they" were ambiguous. The head administrator during the poison pen fiasco had moved on. As yet, I had no face for her replacement, or the other building administrators, the corporate office people, or the board of directors. Who were these people? If I knew them and could talk to them, would I be sympathetic to their efforts to balance the care of the residents with the financial reality?

By the end of the evening's discussion Tom's rational approach had helped to quiet the tornadic activity in my brain and heart. I found in the rubble two valuable determinations.

First, I would put faces on the administrators in the building.

Second, I would research the Department of Health website and find out all I could about nursing home surveys.

Third-Floor
Family Meetings

I WAS EXCITED. AS IF ON CUE, I RECEIVED NOTICE that a new layer of communication with families had been added. As a family member/resident representative I received an invitation to a third-floor family meeting, the first of what was to become a monthly gathering. One purpose of the meeting was to meet the new administrator of the building, Beverly Pierce. I loved her already, simply because she was reaching out to the families and establishing a communication link.

In a conference room with circled tables, the meeting began with welcoming remarks from the third-floor staff. Next, the chief administrator was introduced. Inviting the attendees to call her by her first name, Beverly spoke of her gratitude and enthusiasm for being named head of the "Cadillac of nursing homes," her description of Riverside North. She then articulated her focus: providing great care for our loved ones. Music to my ears! She followed with an agenda that included general information as well as an announcement that the building was about to enter an expansion phase, details to be forthcoming at subsequent meetings.

About ten third-floor residents were represented by attendees, and we listened attentively as we munched on goodies. Although I often exchanged greetings with many of these people in the hallways, the gathering was my first opportunity to sit down and converse. The barrier of isolation quickly lifted as we shared common concerns for our loved ones.

A time for questions followed the prepared agenda, and I settled in and listened. The opening questions related to the upcoming building renovation and construction. But, as the Q and A session progressed, several people described lapses in their family member's basic care. Although it was somewhat comforting to hear that ours was not the only family with care issues, the universality of some concerns disturbed me. Several people referred to the long waits before call lights were answered, causing exasperated residents to attempt bathroom trips unassisted.

One person voiced concerns about slow responses during medical emergencies.

My thoughts turned to Mom, who had never been able to activate the call light above her door. Did overworked aides attend to her on time, especially considering that their only reminder was written in her care plan, a folded sheet of paper that ended up in a pocket?

Understaffing in the dining room during mealtimes was another common thread of concern. Silent until now, I added my thoughts to this discussion by explaining my concern about understaffing and its effect on those needing assistance at mealtimes. The new administrator assured the group that this concern was being addressed.

Surfacing next were issues with laundry services and menus followed by scary problems involving medication. I continued to listen, thankful that Mom's prescription medication now only amounted to Prevident toothpaste and Ativan before her weekly bath.

What astounded me was the degree of pent up frustration that had been uncorked among this small, friendly group of family members. Pressure obviously had been building for others, too. The meeting continued until everyone had received a chance to air concerns. Finally, after listening to them all, Beverly Pierce responded.

"Even the Cadillac of nursing homes can have a flat tire once in a while," she said, after thanking family members for sharing their concerns. She guaranteed that each issue would be addressed and then concluded the meeting. After the family members exited the conference room, the door was closed, and the third-floor staffers remained behind with their new head administrator.

"Oh, dear," was what our sideways glances said to one another as we continued down the hall, realizing that the "meeting after the meeting" was underway. The buck was on the move and looking for a stopping spot for each of our categories of concern.

I left the building grateful for the sign that someone outside of third floor was interested in the families' input. I hoped that the chief administrator would become personally accountable for what happened to our loved ones and not just toss the buck back to the staff on third floor.

...

ANOTHER MONTH, ANOTHER THIRD-FLOOR FAMILY MEETING. This time I attended with a request in mind. Considering the likely connection between the onset of my mother's UTI's, her inability to request water, and understaffing in the dining room, I intended to request that Mom's fluid intake be monitored for a while. Had all the staff received the care plan's message about the importance of fluids in Mom's diet? My intention was to find out.

Prepping myself for the next meeting, I gathered information from my trusty spy, Pearl, Mom's mentally sharp, verbally skilled, and compassionately astute tablemate. Pearl had become Mom's advocate, and now with Esther and Mary gone, she focused on my mother during mealtimes. Pearl was not shy about informing whomever had been assigned to feed Mom that yes, now that her case of thrush had healed, my mother did eat all foods except sauerkraut; yes, she did like to chew her food thoroughly so be patient; and yes, a straw helped. Furthermore, Teen would drink all her fluids if she was given time.

According to Pearl, Mom's food and beverage intake during supper and weekends directly correlated with the conscientiousness of the staff person doing the feeding. Reality, however, was not always comforting. Too often, she informed me, a staff person aborted his or her feeding responsibility before Mom, the slowest of all chewers, completed her meal and drinks.

Third-floor families and staff gathered once more in the same conference room on first floor. Perhaps word of this opportunity had spread because several more family members/representatives took seats around the circle. Soon it became obvious that Beverly Pierce would not be attending the meeting. In her place was the facility's director of nursing, and he offered a few remarks about the changing responsibilities of the nursing staff. Instead of TMAs, nurses would be dispensing all medication, he informed us. According to him med-passing by nurses would promote more interaction between the nurses and residents. TMA positions would be eliminated, and job shifting would occur.

"How can nurses dispense meds at mealtimes and feed residents at the same time? Won't this change create more understaffing in the dining room?" someone asked before I had a chance.

The director responded with a series of explanations and pleas: We have many residents needing feeding on third floor right now and that reality is throwing off the schedule. We are looking for more people to help feed. We ask for your patience.

What was I hearing? A month had passed since Beverly told us they were working on dining room staffing, and we were still talking about unresolved issues of feeding residents? *Ask me to be patient for maintenance repairs to be made to Mom's room, and I will not complain. Ask me to walk flights of stairs when the elevator malfunctions, and I won't bat an eye. But don't ask for patience when understaffing in the dining room results in rushed meals, tepid food, or an aborted attempt to feed when my dementia-stricken mother appears disinterested.* Temporarily I kept my comments to myself and looked for an opportunity to address my issues regarding feeding and liquid intake.

The director blamed governmental underfunding as a prime culprit for understaffing. Unasked questions swirled in my brain. *What about the $6,000 we are paying monthly? Doesn't that guarantee that three meals a day will be fed to my mother? Even if she were on government assistance, shouldn't she have the right to be fed? What is wrong with a system that can't guarantee this simple act of human decency?*

Finally, I asked my first and what turned out to be my last question.

"I'm concerned about my mother's reoccurring UTIs," I began. "Since there is a correlation between this type of infection and lack of fluid intake, would it be possible to find out how much fluid she's actually drinking during the course of a day?" Before I could express my concern further, I was interrupted.

The director jumped in like a superhero thrusting himself between his overworked nurses and me. "If we had our nurses recording everyone's fluid intake all day long, they wouldn't get anything else done," he responded with a tone of indignation at my presumptuousness.

Question answered. Case closed. Subject, and me, dismissed.

Stunned, I sat in silence like a scolded child, while another question carried the discussion off in another direction. The director's rude dismissal of my question sickened me.

As the discussion in the room centered on food service issues, I held court with myself. If Mom were a diabetic, wouldn't a nurse monitor her diet and check her blood sugar? The director of nursing must know that in the case of any elderly person, a UTI could be not only discomforting, but also deadly, especially for someone like Mom who was now antibiotic resistant from repeated treatments. Yet, my request for monitoring fluid intake was considered ludicrous if I read his tone correctly. My mother was just one of over 200 needy residents in a building too large for individualized care. Without any attempt to understand her situation, he slammed the door on my request.

Even on an impersonal level, wasn't the director interested in investigating the cause of an infection that often directly related to the quality of care given to a resident? (Perhaps so many of the nursing home residents had UTIs that he envisioned his nursing staff swamped with calculations of CCs!)

As I listened to his responses to other questions, an image emerged, a man with only ten fingers, unsuccessfully attempting to plug holes in a leaky health care system from which quality care was gushing away. If I hadn't been so distressed, I would have smiled at the irony. He was trying desperately to keep erosion at bay, and I was trying just as desperately to exert pressure so water could come in—into Mom's body to wash out her infected system.

After the meeting Julie, the community coordinator, motivated perhaps by an understanding of Mom's treacherous battle with UTIs, caught up to me and assured me that the staff would push fluids. I appreciated her comment, but "push fluids" had been on Mom's care plan for months, even during the four-month bout of urinary tract infections last winter, her eventual MRSA (methicillin-resistant staphylococcus aureus) diagnosis (finally, a nurse has shared the paperwork with me), and her resulting $1,700 course of Linezolid. I did not believe that Mom would get the fluids that her body needed unless someone was required to document them. Furthermore, my first impressions of the new director of nursing were disappointing. He certainly was not the residents' knight in shining armor.

In the parking lot, I climbed into the van and stared at the peaceful pond twenty feet in front me. The serenity of the water disappeared. I saw nothing but memories of the Gardens, and the Meadows before that. What had happened to this health care system? The Meadows, the Gardens, Riverside North—all within a continuum of care provided by Riverside Homes. How could the resident-centered care, so natural so compassionate, so commonplace at the Meadows and the Gardens, dissipate so completely once Mom moved to her final home? Financial realities, not resident care, seemed to drive the nursing home system, and the director of nursing appeared to be caught in the middle. Yet, his abrupt, condescending tone removed any sympathy he might have garnered from me. Instead, I chastised myself for crumbling like a tea cookie when he discounted my request. Why hadn't I asked for clarification and demanded accountability?

However, this wasn't about an arrogant director of nursing or my cynical reaction to him. This was about the realization that Mom might not live through her next infection, and no one seemed willing to take simple steps to pinpoint the possible cause. Instead, I was smothered by a commonplace attitude: this was a nursing home; people died within its walls; that was what they did. It was not commonplace for me, however, to think of Mom as just another death around the corner.

Nor did I see the humor, a few days later, in a comment made by one of the third-floor nurses as she explained to me that nurses were not happy about having to dispense medication as the new protocol dictated.

"Many of the meds have to be passed at mealtime," she shared with me. "So we won't be available to feed residents like we did before. It will be awful on the weekends. The joke in the staff room is 'we better stuff the residents on Friday noon because they won't get much more to eat until Monday morning.'"

I was blown away. The horrible truth behind the joke was only worsened by the insensitivity of sharing it with me, a family member. It confirmed what I had suspected. Serious understaffing negatively affected the feeding of residents in the evenings and on weekends. And it also provided disconcerting hints regarding why Mom, who had a full set of teeth and an appetite of a lumberjack, was surprisingly given an occasion nutritional supplement in the form of a milky drink. Weight loss would indicate poor care. I wished the same concern was given to one of Mom's last remaining enjoyments in life: meals highlighted with fresh, crunchy vegetable salads, sweet desserts, and glasses of cranberry juice and water—simple, life-giving water.

The Ring

IF WEEKENDS WERE HIGH-ALERT TIMES due to understaffing, then holiday
weekends were even scarier. This became alarmingly clear on the morning
following Memorial Day 2005 as I glanced down at Mom's hands while I
fed her lunch. On the ring finger of her left hand sat her wedding band,
unaccompanied by the diamond engagement ring that for sixty-five years
had never left its side, until sometime recently. Frantic, I jumped out of
my chair and raced over to James who was feeding another resident at a
table on the other side of the dining room.

"James, Mom's engagement ring is not on her finger!"

James's response startled me and was the first clue that something
was definitely amiss. He jumped up, obviously agitated, and growled short
phrases like "not again . . . I told them . . ." Then he regained his composure
and turned his attention back to me and suggested that I check with Delores, Mom's nurse, to see if perhaps she had locked the ring away. I sought
out Delores, who checked the logical places for items that needed safekeeping. But the ring was nowhere, and we agreed to meet in Mom's room
and continue with our search after the residents had been fed.

Later, we tore the bed apart and searched through the sheets and
under the furniture. All the while I was trying to convince Delores that in
no way had my mother's ring accidentally fallen off her finger, thanks to
her enlarged knuckle. Zippy arrived and joined in the search, while Delores
continued to check off the list of other places where the ring may have disappeared, such as the tub room, even though Mom had not been given a
bath in several days.

Slowly and sadly I realized what I actually had known from the first
moment I saw the space on Mom's finger. Her engagement ring had not
come off accidentally. Unfortunately, the only way to guarantee her safety

and the security of her wedding band was to remove it and take it home. That thought broke my heart.

For two reasons I asked Delores to accomplish the task of removing the wedding band. The first was purely emotional. In no way could I separate my mother from something that connected her so deeply to my father. I could only hope that dementia had dulled her sentimentality. My second reason had ulterior motives. I wanted someone from the nursing home to experience the difficulty of removing a ring from my mother's finger.

Removal of the wedding band was not easily accomplished. After several attempts, much lubrication and turn after turn, finally, Delores with Zippy's help removed the wedding band and handed it to me. Delores' words, "No way could that ring have fallen off accidentally" were accompanied by "a police report will be filed."

The missing ring was beautiful, but in my heart I knew it was gone. Although not extravagant, it was priceless, a small diamond in an antique setting, purchased by my father in 1939 and given to my mother during their senior year at Hamline University. In fact, the eight-by-ten photograph that I chose to hang outside Mom's nursing home door pictured her and Dad at what Mom called "proposal rock" on campus shortly after she was given her special ring. The photo was taken for Hamline's newspaper, *The Oracle*, announcing the engagement of the class president of 1939 and the Winter Carnival queen. She was standing on top of the rock to bring her head closer to that of her tall, lanky fiancé.

She cherished her ring, and I could not recall a day when I had not seen it on her finger. Along with her wedding band, those two rings were the only pieces of valuable jewelry that accompanied her to the nursing home. Dementia or not, I held on to the hope that the rings brought her comfort and perhaps elusive memories of better times. Routinely I rolled them around her finger to check her skin underneath. Between two knuckles they moved easily on a segment of her finger that they had become permanently indented over the course of six and a half decades. During my checks, I confirmed that her aged and considerably larger middle knuckle continued to barricade the tiny size 4½ rings from accidentally slipping off.

I thought they were safe.

Delores's extensive efforts in removing the wedding band confirmed what I already knew. The ring had not accidentally "slipped" off Mom's finger and Mom, unable to use her opposite hand at all, was incapable of removing it. What did that leave?

I was stricken with a mixture of anger and sadness, and I found myself hoping that Mom's illness had progressed to the point that she did not understand the events that were taking place. I imagined her alone in her room, being victimized, not able to communicate. I feared for her. I feared for others on her floor, so many vulnerable people.

James was not the only person upset by the disappearance of Mom's ring. Val, the clinical coordinator, asked me to pinpoint the last time I had seen it. Was it on her finger yesterday? Could it have been gone and I didn't notice? I explained to Val that sometimes the stone turned to the inside so the ring wasn't always as noticeable. Why hadn't I paid attention yesterday?

"So the ring is loose," she said, latching onto my comment that the stone turned to the inside.

"No," I responded. " It moves around her finger, but her knuckle prevents it from sliding off. It couldn't just have slipped off. Ask Delores. She took off the matching band. She knows how difficult that was." I was upset. Babbling. "The last time I can remember specifically checking the ring was the end of last week. I was out of town over Memorial weekend and didn't visit on Saturday or Sunday."

She assured me that all staff who worked with Mom would be contacted to see if they could remember "seeing the ring."

Arriving home I called a pawnshop and asked about the procedure for pawning jewelry and how I might reclaim jewelry that had been stolen. After being told that a police report was required to recover stolen property, I called Val and confirmed that the police had been contacted. Then I recalled James's angry comments. Had other personal items disappeared recently?

Memorial Weekend, a holiday, a very costly holiday! We had lost a precious heirloom, but more critically, Mom's safety had been jeopardized.

Over the last three years I had intentionally shielded the grandchildren from many of the day-to-day disappointments and fears that I had experienced. However, this latest security breach in their grandmother's care called for family attention, and the troops were gathered.

It was my nephew Clay, a police officer, whom I called with concerns over the police report that I had picked up at the sheriff's department. Clay met me at North, and together we discussed the deputy's upsetting narrative:

> *Johnson is a residence of the home. Last week on a Wednesday or Thursday, she miss placed half of her wedding band. The half missing is gold with diamond chips. The other half still sits on her finger is the gold band. Nothing further was learned. The staff at the home has been checking into the loss.*

I was stunned, flabbergasted, angry. The rough report portrayed Mom as a senile, old lady who absentmindedly took off her own ring, wandered down the hall, and left it somewhere. That was the Mom of two years ago. Her disease had progressed well beyond those simple days when she was able to stroll around The Gardens, deposit her teddy bear in a planter and aimlessly walk away. Not one word was written in the report about Mom's current condition: that she was disabled to such a degree that she had all her cares performed by others, that she was no longer ambulatory, or that she was incapable of using her right hand to take the ring off of her left ring finger. Nowhere was there a mention of the difficulty a nurse had in removing the remaining ring.

Nothing further was learned? How could that be? Why were Delores's observations absent from the report?

Clay was unhappy with the report as well and suggested that I talk with the deputy in person and have it amended. He described the APS (automated pawn system) that matched people's names with their pawn activity and requested a list of names of people who were working at North over the weekend so they could be run through the system.

For Clay finding out who manhandled his grandmother was as important as finding the ring. He was as furious as he was sad, just like Mom's granddaughters when I communicated with each of them. "What is being done?" they both asked, and all I could say was that they were investigating. The family focused on common threads. Since the facts led us to believe that Mom, a vulnerable adult, had been victimized, we agreed that violations of human decency and the law had taken place.

The following day Val supplied a list of staff names as requested, but the list was of third-floor staffers only, and it was filled with misspellings and missing last names. When I asked for clarification, she appeared very distressed. She didn't know the last name of one temporary worker from an outside agency. I cleaned up the list of names as best I could and faxed it to Clay.

Jeanine, Mom's p.m. aide, returned to work after a few days off, and when interviewed, confirmed that she had seen Mom's ring while doing hand care on Sunday night. Thanks to Jeanine, we had a definitive timeline, a short window from Sunday night to Tuesday noon when the ring "disappeared." Memorial Day was right in the middle, a holiday requiring supplemental staffing from an outside agency.

Val was handling the investigation as a "lost" ring, and it mystified and scared me that the administration was not considering this incident a major breach in security. So, for the first time since the poison pen note, I descended to the bowels of the building to the administrative offices.

I asked to speak to the administrative head, Beverly Pierce. My purpose was to emphasize the implausibility that Mom's ring disappeared in any way other than being forcibly removed. I explained the alternatives: that Mom took the ring off herself (but she was incapable), that the ring was removed for hand cares (but Jeanine saw it on her finger DURING hand cares), it fell off accidentally (which was proven ludicrous by Delores's difficulty in removing the remaining ring) or it was taken off deliberately and probably painfully by an unknown thief, perhaps an employee. The choices were quite revealing.

I asked her to not overlook the security issues that surrounded this incident and to warn other families. She responded with sympathetic comments regarding Mom's loss and indicated that she understood my frustra-tion. Then she mentioned that, when warranted, hidden cameras had been used in the past. (Oh, yes, the hidden camera. My mind rewound. Beverly must have been unaware that our family had gone that route with the poi-son pen note.) I pressed again for open and clear communication about security issues during the next third-floor family meetings, so other families could be warned.

Our conversation ended when Beverly employed the same technique I used when ten-minute parent-teacher conferences had to end to accom-modate the next set of parents waiting outside the classroom door. This time it was Beverly, not I, who stood up and moved around her desk to the door. I realized my time was over, and that it had been presumptuous to arrive at her door without an appointment in the first place. I followed her lead and rose. I saw no one outside her door waiting for her attention, yet I suspected that she had pressing details to attend to.

I hoped that they involved security.

The Murphy Family

At the sheriff's office, I was greeted by the officer who responded to the call from Riverside North, interviewed a staff person about the ring's disappearance, and filed the police report. Then he escorted me back to a conference room. As we talked, he shared that he had not observed my mother during the police call. Nor had he been informed of Mom's condition, that she was wheelchair-bound and 100 percent dependent on others for her cares. He was unaware that a stroke had disabled her right hand making it impossible for her to remove the ring from her left hand and "misplace" it as the report suggested.

The report was formulated from information that was gathered during his interview with a representative from Riverside North by the name of Val, he explained. He willingly amended the police report to reflect the new timeline as redefined by Jeanine's assurance that the ring was on Mom's hand during hand cares on Sunday night. A more accurate description of the ring was added as well as the fact that the matching wedding band was removed by staff with great difficulty, adding "It is the feeling that the missing ring had to be removed with the same difficulty."

He suggested that I request an Incident Accident Report for Mom's address to verify other police reports for thefts. Fifteen minutes later, that report and an amended police report were in hand when I left the sheriff's office.

"I definitely sense damage control rather than full disclosure from Riverside North," I shared with Clay when I called and updated him on the new window of time in which the theft occurred.

"Now we need a list of ALL staff in the building during that window," Clay responded. By now it was Saturday and the only persons that could provide this information were gone for the weekend. Of course!

At the same time Krista researched resources on eldercare and legal rights. She sent an email filled with excerpts from the Minnesota Statutes regarding protection of vulnerable adults and compliance regulations as well as web links to the state office of Ombudsman for Older Minnesotans, the National Center on Elder Abuse, the Minnesota Health Department State Surveys for Riverside North as well as "Complaints" filed against Riverside North. She ended the email with "Poor Grandma! How rotten to be dealing with this. Maybe now they will do something to prevent victimization of other residents." She buoyed my spirits. Angie called and encouraged me to "stay tough."

At the end of the day a question appeared in my journal entry: *Is there some way that something positive can come out of this?*

On Monday morning I requested from Val the list of all staff on duty during the time Mom's ring disappeared. We discussed the police report, and when I described the officer's surprise at the severity of Mom's condition, she blamed the officer for not listening while he was gathering information. Recently promoted from nurse to clinical coordinator of the entire floor, she admitted inexperience with this type of reporting and stressed that any omissions on her part were unintentional.

The list of staff was ready for me on Tuesday, but it wasn't until I am standing in front of a fax machine at a nearby Kinko's that I realized that no auxiliary staff (laundry, kitchen, housekeeping) were included. I threw up my hands and faxed what I had.

On Wednesday, Val offhandedly mentioned to me that in a discussion with the director of nursing, she had referred to our family as the Murphy family. "As in Murphy's Law," she clarified. "If something can happen to a family, I told him, it has happened to yours."

"I don't see Murphy's Law at work here. Mom's issues are shared with many residents," I replied with an arm gesture that swept out to include all the wheelchair occupants patiently awaiting dinner. "What is different is that I'm here almost every day, so Teen Johnson's problems get noticed."

Perhaps Val would rather believe that Murphy's Law was at work here. Wouldn't that be simpler? One family with all the problems.

I looked around the dining room. Besides Mom the only other residents with visitors were a married couple with a daughter who arrives almost daily; a gentleman tended by his lovely, silver-haired spouse and an independently hired personal attendant; and a frail, elderly woman with painful-looking facial bruises who was being encouraged to eat by her daughter.

Perhaps the other fifty-five residents would have visitors in the evening.

One could only hope!

A Floorful of Murphys

Still pondering Val's "Murphy family" comment, I returned home to formulate my thoughts for the third-floor family meeting scheduled for later in the afternoon. Recalling the brush-off I received from the director of nursing at the previous meeting, this time I wanted to be prepared to share security concerns with other families and administration. No more relying on extemporaneous speaking. No more sitting tongue-tied until hours later, when I finally arrived at what I should have said. This time I would arrive prepared.

I sat down at the computer and formulated my thoughts, concerns and hopes. I returned to the nursing home with a three-page word document.

My written thoughts began with the distressing disappearance of my mother's ring, why I had allowed it to accompany her to the nursing home in the first place, and the improbability that it disappeared accidentally. Then I described my dreams of improving residents' security through teamwork.

In my vision of a safer environment administrators would acknowledge suspicious activity, communicate honestly with families, and create an easily accessed process for residents and families to report and document all missing items. Besides marking personal items, families would be encouraged to inventory, photograph, and assess their loved ones possessions, and to report all missing items so patterns could be established, and recovered items reclaimed. In other words, families and administrators would work together to strengthen the security of the residents.

My final dream was the installation of hallway cameras much like those in Mom's assisted living building. Not just to thwart thieves, this proactive technology would benefit residents and staff in a myriad of ways.

Now with building renovations in the works, wouldn't this be the perfect time?

Family members, including several newcomers, gathered around adjoining tables. The floor staff was also in attendance. Beverly Pierce did not appear, but the director of nursing sat down and handed out the meeting's agenda. I quickly scanned it and realized a critical missing link: "Security" was not listed. My plea to alert families had been ignored.

However, the new Nursing Home Report Card was on the agenda, and it was the director of nursing who presented this report. He described the new evaluation system that would be conducted by the Minnesota Department of Health. All nursing homes would be ranked with one to five stars in seven categories:

- Resident Quality-of-Life Ratings
- Minnesota Quality Indicators
- Hours of Direct Care
- Staff Retention
- Temporary Staffing Agency Use
- Proportion of Single Rooms
- State Inspection Results

He handed out informational sheets that described each category. Under the first category, I read, "Resident satisfaction/quality-of-life ratings is a measure based on actual interviews of nursing home residents." A sample of residents in each home would be asked to "rate their facility on numerous factors, including . . ." and within the list of twelve factors one in particular jumped out at me: "security"!

Silently, I listened to both the questions proposed by family members and the nursing director's responses.

How would information be gathered from the residents?

Privately and anonymously.

Who would be asked to complete the survey?

The state would choose.

Then came a pep talk. The higher the star rating the better for Riverside North, the director said, and he mentions the word *money*. I was confused. I felt the implication that team playing was important financially. I remained silent. *Pick your battles.*

Next on the agenda was big, exciting news. The facility was about to begin its construction/remodeling phase, and plans and processes were shared: improvements on each floor, new construction for additional space, replacement of elevators, an expanded footprint of the building, the gathering of input from staff, visuals, floor plans—excitement! During the presentation I looked for improvements that would create more intimate settings, a greater sense of "home" and less a feeling of "hospital." I listened for additions that addressed security issues but heard none and remained silent. Everyone was excited. I sat.

Finally, we reached the last item on the agenda: Miscellaneous.

I raised my hand and took out my copy of concerns. I began with the announcement that my mother's ring had disappeared and my fear that it had been stolen. Before I could continue, a woman at the end of the table chimed in: "My mother lost a ring, too, and it was taken right off her finger!" Then she emotionally described the details including physical harm, as well as her frustration and dissatisfaction with the resolution of the investigation. The floodgates opened, and other family members added to the inventory of personal items that had "walked away" from their loved ones rooms: clothing, jewelry, beauty products. The list was long and varied.

I abandoned the first sheet of my prepared thoughts. No need to convince this group that Mom's ring might have been stolen. When a lull in the discussion occurred, I focused on the teamwork approach described in my notes and butted heads with the nursing director at every juncture.

I encouraged the family members to be vigilant, to report missing items, to initiate police reports. He reminded everyone that the family should take the responsibility to remove all valuables to prevent loss. I explained that if I had known about the previous ring theft, I would not have been so naïve. I had been thinking that Mom's rings were safe as long as they were on her finger and not in a jewelry box, especially since they couldn't slip off her finger. The fact that someone might forcibly remove them was a new reality for me, and that was why I was sharing our family's story, I explained. He responded that North addresses security issues and that "vulnerable adult" reports are submitted to the state. I requested a copy of the VA report submitted for my mother's incident. He agreed to make a copy for me.

I asked the administration to work together with the families, to be forthright with issues of security breaches, to consider adding state-of-the-art security measures to their construction plans, to allow us to be part of a team to improve security for our loved ones. I was told that the building's planned improvements did not include hall cameras, but that my concerns would be shared with Beverly Pierce.

When I suggested a bulletin board where family members could post announcements of missing items, a third-floor staff person expressed concerns that a public display would create a HIPAA infraction. I wondered how something initiated by the family could be a HIPAA problem, but admitted to myself that I needed to research privacy protection of the Health Insurance Portability and Accountability Act before reacting, so I sat quietly. Someone suggested a "missing item" notebook that could be kept at the reception desk. Nothing was finalized.

Discussion continued. Comments brought the discussion back to the Nursing Home Report Card and the first category, resident quality-of-life ratings.

"It is disconcerting to me," I began, "that because Mom cannot speak, she will be unable to be interviewed for this survey, especially since security is a listed quality-of-life factor. It seems that the most vulnerable people will not be asked to offer input, because they are incapable of giving it."

The nursing director responded that the State was running the survey, so he had no control how it was done.

"Could family members be interviewed. I'd like to be interviewed," said the woman who had related the disappearance of her mother's ring.

He replied that he would find out if that was possible and get back to her.

"I would like to be included as well," I added and he nodded in my direction as he organized his papers for departure. He jotted no written reminder of our request, so I was left to assume that his memory was better than mine. When the lengthy meeting finally concluded, he exited quickly, while several family members thanked me for my efforts.

On the way out to my car I walked with the other daughter whose mother had "lost" a ring, and I asked her if a police report was filed for that incident.

"I believe so," she answered.

Yet, I knew, from the Incident Accident Report from the sheriff's office, that unless her mother's ring disappeared on February 23, almost four months earlier, then no report was filed. Amazingly, after all the "disappearances" reported during the meeting, the February 23rd incident was the only one to date, besides my mother's ring, that was officially documented by police in 2005.

...

I RETURNED HOME AND FOUND TOM WAITING to hear about the third-floor family meeting. With a voice escalating with each word, I began. "Mom is not the first resident to have a ring stolen right off her finger. Not out of a drawer or jewelry box, mind you, but right off her finger!" I related every detail of the meeting before typing it all into my journal.

An hour later, still angry that the meeting's agenda clearly demonstrated that staff had no intention of addressing security in any organized fashion with families, I found myself back at the computer this time spilling out my rage and disappointment in a pointed letter addressed to Beverly Pierce. I filled the scathing first draft with questions such as "Did not one person at North consider warning residents and families after the first ring theft had taken place?" and "Where are the 'reasonable preventative measures' of protection that are promised in your advertising?" I was surprised that smoke and flames did not emanate from my keyboard as I punched out each sentence.

Finally, I printed a copy of the letter. Deciding, neither to mail it nor burn it, I filed it in my nursing home journal along with the copy of concerns that I had written to prepare for the meeting. My simple journal, at first a factual day-to-day account of Mom's cares, had taken on a life of its own. Documentation of the obstacles and my emotional reactions, it has become an expanding depository for all the curious insights and crazy realities of each struggle along Mom's journey through nursing home care. Before closing the file that contained my journal I typed one last comment:

> *Tomorrow I will start another three-ring binder for resources and whatever else I find when I go online to check out the websites that Krista recommends, including the 2005 State Survey results for my mother's home.*

Lifting the Veils

I AWAKENED THE NEXT MORNING WITH A SICKENING HEADACHE. Wishing I could visit Mom without stepping inside the nursing home, I executed a plan for the next best thing. I stopped at McDonald's on Silver Lake Road, picked up cheeseburgers, fries, and chocolate malts and then entered the building only long enough to whisk her off the floor and outside for a makeshift picnic.

A picture-perfect summer day! Warm in the sun or cool in the shade, we had our choice. I chose sun and positioned Mom so its rays warmed her cheeks beneath her sun visor. I placed her wheelchair right next to a park bench and plopped myself down with my back to the nursing home entrance. Facing the pond which was aerated by a mechanical water fountain, we enjoyed lunch together. Mom's relaxed smile and hearty appetite helped me relax and relish the quiet moments together.

James was on duty. Mom was dressed neatly, no twisted pant legs or soiled top. She was sitting upright, squarely seated in her wheelchair with the small of her back supported and her stiff leg fitting nicely on the extended footrest. Such simple, basic essentials contributed to Mom's contentment and filled me with gratitude. Five days a week, when James was working, Mom was assured these simple pleasures, and even on the other two days her appearance and comfort were strikingly better than during those first, agonizing months.

I offered Mom a bite of hamburger and she methodically chewed. "We must picnic more often," I said, as I continued my endless monologue about anything that might stir a reaction, a little spark in her eye, a twitch of a smile, a word. Oh, a word! I talked about Krista and Steve's upcoming fall wedding.

"Krista insists that September 16 will be gorgeous, as if she has some direct line of communication with the weather maker. You'll be going, you know—your granddaughter wouldn't have it any other way. We have the van already reserved." I prattled on and on and tried to imagine how she might have responded had her brain been capable of composing simple sentences.

Out loud I read Angie's latest quirky email along with a published story that she has written about Korean-American singer-songwriter Susie Suh. Amazingly, Mom gave me full attention as if she was honing in on each word. Mom, the English teacher, would have been so pleased to see her granddaughter's growth as a "word artist," the profession listed on Angie's business card. In a flash of lucidity, as I reached the end of the article, she nodded her head and "ahhh," escaped her lips. Was that a beam of pride I saw? The forty-five-minute monologue had produced a precious reward. As swiftly as a flash of lightning illumined a stormy sky, Mom's veil lifted, offering me a brief, familiar glimpse, before she resettled behind a haze of silence.

"Clay's coming tomorrow," I said, hoping the mention of her grandson's name would raise the veil again. Not today. I did not mention the pawn sheets that he would bring, yet wondered what information they might contain as I gazed down at Mom's vacant ring finger. Did she notice its emptiness? Well-meaning people had suggested I buy an imitation ring to replace her missing diamond. Would it offer her comfort? Would another ring on her finger, no matter how inexpensive, increase her chances of being re-victimized? My trust was gone. The thief had stolen much more than a band of gold and a sparkling stone.

We sat. I talked. She smiled. Then, with cheeks lightly blushed from her stint in the sunshine, I repositioned her in the shade to enjoy a few more minutes of fresh air. I became as silent as she and stared at the pond. The rhythmic dance of water from the fountain lulled me into thoughts as reflective as the water's surface to the sun's rays. How many times had I walked past this pond and into that red brick building hoping to find Mom in a state of dignity? For months I was disappointed, angered at her constant discomfort and dishevelment. Thankfully, her morning care had become reliably dependable lately, at least five days a week.

I pondered new questions. Can't I just relax now? Do I have a veil that I can hide behind? One that can separate me from the many systemic problems of nursing home care that become amazingly transparent when one truly pays attention? Staff shortages with high turnover. Burnout. Residents arriving at nursing home doors under increasingly needy circumstances. Complications due to financial cutbacks and government reimbursement. Trust issues that arise when administrators believe so naively in the messages of their own glossy promotional brochures that they refuse to discuss openly the possibility that a thief exists under their watch and preys on the vulnerable. Eldercare, the perfect storm, as uncontrollable and unpredictable as the weather on the evening of September 16 when Krista and Steve will exchange their wedding vows outside.

Just give me sweet days with Mom like today, I pleaded to a faceless system of eldercare, and let me close my eyes to the rest, to all the questions that come with no easy answers. Can I just trust that all will be well? Can I? Maybe I could have, before the meeting. But, *security* wasn't even on the agenda.

Instead, faces reflecting a broken system began to appear, faces of those in power behind the red bricks. Now I sensed with a heightened degree of disquietude that my advocacy for Mom was no longer contained on third floor, and no longer just about her, but expanding to include the other 200 plus residents who shared her same address. The thought was exhausting. I did not want to go there. If only administration had shown a willingness to place *security* on the agenda.

...

I TIMED MY VISIT ON FRIDAY TO COINCIDE WITH CLAY'S ARRIVAL. At 4:00 p.m. third floor already echoed with weekend stillness. Rebecca, the only Monday-Friday employee still around, handed me an envelope containing the Vulnerable Adult Maltreatment Report that the director of nursing had given her to deliver to me.

I found Mom in her room with Jeanine. "How's your Mom doing?" she asked referring to the emotional trauma of losing her ring. I was touched by the genuine kindness of her question, a question so rarely asked and one I needed to hear. Such a simple, decent question!

It had been ten days since the ring disappeared, and the people who had asked this question out of concern for Mom were cherished. Several were predictable: the people who always treated Mom with dignity. Others were wonderful surprises like a high school student who worked evenings setting tables and serving meals. She casually commented that she hoped Mom was recovering from the experience. All received five-star ratings in my grade book. Disappointing was the absence of this question from the administrative wing.

I opened the envelope and read the copy of the VA form that was received by the Minnesota Department of Health on June 3 detailing the ring incident. The narrative was interrupted with an arrow that directed the reader to the back of one page, but my copy was blank. Obviously, a page was missing. An inaccurate date also added to the confusion—I reported the ring missing on May 31, 2005, not March 31, 2005.

Clay arrived! His appearance usually sparked a visible response from Mom, and today was no different. She smiled broadly and reacted comfortably to his hugs. We took her outside until a summer shower drove us back indoors to a private corner of the first-floor lounge. Clay educated me on the capabilities of the automated pawn system and turned over a huge stack of pages detailing the most recently pawned jewelry in the State of Minnesota. In exchange, I gave him the list of names of the people listed in the VA report to cross reference with computer-accessed pawn histories. However, spelling of names must be accurate for the computer program to do its work, and again I noted discrepancies between names in the report and those on the staffing assignment list that was posted on third floor. While we discussed our next move, Mom sat in her chair and smiled at her grandson. It was our hope that she was oblivious to the content of our conversation. We intentionally kept our emotions in check and our voices even.

Clay left for a late shift of work, and I returned Mom to third floor and assisted her with supper. A worker pushed a cart with a huge pot of delicious-smelling split-pea soup around the dining room and served the residents who were able to feed themselves. She handed me a bowl of soup and crackers for Mom who enthusiastically downed each spoonful. Those needing assistance waited for their food until an aide or nurse brought them a tray and sat down next to them. Sometimes the worker sought out the soup kettle and added a bowl of soup to the tray, sometimes not. What was the likelihood that my mother's menu included soup on a daily basis? I doubted that it did.

Before Mom had finished her first course, Tom appeared. It was a Friday night, and he slid a chair up to the table and began to relax into his weekend. Together we helped her enjoy the rest of her meal. Sitting on each side of her we exchanged light conversation as she comfortably ate. Jeanine was working. Tonight, life was good.

• • •

FOR THE FIRST TIME IN DAYS I AWAKENED REFRESHED AND EAGER to do something proactive for a change. I searched through boxes and albums of photographs looking for a snapshot that might have captured Mom's hands and her engagement ring. Scanning and enlarging what poor photos I had only resulted in blurred images totally worthless for identification purposes. Next, I checked online and located an advertisement on E-Bay for a ring with a similar style: antique gold with an illusion setting around a small diamond. The image of this ring became the focal point of a "Missing Ring" flyer that I constructed on my computer. Below the ring labeled "similar to the one missing" I added descriptive tidbits, "Size 4½, purchased in 1939" along with a narrative that explained that the ring had disappeared off the finger of a vulnerable adult in a nursing home. My contact information was clearly stated on the bottom of the flyer.

After feeding Mom, I quickly left to reproduce my flyer and headed off to jewelry stores in the closest shopping mall to the nursing home. Sales people readily accepted the flyer, offered condolences, and vowed to keep an eye open in case anyone came in to clean or re-size a ring of this description.

Visiting jewelry stores was familiar. Hitting pawnshops across St. Paul and its suburbs was not. Armed with my flyer, I entered each establishment and found kind and helpful personnel who encouraged me to come back periodically and check their display cases. Not knowing if or when a thief might try to sell a stolen piece of property, I realized that each visit was a crapshoot. Yet, the active search energized me, and I continued on, until my list of pawnshops had been reduced by half. No one has seen the ring. And, the reality that I might never see it again loomed larger with each visit.

Sunday was a self-imposed day of rest. I returned to my normal ritual and headed over to feed Mom after church. The nursing home visit was unremarkable until I bumped into a woman who exited with me. This striking woman visited regularly and always came on Sundays to enjoy dinner with her husband, who was as vulnerable as Mom. Since she had not been present at the third-floor family meeting, I shared my suspicions that there had been a thief on third floor.

"Oh," she replied. "I hate it! You know, my husband had a Pierre Cardin jogging suit taken right out of his closet. I hid it in a box on the shelf, and they still found it! You can't have anything nice around here!"

"When was that?" I ask, wondering if it had disappeared over Memorial Day weekend.

She could not pinpoint the date. She just knew that it was gone, "gone like so many other little things that have simply disappeared."

She and I chatted on the walk to our cars. She was leaving her husband behind, and I was going home to mine. Will nursing home environments change before I have to leave Tom in a place like this, or more likely, he has to leave me? The question haunted me as I slid into the driver's seat and stared ahead at the tranquil pond. The clock is ticking for the next generation, I mumbled as I started my car.

Teachable Moments

June 13, 2005

Although last Thursday's picnic with Mom was semi-sweet, sour is the overwhelming flavor of the day.

Mom sprouted another bruise today, this one about the size of a fifty-cent piece on the inner side of her left arm. I spotted it when I arrived and found her in bed. A pool of bluish liquid mounded under her skin, swelling the area into an ugly mound. Either it was a very recent injury or something worse was happening, so I asked Theresa, to examine it. To rule out a blood clot, she wanted a second nurse's opinion, so Kari, the LPN from the other side of the floor, took a quick "look/feel" before ruling it a simple bruise.

"Looks like you bumped into something, Teen," said Kari, trying to make light of the situation as she gazed down at Mom, immobilized and in bed.

Had Mom not been lying between us, I might have sarcastically asked, "And how exactly did she do that, Kari? It's not like she can move by herself!"

I have become impatient. How refreshing it would have been to witness a nurse taking advantage of a teachable moment. However, instead of reviewing techniques that avoid bruising with Mom's new aide, she tritely passed off the mound of blue as Mom's fault. Since Mom was not one of her regular assignees, after her declaration she hurried back to the residents under her care at the other end of the floor.

Theresa, on the other hand, returned with ice and informed me that she had called the nurse practitioner to report the bruise. Theresa, a registered nurse who arrived from the Philippines with fresh eyes a few months ago, has quickly established a reputation of seeing what needs to be seen, doing what needs to be done, and surrounding it all with a sweet compassion. She is a perfect prescription for Mom's nursing home! Let's clone her—along with James and Jeanine and Rebecca and Kate.

Another sour revelation—two of us left last Wednesday's family meeting with the understanding that the director of nursing would pass along contact information for those implementing the new satisfaction survey, the Nursing Home Report Card. It was our hope that we might represent our dementia-stricken mothers. Not only has that not happened, but also I discovered today that the survey team has come and gone. Our request was forgotten, ignored, blown off. I am suspicious. Is there more than just forgetfulness at work here?

I left with a sour taste in my mouth (but only after I routed a request to the director of nurses for the missing page of the VA report). Once home, I resurrected my vitriolic letter to Beverly Pierce, reread it and passed it through the shredder. Then I wrote another, a bit more professional, in which I described my concerns about my mother's wellbeing. I requested additional information and pleaded for open communication. Now I wait. Let's see if I get blown off once again. Sweet or sour, what's it gonna be?

Denial

July 1, 2005

Dear Dad,

I need a sounding board, so I send this letter into the void. Please listen as you have done so often in the past. Today, I try to separate the blessings from the casualties of this whole experience.

I've wrestled again with the option of uprooting Mom and moving her to another facility. I guess as long as Jeanine and James are here, Mom will stay. I fear it would be just too traumatic to move her at this point. Plus, I believe that North is a microcosm of a much larger nursing home business fraught with systemic problems. Where is there a place with resident-centered care?

I look for signs of pain. Thankfully for Mom pain is not a side effect of her disease, unless you count the discomfort she experiences from poor positioning. Now, the good days outnumber the bad, thanks to the two saints mentioned above.

Mom's sweet manner has remained intact. What a blessing! How do families deal with behavioral and personality changes that produce physical or verbal belligerence? I can't fathom it. Mom's lack of affect is heartbreaking enough. I miss her spunkiness, her wit, her charm. The occasional words that escape her mouth now are confined to the socially acceptable responses probably drilled into her as a child. ("Thank you" or "Fine" when asked how she is.) She still lights up when we come, and I offer thanks for that. Angie's comment sums it up: "I miss the Grandma that she used to be, but I also love the quiet, little lady that she has become."

Dad, I'm looking for the positives amidst the chaos. I know that the third-floor clinical coordinator and the community coordinator are caught in a terrible predicament. They have open hearts for each resident, all sixty under their wings! Sixty! So many! Too many! Some suffer from end stages of an endless array of chronic and acute diseases; others are just too old or too feeble to live alone any longer. Dealing with theft is a lousy part of Val and Julie's job descriptions! The investigation of the "missing ring" took precious time away from the other residents. I wonder if they feel caught between advocating for the residents and aligning with supervisors who seem to prefer to sum up loss by theft as the family's irresponsibility?

The family is to blame, I hear, for allowing Mom to wear her ring in the first place. Blame the victim! Much like a rape victim is blamed for dressing provocatively, I guess. Mom was asking for it by wearing the rings that symbolized your love and commitment to her. Let's blame her for "misplacing half of her wedding set" as the first police report suggested. Let's ignore Delores's testimony that the remaining ring was "very difficult to remove." Something is so very wrong here, a veil of secrecy, and I sense an unease when my questions attempt to shed light. At the family meeting I urged, almost begged, for open communication so family members can be part of the team to increase security. Yet, no open discussion can be held if the family's only contribution to the team is to strip our loved ones of everything valuable. Haven't they lost enough?

For the most part, I guess, I have made peace with third floor. I am well aware that I have no idea of the complexities I would encounter if I walked in the shoes of those in charge. Nonetheless, I am grossly disappointed. I'm still waiting for any kind of acknowledgment from Beverly Pierce that she has received my questions. Just a simple, "I got your message and will get back to you" would be appreciated. If I can't even get that after two weeks, are answers to my questions coming at all? I was hoping, expecting actually, a more compassionate response to the issue of Mom's missing ring. Proof "beyond a shadow of a doubt" is needed here, I guess, before any acknowledgment that theft really does occur. I can sum it up in one word: DENIAL. Perhaps administrators have been stricken by the same affliction that beset me for years as I watched Mom's memory fade. In response to dreaded reality, denial insidiously germinates and grows. Such was Mom's increasing dementia and my blindness of it. And now I see it here: issues of security denied by administrators. (I picture lawyers, fearful of litigation, huddled around tables advising against the ethical response of admitting culpability.)

Are these the rants of a paranoid lunatic? Perhaps, but the administrator's unresponsiveness to my letter is fertile ground for suspicion and doubt. Scariest of all, somewhere an unidentified thief has discovered a fruitful playground where supervisors turn their heads.

As you can tell, every aspect of this ring incident has left gaping wounds of mistrust. Thanks to scar tissue left behind, this daughter of yours, the one who hates confrontation, has developed a thicker skin. I just may need that extra layer of protection in the days ahead. Thanks for listening, Dad.

Love and miss you.

J

Blindness

WHEN I PULLED UP A CHAIR NEXT TO MOM so I could assist her with meals, I always sat on her left side. For a right-handed person like myself, the position was a bit awkward, but my reasoning was sound. The vision in Mom's left eye was much better than her right, thanks to cataract surgery shortly after Dad passed away. So, when I sat to her left, her good eye kept track of me, just like she had done all her life. That was comforting for both of us.

Five years had passed since my mother exited Central Medical Building with a patch over her eye and post-surgical instructions that I knew she had forgotten a second after they were given, even though she nodded in agreement to the nurse who requested that she follow them to the letter. Aware that she needed companionship and supervision for twenty-four hours, I returned with her to her apartment at the Meadows and joked about our planned sleepover. After we shared a light evening meal, I crawled into the queen-size bed next to her. Fearing that she might wake and rub, or in some other manner, injure her eye, I switched on my internal alarm clock and awakened with any movement coming from the other side of the mattress. She awoke the next morning totally refreshed, and I rose, exhausted from a fitful night. I delivered her to the clinic for a follow-up appointment, and we received the good news. What had been Mom's bad eye was now her good one. The operation was successful. The opaqueness had been removed, simply and cleanly, in a day's time.

Wishing all sight could be restored as easily I contemplated the causes of blindness:

Perhaps the mental turning of a blind eye grows from the human condition of preferring to screen life through an opaque filter. Every-

one is blind to something: blind to our own feelings, blind to painful realities, blind to prejudice and injustice. Our blindness is as unique as our personage. Some people prefer the blindness of denial, while others suffer blindness as a natural outcome of fatigue, anxiety, or simply, lack of focus. Sometimes we grope around in the dark, inattentively sightless.

At times I have pulled down the shade, intentionally separating myself from simple truths: the truth that Mom and Dad were no longer capable of living independently, the truth that Dad's disease would take his life and that Mom's will rob her of almost everything before it comes in for the final kill. These are ugly details, so I unintentionally blinded my vision until their realities screamed for my attention.

Ironically, the lessons of the missing ring opened my eyes. I arrived at the nursing home each day with a keener vision, and what I discerned were troubling examples of blindness. I watched an aide, someone from a temporary agency, prepare Mom for transfer from her bed to her wheelchair. While attaching the Hoyer straps to the mechanical crane he failed to cross them between my mother's legs, a critical safety measure that prevented her from dropping to the floor during transfer. A second aide, one who occasionally worked with my mother, entered the room to aid in the transfer and understandably didn't notice the failure of protocol that had already taken place before her arrival. How might this story have ended if I had been blind as well and hadn't interrupted the transfer and insisted that the straps be crossed?

I arrived at noon and found Mom already eating, but her body was positioned so badly that she was listing over the right armrest of her wheelchair. Her head was no longer supported by the headrest, thus her mouth was angled at such a slant that food dribbled out the lowest corner. To make matters worse, she was being fed by a nurse, someone responsible for supervising the correct positioning of residents. What had made this nurse so blind to Mom's discomfort?

How blind was I to think that perhaps my security concerns were shared with the building administration. I had finally received a complete copy of the Vulnerable Adult Maltreatment Report that documented both inaccuracies and great stretches of the truth. (Mom was not admitted to Riverside North on July 20, 1998, as the form stated, but four years later on August 1, 2002.) "No incidences of missing valuable items have occurred in the other three communities at Riverside North," the form stated. None substantiated, perhaps, but plenty were discussed at the June family meeting. Yet, the state used this report as its basis for its conclusion that "no further action from this office is necessary at this time." Case closed.

Tom listened to my daily harangue about the staff's unwillingness to note anything in the VA Report that would consider the possibility that a thief may have taken Mom's ring.

"That would make them culpable," he explained.

"That would make them honorable," I replied.

To prove his point and to witness for himself the demeanor of the director of nursing, the man who had stirred great ire in his wife, he took an afternoon off from work and accompanied me to the July third-floor family meeting. When the issue of missing items was addressed, I referred to the "theft" of the missing ring.

The director scolded me for using the word "theft" because "theft has not been proven."

Tom spoke up. "No, what we should be talking about is way more than theft—it's assault—of a vulnerable person."

I watched in stunned amazement as the director immediately backed away from the aggressive posture he had held only moments earlier with me. Now he made pacifying remarks to Tom about the commitment of the nursing home to keeping residents safe. I was awed at the power of the word *assault* and saddened that it took a power play to bring about a discussion regarding theft.

Even though our family had no interest in pursuing the incident legally or asking for restitution, I was angered that because no one was caught in the act, the investigation was over and the incident dismissed. The meeting ended, and Tom and I left.

We simply had wanted all families to be warned that snug rings weren't safe rings.

•••

SO, THE CASE OF THE MISSING RING WAS CLOSED, but before business could entirely return to normal, an ironically timed incident startled nursing home staff. During Mom's July care conference her care team informed me of the theft of credit cards from the purses of staff people during a recent electrical blackout. Within a couple of hours, the cards were used for large purchases in stores on the southern edge of the Twin Cities. Voices registered shock, disbelief, and anger as they related the details of the brazen crime. Where was all this indignation when the residents were the victims, I wondered?

"Have you seen the memo warning staff and families to secure their personal items?" asked Val, surprised that I hadn't seen it. "It's posted on third floor." *Communication at last! How could I have missed it?*

After the conference, Val led me upstairs and showed me the memo dated July 6, a week earlier. It was taped to the counter of the reception desk, unfortunately hidden under the resident sign-out notebook, but communication nonetheless. Progress comes in baby steps, I surmised.

I left the building, not enjoying the fact that hardworking people's identities had been stolen, but hopeful that the latest thievery might have given administrators a symbolic rap on the head, forcing eyes to open to the realities under their roof.

It wasn't until I began backing out of the parking lot that I saw the parallel. The date of the memo: July 6. When did the blackout and credit card theft occur? During the July 4 holiday? Hmmm, Memorial Weekend and Mom's ring. What was it about holidays? Understaffing? Staffing from outside pools? Definitely a reminder in the future to vigilantly approach holidays at the nursing home as high-alert times and to visit often with open eyes.

•••

THE THEFT OF STAFF MEMBERS' CREDIT CARDS had not been the only eye-opening revelation gleaned from the day's care conference. As I typed the details into my journal, a reoccurring theme became apparent:

> Most of my present concerns are issues over which the three people who joined me around the table today have little control. Val, the clinical coordinator, Julie, the community coordinator, and Kate, the recreational therapist, all know Mom and her needs well, and all three were willing to listen as I poured out my frustrations, but they have little clout when it comes to addressing building-wide issues.
>
> After providing an initial update on Mom (status quo), they asked for my concerns, and I spilled them out one after another: my disappointment in the response to Mom's ring disappearance, the refusal to even acknowledge the possibility that it might have been stolen, the missing page from the VA report, the lack of response from Beverly Pierce to my written concerns, the Nursing Home Report Card fiasco, the reluctance to talk openly to families about security concerns. All are issues that directly relate to the organization and philosophy of the nursing home system.
>
> Everyone acted surprised and disappointed that I have not received a response from Beverly Pierce to my written concerns.
>
> "How did you send it? Did you mail it?" Val asked.
>
> "I was directed to place it in the wire basket behind the reception desk," I said.
>
> Val was quick to offer a possible explanation. "Sometimes I see residents going through that basket. Maybe something happened to it."
>
> In her haste to cover for her administrator, she opened another "can of worms." For someone discomforted by the building's security in the first place, to hear that residents often rifle through inter-facility mail was not reassuring.
>
> One other disturbing bit of information was given in response to my request for open communication with families.
>
> "I have received notes," Val said, "from family members. They say they don't want to know about bad things. It makes them fearful."

"*You have received notes?*" I pressed. "*Out of the blue, you have received unsolicited notes?*" I was incredulous. "*Well, let me go on record,*" I added. "*Teen Johnson's family would like honest and open communication of the bad as well as the good.*"

...

AS I FINISHED MY JOURNAL ENTRY A BRILLIANT MOMENT of clarity solidified my resolve. If the philosophy of blindfolding the families was being promoted on third floor, then I needed to get off third floor and down to the administrative bowels of the building if I wanted to have our family's voice heard. I had one request for information down there already (if the wire basket wasn't vandalized). I prepared a second.

July 15, 2005
Dear Ms. Pierce,

A month ago I requested information pertaining to safety/security issues concerning my mother Ernestine Johnson. To date I have received no reply, so I am including another copy of my original letter to you.

I would appreciate hearing from you.

Thanks for your attention to my concerns.

After adding my contact information and signature, I copied the correspondence for my records and then sent the original via the U.S. Mail.

State Survey, 2005

WITH A FAIR AMOUNT OF TREPIDATION, I decided to resurrect the web-sites that Krista provided me and to begin a process of self-education re-garding the state's evaluation of my mother's home.

With iced tea in hand, I settled in front of my computer and logged onto the Minnesota Department of Health home page. It appeared with links to a wealth of information related to Minnesota nursing homes. Mak-ing a mental note to check out "Facility Complaints" on another day, I continued my search for the latest survey results by following simple links. After a few clicks of the mouse I entered "Riverside North" in the search engine and—Voila! What materialized on my computer screen was a lengthy report, the 2005 State Survey Results.

Downing a cold swig from my sweating glass of iced tea, I began my investigation of the correspondence between the State Department's Di-vision of Compliance Monitoring and the administration of my mother's nursing home. I learned that surveyors from the department completed its initial survey in January and found the facility non-compliant in several areas. A plan of correction was submitted by the facility and two revisits from the surveyors occurred two months later, when finally, the facility was found to be in "substantial compliance with federal certification regula-tions." I read each page with detached interest.

Then, a wave of nausea grew as I continued through the pages. Fed-eral requirements and summary statements of deficiencies filled the left side of many pages, and the facility's plan of correction occupied the right.

"QUALITY OF LIFE" was the first heading. Listed below was docu-mentation from the minutes of resident council meetings. It indicated that for several months residents had complained about an excessive wait for call lights to be answered. The State was expecting accountability, and I read in the right column about the facility's plan of correction: "call light audits." Yet, judging by the complaints during the third floor family meetings, audits definitely had not guaranteed any lasting improvement. I read with interest:

> *A family member visiting indicated a concern regarding her family member waiting for call lights to be answered on the third floor. The family member indicated it was worse on the weekends, but occurred frequently during the week . . .*[1]

Worse on the weekends, not surprising at all to me - I continued reading.

The next QUALITY OF LIFE deficiency struck like a fist to the heart. I read the regulatory information first:

> *A resident has the right to reside and receive services in the facility with reasonable accommodations of individual needs and preferences, except when the health or safety of the individual or other residents would be endangered.*
>
> *This requirement is not met as evidenced by: Based on observation, interview and record review, the facility failed to provide adequate positioning in wheelchairs for 2 of 6 residents . . .*[2]

Further down the page I zeroed in on one particular case:

> *Resident #11 was observed to slide forward in her wheelchair... she would also lean out over the right side of the wheelchair. She appeared uncomfortable . . . resident #11 was repositioned at the request of a family member. After resident #11 was repositioned, the family member asked resident #11 if she was more comfortable. Resident #11 did not answer verbally, but smiled in response.*

Had I not been on an airplane on the day of this incident, I might have thought that resident #11 was my mother and I was the family member asking for repositioning. Hadn't I repeatedly made that request? Hadn't I felt like a whiny annoyance, a demanding troublemaker, when I repeatedly pointed out the problem? Now I saw clearly that my mother's lack of correct positioning amounted to a deficiency in care that could interfere with state licensure. So, why didn't a nurse, any nurse on the floor, step up, spot a repositioning problem and consider it important enough to immediately correct? I turned back to the facility's plan of correction to see what changes had been instituted and found it almost laughable, in a sad and scary way:

> The facility has a program to review all resident positioning needs . . . resident #11 (was) reassessed, and positioning instructions . . . were implemented in the plan of care . . . Clinical coordinators to monitor for compliance by reviewing weekly audit results and direct observation . . .[3]

Putting it in the care plan? Direct observation?

Laughable, yes, especially when under RESIDENT ASSESSMENT the facility took another big hit when the surveyors' observations, interviews and record reviews found that the facility failed to ensure that care plans were followed for several residents. Strikingly, four out of four residents, dependent like my mother, were not repositioned according to their care plans. The facilities plan for correction stated:

> Clinical coordinator and community teams to monitor for compliance by direct observation, audits and timely and proper positioning and repositioning of all residents according to the plan of care.[4]

"Hmph" escaped my lips when I read the words *timely* and *proper*.

Page after page I scoured, finding parallels too numerous to believe. Inappropriate treatment and services to prevent UTIs . . . failure of a splint to be applied even though the treatment sheet signed by a nurse indicated that it had . . . understaffing given as a reason for lack of range of motion activities . . . a citation for having resident charts on a moving cart in the resident hallway rather than safely locked away . . . no evening snacks offered to residents . . . on and on, pages and pages.

Here was a list of deficiencies that paralleled my journal's documentation of my mother's care, the breaches that were labeled "Murphy family" anomalies by the third-floor clinical coordinator.

The saddest part of the survey, however, spared Mom. It documented the environment on another floor that to my surprise housed twelve more residents than my mother's! Even more unfortunate, this floor, whose image was sorrowfully tarnished by the findings of the State surveyors, was designated for cognitively impaired residents, the floor that I had observed during my first visit in 2002. It was exposed as a place that failed repeatedly to provide activities that met the needs of this unique population. Pages of heartbreaking examples made me thankful that even though Mom's cognitive impairment made her a candidate for this community, I had not placed her there.

Internal questions bubbled. How could The Gardens and the nursing home floor be run by the same health care system? Was there a presumption that as a person's cognitive abilities waned, so did his or her right to quality-of-life? How could Corporate justify moving someone from a nurturing environment to the one described in this report?

As I closed the website and shut down my computer, a disturbing reality surfaced. I knew that Mom's facility primped for company. I had felt the high-alert atmosphere kick in, and I had witnessed the desire by all to perform at their peak in front of the surveyors. Yet, the pages in front of me revealed serious breaches, even when staffers worked with a focused desire to excel. What about the state of resident care on days when the State was inspecting some other facility, or on weekends with skeleton staff, or even worse, on holidays when temporary staff from outside agencies filled the holes?

July 23, 2005

   Each request to have Mom repositioned—each urinary tract infection—each complaint about a missing wheelchair tray, splint, elbow pad or headrest—our family's experiences should have illu-mined the warts in the system well before the state's arrival. What systemic problems are at work here? Blindness? Burnout?

Thank you, State, for demanding that North take a better look. You force a raising of the bar, because you have clout. Your Medicare/Medicaid dollars have a way of getting the system's atten-tion. I hope to see you the next time you come. Perhaps we can talk!

Poison Pen Resolution

I GUESS IF ONE WAITS LONG ENOUGH, and if a loved one outlives the average stay of a nursing home resident, some questions are answered. Two years and two months had elapsed since the discovery of a poison pen note in my mother's laundry. Finally, on a sultry July afternoon a bit of closure arrived by way of a side comment from the head administrator, who called in response to my June 15 letter.

> *Wednesday, July 27, 2005*
>
> *Received a call from Beverly Pierce today. Finally (after six weeks) a response to my letter about security concerns! She apologized for the belated contact. We talked about security cameras (perimeter cameras that are present and hall cameras that are not) and the "black hole" into which families' concerns seem to disappear. I explained that Mom's missing ring was our family's second major security problem that has had no closure, and I mentioned the poison pen letter of May 2003. Curiously, she responded that she had been unaware "that anyone BE-SIDES STAFF had received anonymous messages." She assured me that the culprit had been identified, and because of the "terroristic" nature of the notes ("do this . . . or else"), firing had taken place.*
>
> *There it was, finally, more information about the poison pen author than I had ever been given, and it was disclosed sideways. If Beverly could have seen the stunned look on my face! The note to our family had been one of a series—others had been sent to staff— two bits of information that were never divulged by Beverly's predecessor during those horrible weeks in 2003.*
>
> *I barely connected with the rest of our phone conversation. Beverly invited Tom and me to check out the security cameras that record*

activity around the perimeter, and we set a date. The conversation ended, and I sat silently in disbelief, recalling the pain and fear generated by a cryptic message scrawled in pencil on a white sheet of paper.

Other messages had been sent! Is this why the administrator who interviewed me back in 2003 could so confidently state that the note writer "was probably doing the worst thing that he or she could think of"? What made her so sure that Mom was safe, I had wondered at the time? Now I wonder why, if she was aware of a pattern, she had not considerately informed me that Mom was not the only target? There would have been some reassurance in knowing that our family's involvement was only a single piece of a much bigger problem.

Couldn't someone have informed us when the author had finally been identified and fired? Weren't we allowed to know when the threat was over? Did no one care about easing the family's concerns?

Or, is something more deplorable at work here? Is "hush-hush" the name of the game for anything that will tarnish the reputation of the "Cadillac of nursing homes"? Does image trump resident advocacy once again?

Or, is this just one more example of the right hand not knowing what the left hand is doing? How sad that if I give the benefit of the doubt, this becomes the sorry conclusion.

Cameras, Cameras, and Please, More Cameras!

I TURNED MY ATTENTION TO MORE IMPORTANT DETAILS than the workings of the perimeter cameras of Riverside North. Mom was turning eighty-eight, and the family was ready to celebrate her special day. I brought doughnuts to the staff in Mom's honor, spent the morning with her and then returned home to pack up a hot Italian birthday dinner for delivery at 5:30 p.m.

Mom's spaghetti was legendary. Spiced with thick slices of pepperoni and a hint of sugar, it simmered for hours on the days I arrived home for college breaks. I could almost smell that bubbling sauce as Tom and I crossed the township line into White Bear Lake. No matter what time of the evening we pulled in, Mom had a delicious Italian dinner on the table in the ten minutes it took to boil the pasta. It was tradition.

Today I prepared the sauce for Mom in hopes that its unique flavor would trigger a sensory connection to her past. While I retrieved her from third floor, Krista, Steve and Tom decorated a round table in the empty, first-floor snack area.

She smiled at Tom and then focused on Steve, who stood as tall, strong and handsome as the man she married so many years earlier. What would she say to Krista's future spouse if she could only speak? Would she commend him for choosing her granddaughter as his life partner? Would she banter with him about marrying into a crazy family? I could almost hear her saying, "Steve, look what you have gotten yourself into! Having to give up a perfectly good July evening to celebrate with me!" Then she would tell him how much she appreciated his easygoing attitude, his quick wit and his devotion to "family" before thanking him for helping to make her birthday special. That's just the way she is/was.

The gracious woman who loved to converse was gone, and the anniversary of her birth probably didn't register. Instead, she smiled broadly at her company before settling her gaze upon her granddaughter, who sat to her left and assisted her with dinner.

With no one rushing her, Mom munched a tossed lettuce and veggie salad, a slice of buttered garlic bread and a generous portion of spaghetti, then eagerly greeted the birthday cake and ice cream. Cameras appeared from pockets and purses to record the evening. Slowly Krista unwrapped her grandmother's birthday gifts and held them up for her to see—a CD of soothing music that Angie had mixed and sent from California, a navy blue sweatshirt with red cardinals, a rainbow-making prism for her window. While we focused cameras on Mom's face, she zeroed in on the face of her granddaughter and mimicked her, smile for smile and laugh for laugh. These were her gifts to us.

Happy eighty-eighth birthday, Mom!

• • •

FIVE DAYS LATER TOM AND I MET BEVERLY PIERCE for our tour of the security cameras. She introduced us to a male employee who led us to a room in the dark recesses of the basement, where he showed us the monitors that recorded activity in the parking lots and around the building's entrances.

I quickly realized that Beverly defined "security" differently than Tom and I. She wanted to show us how great the perimeter cameras worked; we wanted her to consider adding cameras to hallways on each floor, not only to deter crime, but also to alert staff to the needs of residents.

"Does someone sit down here and watch these monitors?" asked Tom while activity in the parking lot and around the front door appeared on the screens. I saw the wheels turning in his head and waited for the response. No. The cameras recorded on a loop, so if necessary, the tapes could be replayed during investigations of security breaches.

"Like the incident of stolen credit cards from staff purses?" Tom pursued.

Those thefts occurred during an electrical blackout, so the cameras were not running at the time of the theft, we were told.

Now I took a turn and directed my question to Beverly Pierce.

"Wouldn't this be a perfect time to install hall cameras, since the building is being remodeled?" I asked.

"Unfortunately, we are already over budget," she replied. "Besides, hall camera won't necessarily catch thieves."

"No, but they can aid staff in supervision of residents," I responded, thinking back to Mom's previous facilities. "Aren't cameras becoming commonplace in newer facilities?"

She was unsure but offered to investigate.

Our short tour completed, we exited the building with Beverly Pierce's business card, her promise to check out the use of cameras at a newly opened nursing home within the health care system, and directions to contact the community coordinator on third floor with any future concerns.

Tom and I headed to a nearby restaurant to discuss security over chili and cornbread.

"Imagine how great it would be to have hall cameras on third floor," I began. "Monitors could help nurses see around corners, spot call lights, see who's lost or wandering."

Again Tom pinpointed major concerns in a limited number of words. "The present security system addresses who goes in and out, but not what happens in the building. They've got monitors of the perimeter, always running, but not often watched until after a breach. And, it looks like the administration is comfortable with that."

"I go to work every day in a public school, with cameras on the perimeter and cameras in the halls," I replied. "I'm required to stop any visitor without a name tag and escort them to the office. It's just twenty-first-century protocol expected by every citizen who wants safe schools. Shouldn't vulnerable adults in nursing home be as secure as our school children?"

"You're preaching to the choir," Tom replied.

"I just wish nursing home decision-makers would join us in the choir. Right now I feel like our family is singing solo."

Moment of Clarity
August 2005

Defining moments, those brilliant flashes of clarity, make unscheduled arrivals in unlikely locations: airport gates, doctors' offices, and the parking lot of Fridley's Pawn America.

Forever emblazoned in my memory was the vision of a tiny five-month-old, dressed in Korean pajamas, with bare feet and a flurry of black curls framing an inquisitive smile and almond-shaped eyes. Our flight aide, holding Krista upright and visible, exited the jetway on that April day in 1979 and headed directly toward us. The moment she handed our daughter to us, our dream of becoming parents to a child we had only seen in photographs became a reality. Our lives and family tree blossomed in this one defining moment. Two years later, almost to the day, we repeated the experience and met another plane at another gate and welcomed Krista's baby sister, Angela. Both events–joyous occasions–defining moments.

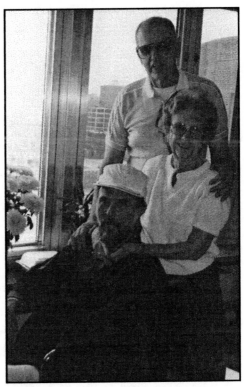

Mom and Dad with Jim after his brain tumor biopsy.

Another defining moment incarcerated us in dreaded reality. In 1989 a surgeon, skilled with a knife but blunt with information, blindsided our family with a dire prognosis after my brother Jim's brain tumor biopsy. "Twelve months to live if he undergoes surgery and radiation," he calmly stated. "Four months without. Less than one-percent survival rate either way."

As Tom and I sat in our car in the parking lot of Pawn America, the events of the summer coalesced into one more defining moment. With neither jubilation like that felt at our babies' arrivals, nor numbing grief that accompanied a terminal prognosis, the fog lifted and clarity remained.

Thirty minutes earlier a call from Clay had set everything in motion.

"Hey, Aunt Jackie. The APS got a hit," he said, referring to the Automated Pawn System used by law enforcement to track pawned jewelry. "Someone who worked the weekend Grandma's ring disappeared just pawned one. In Fridley. At Pawn America. I've put a hold on it."

"Yes!" I responded as I triumphantly gestured to Tom. "Tom's here. We'll go right over."

"It looks like this guy has a pretty extensive pawn history," Clay added.

Thinking we finally had identified the guy who preyed on vulnerable adults, my excitement revved until Clay with cop-like objectivity reminded me, "Remember, pawning jewelry is not a crime. Maybe the guy needed to pawn his own stuff to buy medicine for his mother."

"I just want to get the ring back," I said.

"You want to find the ring," Clay replied. "I just want to find the guy who assaulted my grandmother. But there's a good chance it was sold on the streets the first night it was taken," he said, referring to the ring. "So don't get your hopes up."

Tom and I, armed with the police report, jumped in our car, drove across highway 694 and exited on Central Avenue. Entering Pawn America we took our place behind a line of people pawning an assortment of tools, jewelry, guitars and stereos. A couple directly ahead of us pawned the young woman's ring. Appearing crestfallen at the appraisal, they pulled another ring off her finger and added it to the first.

Finally, we arrived at the front of the line. When I requested to look at the ring that had been placed on hold by the police, the manager was summoned. He disappeared into an office area then reappeared with the ring and laid it on the counter between us. The ring was a beautiful solitaire. Not a vintage 1939 engagement ring.

"I'm sorry," said the manager when he saw my disappointment. "Next time you come in to check, don't wait in line. Just ask for me."

I thanked him for his time. Tom and I left the building and headed for our car.

...

So here we sat. The key was in the ignition, but Tom hesitated and turned to me instead of starting the engine.

"Maybe next time," he offered.

"I won't be back," I told him. "Mom's ring is gone, and I don't know what else I can do to find it." We sat wordlessly, and I expelled a long, deep, audible sigh. "Everything is out of my control."

"Everything?" he asked.

"I can't guarantee that Mom is fed, that she is given enough fluids to prevent UTIs, that she is safe from bruises, sprains, predators. All I hear from the staff is be patient, be patient, we're working on it—if there is any acknowledgement of a problem in the first place."

"So what can you control?" Tom gently prodded.

"Nothing," I said.

"Not necessarily," he said. "Unlike your mother, you have a voice."

"What good is a voice if no one listens?" I asked.

"You have no control over whether they listen," he said.

"Tell me about it! How can I expect administrators to listen when their ears are filled with the sand their heads are buried in?"

"Maybe you just need to drop the expectations," said Tom.

Then, in the parking lot of Pawn America, I cleaned the sand out of my own ears and heard Tom's message. I returned home, opened my journal to the documentation of three long years of nursing home living and scanned through my entries. Turning on the computer I opened Word and created a new document. I was not sure what I would say or how I would say it, but, recalling my final assurances to my dying father, I typed the title: *A Daughter's Promise: Taking Care of Mom in the Twenty-First Century*. Perhaps no one would listen to my story of trying to advocate for my mother in the confusing world of eldercare. That was out of my control. But I could speak, and I'd do so in the way that I knew best, the written word.

And I began to type.

Golden Threads

GOLDEN THREADS, SMALL BITS OF RADIANCE, are woven into every person's life, according to Mom who explained her philosophy to me in 1990 during the final year of my brother's life. "In times like these, in the darkness of despair," she said, "they shine most brilliantly."

Mom was always on the lookout for golden threads. Because Jim's tumor and surgery took its toll and he could no longer negotiate the steps to his apartment, two golden threads surfaced: his willingness to come home; and Mom and Dad's physical ability to care for him there (with the help of hospice) until he exhaled his final breath.

For months, Jim's need for round-the-clock assistance prompted my parents to alternate caregiving shifts throughout each night. Although exhausted, Mom uncovered the golden threads. She saw this vigil at her son's bedside as an opportunity to be available for spontaneous heart-to-heart conversations any time either he or she needed a chance to say all that one might wish to convey. "Some people never get this chance," she reminded me.

I watched Mom and Dad grow weaker and thinner as the year progressed. I worried about their health, but Mom found comfort in the assurance that Jim would not die alone. He was home, and my parents were determined that he would stay there.

I wondered about the source of this positive spirit. Grandma Young, Mom's own mother, might have been the inspiration. Grandma Young was even tinier than Mom. Less than five feet tall, trim, meticulously groomed with dark hair and flawless complexion, Grandma's unqualified spirit rose above the difficulties of life.

"It was common for the times, Honey," I remembered her saying matter-of-factly as she wove stories of loss among recollections of happier mo-

1919 - Teen with big sister Gert and parents Margaret and Ernest Younng.

ments as a wife and mother. Grandma's first child died shortly after childbirth. She then nursed two of her four other children, all daughters, through serious bouts of polio and spinal meningitis. In 1939, she lost her husband only two weeks after the family gathered at Hamline University to celebrate their daughter Teen's graduation from college. Ernest Young, the grandfather I would never meet, was tragically electrocuted during his work as lineman for the Milwaukee Road Railroad. Severely burned he remained alive in a hospital bed in Webster, South Dakota, until Grandma arrived to say goodbye. He must have been one special guy. Grandma left the Catholic Church to marry this non-Catholic, back in a time when such an act was considered a mixed marriage.

For me, the fact that Grandma Young chose love over convention added to her charm and pointed to her grit and determination, both of which were sorely needed in the remainder of her life. Grandma, widowed with two daughters still in high school, ran a boarding house to support her family before returning to school to become a registered nurse. Then until retirement, she compassionately cared for many people in a dismal facility know then as the Ramsey County Old Folks Home in St. Paul.

Grandma appeared very comfortable in a setting that I found sad and unsettling. As a nurse she lived in a small room on the premises with her worldly possessions whittled down so they could be neatly stored in her tiny closet. Grandma was a valued employee thanks to her compassionate nursing skills, her proximity to the residents, and her willingness to work long hours and holidays. During visits Grandma escorted us around the wards until we found the "doll lady" whose days were filled with childcare tasks for pink, plastic bodies covered in an odd assortment of knitted outfits, hats, and booties. Often my mother would add a hand-knit creation to the wardrobe.

I relished listening to Grandma's life stories. The best storytelling sessions occurred after her retirement when she and her four daughters, Gert, Teen, Betty and Max, and offspring gathered from four different states for a reunion. I loved the stories of raising a family during the 1920s in Murdo, South Dakota, the antics of my mother and my aunts during their childhood, and the cultivation of courage and resiliency on everyone's part during the Great Depression. Grandma and her four daughters, all small in frame, were living illustrations that women's strength comes from the core, an internal source that mystified me on one hand and inspired me on the other.

Suffering from severe dementia, Grandma died at the age of ninety-three in a nursing home not far from the house she shared after retirement with her daughter Gert in South Sioux City, Nebraska. I

1991 - Warren and Teen (center) with Teen's sisters Maxine (left) and Betty (right).

recalled Mom's long drives to visit my grandmother, her consternation over living so far away when Grandma needed her most, and her agonies over the disappointing condition in which she often found her during visits to the nursing home back in the 1980s. Most upsetting to Mom was the incongruity between the nursing home care that Grandma provided others for decades and that which she received during her final years of life.

Now my mother was the one suffering from dementia, the one living in the nursing home, and the one whose care fluctuated from wonderfully skillful and compassionate to a 1980s version of inept and neglectful.

Observing the current nursing home situation for people with dementia was like witnessing a tragedy in slow motion and being helpless to change the tide. It reminded me of sitting under a beach umbrella and spotting a rising set of giant waves approaching unsuspecting waders with their backs to the ocean. Nothing could lessen the power of the waves, but someone could call out a warning that might or might not cause the waders to turn and spot the oncoming swell in time to dive under the crashing surf.

Until now I had been expending my rapidly depleting reserve of emotional energy in an attempt to effect changes in the way nursing home administrators viewed consistency of care, security, and communication with families. Results had been disappointing. But writing my essay, *A Daughter's Promise*, was cathartic. It simply told our family's story, calling out to policy makers and caregivers to turn around and observe with open eyes the disturbing realities of long-term care from one very ordinary family's perspective. In addition, it offered a prediction: An oncoming wave of babyboomers is poised to descend on nursing home nationwide in search of long-term care for their loved ones or themselves. Most, like me, will be dissatisfied with business as usual in a place that has not kept up with advances in the outside world. The collision of expectations and reality will most likely reverberate in an undeniable crash.

Organizing my thoughts for the essay blessed me with a surprising gift. As I contemplated, analyzed and organized the events of the last few years, the golden threads gleamed from under the matted inter-weavings of disappointments and frustrations that had become so toxic to my outlook and attitude the previous three years. They had been present all along, the golden threads, the blessings covered over by layers of grief and frustration.

My essay personified the golden treads. Innumerable faces of health-care workers and administrators at the Meadows and the Gardens shone. How they rescued my parents when their independence waned! With dignity intact, Mom and Dad thrived in their assisted living apartment. After Dad passed away, Mom became the recipient of conscientious care from compassionate souls who understood the importance of community, dignity and simple pleasures—a lemonade break in the afternoon—an after-dinner gathering in the courtyard on a summer's evening—a homecoming for a stuffed teddy bear inadvertently misplaced. Golden threads!

And, of course, Zippy. To see Mom brighten in the company of this remarkable woman confirmed that Zippy had become a cherished golden thread.

My essay uncovered golden treads in the nursing home, too: the many aides in addition to James and Jeanine who treated Mom with tenderness and respect; Kate, the recreational therapist, who assisted with feeding in the dining room every lunchtime (whether the State surveyors were present or not); the music therapist who sang directly to Mom and connected with her in one of the few remaining ways; and so many others who worked tirelessly doing what they are asked to do in an environment where available time never equated with expected work. Many of the most glorious of the golden threads had been the other residents who daily summoned courage and humor to deal with painful infirmities and even less promising futures.

My essay, A Daughter's Promise, helped me reclaim the golden threads often overshadowed by frightening realities. My essay gave me a voice, and in some ways restored a bit of Mom's. It provided a forum to describe eye-witness snapshots of Mom's quality-of-life as she progressed through the continuum of care provided by a care system reputed to be one of the best. Thanks to Tom's simple reminder, I wrote it without expectation that it would spawn improvements in eldercare. That was up to others. The rough draft was completed. Revisions, however, were needed, giving me time to contemplate my next decisions: to whom would I choose to tell my story, and when?

Another Wedding

To an extent, writing the first draft of *A Daughter's Promise* calmed my soul. Now anxiety over the weather on September 16 was my biggest hurdle, even though I was fully aware that nothing I did could affect whatever conditions the day decided to deliver.

Krista and Steve's wedding would be held outdoors, in the beautiful backyard of a home on Summit Avenue. The plan was set. Guests would fill the white folding chairs, the bridal party would follow a trail of rose petals strewn down the center aisle by a charming flower girl, and Krista, on her father's arm, would join Steven Freier under a floral arch where they would exchange their wedding vows. Krista, master organizer, had superbly coordinated all the details for both the ceremony and the reception. More confident than I, she had made one thing perfectly clear: no rain would fall on the afternoon and evening of September 16.

Krista's request was equally adamant. She wanted Grandma in attendance. No amount of worry would control the weather, so I focused on the necessary logistics for Mom's inclusion in the celebration. Mom's formal outfit was resurrected, and transportation services were re-

Krista and Steve on September 16, 2005

served. Kate, also engaged and planning an October wedding, volunteered to team up with James to prep Mom for the event.

September 16 arrived, and as Krista had predicted, the weather was spectacular—sunny, calm, and comfortable. On schedule her grandmother arrived by van, dressed once again in black and silver, reminiscent of her appearance two years earlier at her grandson's wedding. In stark contrast, however, was the physical deterioration that has taken place over that time. With dropped jaw, vacant expression and heavy head plastered against the headrest, she clearly showed the debilitating effects of two additional years of dementia. For a brief period I wondered about the advisability of subjecting her to the long, tiring day.

All reservations were erased in one startling moment. In response to Krista's laughter during the ceremony, her grandmother honed in on the familiar voice and giggled in response. Briefly, she connected. Then during the reception with Clay's help, she smiled and munched on buffet offerings before she was returned to her home on third floor.

September 16, 2005, a picture-perfect day with Grandma in attendance.

Becky, Clay, and Angie with Grandma during Steve and Krista's wedding.

Teamwork on the Third Floor

Dad loved all sports, especially basketball. In his school days he earned a reputation as a stellar athlete and over the years was installed in athletic halls of fame at both his high school in Montevideo, Minnesota, and at Hamline University. Throughout his teaching career he also coached football, basketball and track in Norwood-Young America and Long Prairie, both small towns in Central Minnesota; Crookston in the northwestern corner of the state; and Harding High School in St. Paul.

I don't remember attending any games that my father coached, most likely because the year I turned three, he switched career paths and exchanged the job of teacher/coach for parole/probation agent with the Minnesota Department of Corrections. After training he was assigned to Crookston, and moved the family back to where they had lived before I was born. Although no longer coaching, Dad never lost his love for athletics. Many Friday nights he donned his refereeing uniform and traveled to nearby small towns to officiate football and basketball games. In preparation for football games, he sent me outside to find a rock that he could tie in the red flag that he tossed at each rule infraction.

"Not too big or it won't fit in my pocket," he instructed, "but big enough to bring the flag down quickly."

As a child I thought that my well-chosen rock was critical to the game. I imagined Dad whipping out the flag from his back pocket and sending it high for all to see, before it decisively plummeted to the ground, thanks to the weight of my rock.

My brother inherited much of my father's athletic ability. Three years older than I, Jim played football and basketball and ran hurdles in track. I, being female and at least one decade ahead of the blooming of women's athletics, passively enjoyed sports. When the weekends arrived, I traveled with Mom and Dad to games all over the northwest quadrant of the state rooting for my brother and the Crookston Pirates.

Although I had little opportunity to play basketball in any organized manner, I became the beneficiary of athletic wisdom discussed nightly around our family dinner table. Rules of the game, training regimens and fitness, and teamwork and team spirit were frequent topics, and Dad had a way of expanding their importance to life beyond the football field or basketball court.

Over the years I continued to cheer on hoopsters. Since 1973, three years after our wedding, Tom and I enjoyed season tickets to the Minnesota Golden Gophers mens basketball team. Many a blustery, winter afternoon or evening we warmed our blood in adrenaline-filled Williams Arena, affectionately known as the Barn. Over the years, many great players competed, then graduated. Coaches, popular and not so popular, came and went. Yet, one thing remained constant: the correlation between attitude, teamwork, skill and winning. If the first, second or third component was lacking, the fourth was rarely achieved.

It was during our first season with Golden Gopher basketball tickets that I coined the shortcut phrase, "Remember Furman!" It was not the Furman team that I wished to remember, rather the lesson learned the night the Gophers played them. During the second game of the season, a youthful, underdog Gopher team with freshmen Tony Dungy and Phil "Flip" Saunders rescued a near loss to Furman by scoring several points in the last few seconds of regulation time to send the game into overtime. The comeback was miraculous.

A few pessimistic fans left the arena during the final, fourth quarter timeout only to get to their cars, turn on radios for the after-game wrap-up, and hear the broadcast of the last minutes of the overtime victory for the Gophers. The tenacity of the Gopher players, the wise coaching, and the crowd's thunderous support coalesced into an indomitable union. The Gophers left the court victorious, and I left the Barn having witnessed a living example of my father's life lesson regarding the formidability of teamwork paired with a positive attitude. Over the years I often uttered "Remember

Furman!" whenever I needed a reminder to dig deep and tap that extra bit of heart, before conceding to disappointment and despair.

...

IT WAS EARLY OCTOBER, AND THE TEMPS WERE DROPPING along with the withered leaves stripped by the autumn winds. The basketball season was approaching, but unlike Williams Area, the nursing home was eerily quiet. I switched on the CD player and the gentle sounds of Lorie Line's piano music quietly filled empty corners of Mom's room. She quickly dozed off. Normally that would be my cue to leave, to tackle the errands and schoolwork that I had waiting for me in my other life. But I stayed. I was unsettled and depressed, even though Mom was clearly comfortable and asleep.

I was missing Dad so much—Mom, too, even though her body was inches away. In the privacy of her room I gave way to the sadness of losing the family I grew up in. One by one, first Jim and then Dad—now Mom, inching away, little by little as dementia robbed her of her past, her memories, her faculties, her skills, her dreams, her voice. Dementia was the most formidable opponent I had ever encountered. Why wouldn't it be? It always won in the end, claiming its victim by chiseling away all the preciousness of life. I was tired, so tired of fighting. So depressed. And, if depression was anger turned inward, then I was wrought with anger, too—anger at the disease, anger at the excuses that had become commonplace in this home that I had chosen for my mother—the empty assurances—the roadblocks. I reached into my bag, and pulled out my journal and pen.

> *Dear Dad,*
>
> *The little lady that sleeps so peacefully in the bed next to me has shed almost all remnants of her vibrant personality. Now her disease takes center stage. The mom I love continues to slip away, gently, quietly. Her spoken words are few, most nonsensical. I listen carefully for an occasional lucid comment. Longing to hear her call me by name. Trying to remember the last time she did so.*

I wish I could clone James and Jeanine. Their gentle care of Mom eases my grief. For two shifts out of three, five days of the week, I am comforted by the knowledge that the people closest to her are the best possible. Sounds pretty good actually—until an incident of neglect involving an aide unfamiliar with Mom counteracts all the good.

I am so filled with regret that I have chosen this "home" for her. She deserves to end her life in a place where her final breath means more than an empty bed needing to be filled. She deserves to live each day with dignity until that time arrives. I so appreciate the individuals who express this sentiment with more than lip service.

Dad, how can I respond to a middle-aged aide from Africa who asks me why Americans "throw away their elderly"? "Our families take care of our loved ones," she added. How can I justify this system that Americans call nursing home care? Guilt-ridden, I wait for the day in the not too distant future, I suspect, when my daily trip to this "home" will no longer be necessary.

Will the grief that I now feel be eased when Mom passes? Will the finality of her last breath put closure on this " long goodbye"? When will that come? This week, this year, this decade? How long? Does it feel like a long wait for Mom, too? If there is a compassionate God, Mom's fears and concerns have melted away along with all her cognitive abilities. I need to believe that they have.

How long, Dad? How long? I am just so tired—tired of fighting this system—tired of grieving—

Love and miss you,

J

I closed the journal, exchanged CDs, kissed Mom on the cheek and left the building as inconspicuously as possible.

The following day I was drawn back, and a small announcement posted near the sign-in book changed my life, and certainly Mom's, for the better. The flyer invited interested persons to a gathering in the evening. The program intrigued me: Hospice in the Nursing Home.

After feeding Mom I left, scurried through afternoon errands and dinner preparations, and returned for the presentation. The speakers talked about the philosophy of hospice, of which I was well acquainted, since my family benefited greatly from hospice care during the final year of my brother's life. Hospice care in the nursing home, however, was a new concept for me. So, when two employees from an independent hospice program articulated the prerequisites for hospice care for dementia patients, I paid close attention.

"Certain conditions have to be met," explained one of the representatives. "If a person is incontinent, unable to feed him or herself or take care of basic needs, cannot speak, and cannot walk, he or she would most likely qualify for hospice care."

He continued on, but I was stuck on his last sentence. Mom fulfilled those conditions, and had for several years. Would she qualify for hospice? Wasn't there some restriction, month-wise, regarding the terminal condition of her disease? The men enthusiastically described the hospice services offered through their program, and I patiently waited for a Q and A time so I could ask them to repeat the prerequisites. They did, and when I explained that my mother had met the conditions for years, they encouraged me to call a hospice of my choosing and request an assessment of my mother. I left the meeting wondering why no one from the nursing home has shared this information with all residents that might possibly quality. Shouldn't they have the choice between hospice care and aggressive treatment? In Mom's case, since she was receiving no medical treatments, she had nothing to give up.

A few days later at Mom's care conference I shared the information I received at the presentation and informed Mom's care team that I was interested in having her assessed for hospice care.

"Oh? Really?" Val appeared surprised and asked if I wanted her to relay my request to Mom's social worker Eleanor, who was absent from the meeting.

Wanting to move quickly I declined her offer. "Thanks, but I would like to make some calls first."

I researched programs and discovered that the hospice offered through my mother's supplemental insurance provider was the same one that recently had supported my friend Helen's family during the passing of her in-laws. When I called for further information, I was impressed with the professionalism and patience of the person who answered my questions.

The process began. I turned over the name of the hospice to Eleanor with a request to have my mother assessed. She contacted Mom's doctor for orders and volunteered to be present during the assessment process. Shortly, I received a phone call from a hospice representative, and an appointment was set for the assessment. The positive experience was marred only by comments from nursing home personnel that Mom "certainly won't qualify."

I wrote in my journal at the end of the day: *Perhaps their only experience with hospice has involved residents in the actively dying process, when hospice swoops in for the final days or hours. How sad that those who care for people at the end of their lives do not grasp the gift that hospice can give to residents with dementia ...*

At 9:00 a.m. on Thursday, October 25, 2005, Eleanor, my friend Helen, Jane from the hospice program and I gathered around Mom in her room. Less than an hour later Jane called my mother's doctor to request a change of orders from "assessment" to "assessment and admittance." Eleanor excused herself to attend to other business, and Jane and I finalized the paperwork. At 11:30 a.m., while Helen fed Mom in the dining room, hospice social worker Sarah arrived and described the care team and the schedule. Two hospice nurses would be working with Mom. The law required that they begin within forty-eight hours. We also set up a plan for additional visits from an aide and a chaplain. Sarah assured me that she would check in often. The efficiency of the morning buoyed my spirit.

Then I entered the hallway. The grapevine was operating. One staff person greeted me with "I can't believe your mother qualifies for hospice!" I proceeded down the hall wishing that nursing home personnel had attended the hospice presentation with me.

I made my way down to the dining room and found Mom chewing as Helen patiently waited with the next forkful of lasagna. A lightness of spirit returned as Helen and I exchanged a thumbs up. We laughed. Mom laughed. Relief, finally!

Later, I found myself alone with Mom in her room. I opened my journal, eager this time to write something positive for a change. I scanned my previous entries and reread the depressing one of a few days earlier. I dug in my purse for a pen and open my journal to the first clean page.

Dear Dad,

Remember Furman?

Great news! Mom's care team has expanded! Hospice has arrived with all the elements of the winning 1973 Golden Gopher team that you admired so much: a positive attitude, well-rounded skill and team spirit.

So many people equate "hospice" and "death." Not me! Hospice means life—life for Mom, quality-of-life until her final breath. Now, when her caregivers rally in a huddle, she is right in the middle with all players focused on her needs. Mom's team is incredible. Of course, James and Jeanine are key players in Mom's day-to-day care. I think of them as the Tony Dungy and the Flip Saunders of the squad. Now we have a full lineup of players who round out the squad: hospice nurses, a social worker and a chaplain are starters and other specialists and volunteers are ready to enter the game when needed. I realize now what was lacking on Mom's previous team: an effective coach, someone with authority to call the plays, someone with clout to see that they are executed. In one short morning, hospice has done what the nursing home has been unable to do in three plus years. How can I explain this relief? It feels like a slam-dunk, Dad!

I am very ready to take a seat on the bench and rest for a while.

Love and miss you,

J

Breathe, Breathe . . .

I LOVE A BRISK WALK ON A COOL DAY, but the only running I enjoy is in the opposite direction whenever a well-meaning friend encourages me to take up jogging. The suggestion conjures up memories of the dreaded 600-meter run, my least favorite physical fitness test in junior high school.

Standing at the starting line of the cinder track that encircled Crookston's football field, I cringed knowing that when the flag was dropped, I was expected to race the circumference. Two hundred meters into the race, more relaxed girls easily passed me by. The remainder of the race tortured me as I gasped for oxygen and struggled to the finish line.

It was not until years later that I diagnosed my problem with long-distance running. As the starter announced, "Ready—Set—" I filled my lungs as deeply as possible. With the direction "Go!" I sprinted off, conserving my stash of oxygen by expelling it at last resort and then replacing it with small gasps through a throat constricted with anxiety. In other words, I held my breath.

The same calamity followed me to the nursing home. Often, I was required to remind myself to inhale when anxiety blindsided me. "Breathe! Breathe!" became my mantra as I travelled alongside Mom, not knowing when the finish line of the-long-goodbye would be reached.

Thanks to the presence of Mom's hospice team, I relaxed a bit. Independent of the nursing home, the hospice program was unique. The nurses, social worker, chaplain and volunteers headquartered offsite and arrived at the nursing home periodically, depending upon my mother's needs. Since the hospice nurses had authority to write orders, they quickly addressed my concern that Mom was receiving little if anything to drink between meals. An order for two ounces of a supplemental liquid given two times per day (with specific times for dispensing) was added to her care plan during their first visit.

Unfortunately, when hospice personnel were not in the building, the possibility of breathtaking breaches in my mother's care continued to exist. One afternoon, when I arrived a little later than usual, I expected to find Mom positioned comfortably in her wheelchair and enjoying her dinner in the dining room, thanks to whomever was assigned to feed her. However, it was Saturday, a day frequented marred by understaffing, so I reminded myself to inhale deeply as I stepped out of the elevator and onto third floor.

Circling around the reception desk to the dining room, I spotted my mother's place at the table, but not Mom. Her filled dinner plate, with a fork sticking out of a mound of chicken lo mein, sat on a paper placemat next to full glasses of milk, cranberry juice and water. Alongside was an untouched plate of her favorite vegetable salad, a simple arrangement of tomato and cucumber slices garnished with two black olives. Pearl informed me that my mother had already been returned to her room. I found her there, alone, sitting in her wheelchair, the Hoyer sling underneath her and its straps already attached to the bars of the mechanical lift. She was ready for transfer with no aide in sight. Breathe! Breathe!

I bent down next to her and caught her gaze. "Hi, Mom. It's Jackie," I said. In response, she smiled, but her eyes communicated confusion. "How are you feeling today?" I asked, fully aware that Mom would be unable to articulate an answer. Trying to mask my rising anger at finding her in this condition, I reached up to disconnect the straps of the sling from the Hoyer bars. Simultaneously, a nursing assistant, a newly hired young man, entered the room and recoiled when he spotted me.

"She didn't seem hungry," he explained when I inquired about Mom's early departure from the dining room.

Perhaps the aide didn't realize that although Mom had "lost" many things during her stay in the nursing home, including a pink embroidered nightgown and an engagement ring, she had rarely lost her appetite? The explanation did not placate me. Mealtime to Mom was cherished time, one of her few remaining enjoyments of the day that unfortunately required the willingness of someone to place the food into her mouth. Was it Mom's appetite or the aide's willingness to feed her that had disappeared?

"Is she ill?" I asked, grasping for the only acceptable excuse for prematurely removing her from the dining room while other residents enjoyed their dinners.

"No, she just didn't like lo mein, I guess," he uttered. "But she ate all her dessert," he added with a chuckle tinged with embarrassment, or guilt, or both.

"Really?" I responded with sarcastic undertones. "Strange, there was no empty dessert plate at her place setting. No one has cleared the table yet, so wouldn't it be right there next to the rest of her meal?"

"I guess she didn't get dessert," he replied, realizing his entrapment. A softly spoken "sorry" was his feeble offering for dereliction of duty.

"Do you want me to put her in bed?" he asked.

"Yes," I answered before turning to Mom and adding, "I'll be right back, Mom."

While he transferred Mom to her bed, I returned to the dining room armed with a tray. Mom's meal still sat on the table. Leaving behind the plate of lo mein, now cold and unpalatable, along with the warm milk, I reclaimed the salad and glasses of juice and water and placed them on the tray along with silverware and a napkin. Then I headed to the refrigerator behind the steam tables and scrounged up yogurt, Jell-O, and ice cream before I returned to Mom's room at the end of the hall.

"How 'bout dinner in bed?" I asked Mom as I adjusted the head of her bed so she was in a sitting position. With my assistance Mom munched on cucumbers, tomatoes and olives with the full set of teeth that thankfully had survived the physical breakdown of her body. She enjoyed the rest of her makeshift meal and polished off large glasses of cranberry juice and water. Mom smiled through it all, and I smiled back, masking my contempt at the day's neglect.

I chatted about anything I could think of, the oncoming winter, Thanksgiving plans, until Mom's meal had settled enough so I could lower her bed back to a horizontal position. Shortly after she reclined, her eyes closed for an afternoon snooze. I took a deep breath.

"Ready, set, go!" I muttered as I headed down the hall seeking out supervisory people to report the latest breach in quality care, adding "breathe, breathe," with every step.

The response was predictable.

Mom's nurse, unaware of the events of the day, was apologetic.

Members of Mom's third-floor care team were nowhere to be seen. Oh, yes, it was Saturday!

Things did not improve on Monday when the third-floor clinical co-ordinator heard of the weekend's incident. I vented. She attempted to placate. I found myself trapped in the same dysfunctional cycle.

On Tuesday, Sarah, the hospice social worker, arrived. After hearing about the incident of neglect, she took a proactive stance. "What does your mom need?" she asked.

"Simple things. Meals. Someone to feed her. Time to chew her food. Opportunities to quench her thirst between meals, just like the rest of us," I answered.

She accompanied me to Val's office where she, Val, and I discussed several issues, but one in particular shined a startling light on the difference in focus between the nursing home approach and that of hospice.

During the meeting Sarah and I discovered that Mom had not been receiving the hospice-ordered liquid supplement between meals. Without the required hospice authorization, orders had been changed by nursing home staff. The liquids had been moved to mealtimes!

"Why?" I asked, incredulous that they didn't understand that the purpose of the orders was to give Mom refreshment between meals.

"We don't want your Mom to aspirate. Often she is in bed during the times the supplement is ordered," was the nursing home response.

"Can't the head of her bed be raised when the fluid is given?" was the hospice question.

"It's hard to crank up the beds" was the unbelievable nursing home excuse.

"We can order an electric hospital bed" was the hospice solution.

Sarah suggested a group meeting between hospice and nursing home personnel to coordinate efforts and agreed to set it up. I returned to Mom's room relieved that someone other than me was insisting that Mom's well-being should be the central focus of her care. That evening I included a lengthy paragraph of gratitude for hospice (and Sarah) in my daily journal entry.

One week later the meeting occurred, and firm expectations were established. A hospital bed was ordered. Liquid supplements were reestablished between meals and oral swabs were provided to freshen Mom's mouth at other times. Repositioning would occur every two hours, I was told.

I informed the group that no assumption should be made that my mother would be fed by family. My presence at almost every lunchtime has enabled the nursing home to be neglectful. It had placed Mom in jeopardy of not having a staff person available to feed her on the days I did not arrive.

"My visits will be later in the day," I explained, "when I can spend private time with Mom in her room or on the grounds" *and away from unanswered call buttons, unhappy residents and blind caregivers.*

I was conserving my emotional fortitude for the marathon in progress, fully aware that the race to the finish line might be days, weeks, months, even years away. Thankfully, there was comfort in knowing that hospice would accompany Mom and me each step of the way.

Improvements Come, But Not for All

THE THIRD-FLOOR FAMILY MEETINGS CONTINUED on a regular monthly basis, and I kept attending. I listened and learned. A major discussion led by Beverly Pierce centered on a new plan to alert aides to a resident's need for assistance. In the past, to signal for help a resident depressed a call button inside his or her room. This button activated a light above the resident's door. In the future, aides will carry pagers that will alert them to a need for assistance. After a programmed amount of time, if the call is not addressed, it will roll up to a higher level of authority, then another. Necessary wiring will be installed during the remodeling phase. Accountability will be improved, we were told. Family members frustrated with the current system verbalized enthusiastic comments and questions.

Under my breath I muttered a quiet "Thank you, State," because I suspected that motivation for this improvement may have been encouraged by the 2005 survey that nailed the nursing home on that specific deficiency.

Thinking about other residents like Mom who were either too cognitively or physically impaired to depress a call button at all, I waited for the discussion to wind down, and raised my hand.

"Is there a possibility that these pagers could be automatically programmed to go off every two hours for people like my mother who need repositioning but are unable to depress a call button?"

The building administrator's first response was distressing. She informed me that call buttons would be located in several places of each room to make them more accessible. "Accessibility of the call buttons is not my concern," I tried to explain. "My mother could have fifty call buttons in her room and she still wouldn't be able to depress one," I responded with mounting frustration. Obviously, even after all our dialogue over

Mom's vulnerability during the ring incident, I had not communicated her total helplessness. Beverly Pierce did not know my mother at all.

Then with effort to regain objectivity I added, "Will there be any attention given to improving accountability for the care of residents who cannot use the new system?"

My questions dampened the enthusiasm in the room, and I sensed that *wet blanket* was another adjective being added to my name, right behind *whistleblower* and *troublemaker*. Annoyance registered on several faces. Other family members, however, grasped my concern and waited for the response.

"If repositioning is in the care plan then an aide already knows to go in and take care of that" was the explanation.

"But in case that isn't done on schedule," I replied, "could the pager be used as a prompt?"

The possibility would be investigated, I was told, and the meeting continued with discussion of agenda items. Mid-meeting the facility's chaplain entered, spoke with a staff person, and then as an afterthought directed a comment to me from across the room. "I hear that your mother just went on hospice. We should talk," he said before exiting and leaving me stunned at the disclosure of confidential information in front of the entire group.

HIPAA regulations had been used a few months earlier at a family meeting as a reason to veto a "missing items" bulletin board. Since families would be doing the posting, I saw no confidentiality concerns. My point was lost, however, and HIPAA was one of the fallback rationales for squashing the idea. Perhaps they feared that I would post something like "LOOK OUT! GUARD YOUR VALUABLES! THERE'S A THIEF AMONG YOU!!!" Instead, a "missing items" notebook, discreetly held at the third-floor reception desk, was eventually agreed upon to protect privacy. For the life of me I could not understand how my posting of a notice about my own mother's missing ring could be a HIPAA infraction, yet a staff member could announce my mother's admittance to hospice in front of twenty people. I left the meeting shaking my head.

At the next family meeting, Beverly Pierce delivered an update on the new plan for call lights. No mention was made of any investigation into the possibility of using pagers as prompts for regularly scheduled care of residents who could not access the system. Again I raised my hand and asked if anyone had pursued that possibility. I was told that there were measures in place to make sure that aides followed care plans. They were called supervisor audits. I was skeptical. Certainly, an aide's recent failure to feed my mother under the eyes of all staff in the dining room did not offer assurance that other aspects of the care plan, especially cares done behind closed doors, would be conscientiously followed. Thankfully, at the end of the discussion Beverly volunteered to investigate the possibility of additional programming for the new call system.

Other agenda items were covered by the director of nursing who announced that by the end of December no pool of outside temporary staff would be used. Also, he added, three new nurses had been hired and would arrive soon from the Philippines. I greeted both announcements with jubilation. Perhaps fewer outside temporaries might mean more consistent, safer care. And, if any of the new nurses were anything like Theresa, who had been working tirelessly and compassionately since her arrival from the Philippines a few months earlier, the residents were in for a treat.

The following day I received an email from Julie, the community coordinator. She informed me that as promised Beverly Pierce had talked to the call light vendor and found that "there is a possibility of programming the pagers to go off every two hours for residents who are unable to depress call buttons." She explained, "It can be done, but they found it was not always the most helpful. Probably the auditing piece, to make sure the resident is getting repositioned every two hours would be more valuable."

I was skeptical that audits would ensure accountability and disappointed that the most needy residents would not benefit from the new technology. However, I appreciated the quick response and clear communication. Finally, communication in a completed loop! I dropped the issue, leaving it for other families to pursue when their loved ones became helpless.

My main concern was Mom, and I was overwhelmed with gratitude for hospice and the way the compassionate program ministered to her. Along with Sarah's support as Mom's social worker, topnotch nurses arrived regularly to oversee her care. Greta, the chaplain of the hospice team, visited often. Her flute music soothed not only Mom but also anyone within earshot. Doug, a volunteer, read to my mother, often from the biography of her life with Dad. While she enjoyed both a massage and the energy healing of Reiki, my anxieties diminished as I witnessed firsthand the deliverance of comfort care.

If there had been an evaluation tool, I would have bestowed five stars on every aspect of Mom's hospice care. Pondering that thought in my nightly journal entry I was reminded of the Nursing Home Report Card. A quick check on the Web confirmed that results of the evaluation were still unavailable.

Holidays

Dᴜʀɪɴɢ ᴛʜᴇ ʜᴏʟɪᴅᴀʏ sᴇᴀsᴏɴ ᴏꜰ 2005 Mom arrived safely and comfortably for both Thanksgiving dinner and our family's traditional Christmas Eve celebration. The day before each transport, I lay the groundwork by informing the nursing home of our plans and by setting out an outfit for the day along with Mom's rarely used winter hat, mittens, and cape. At home Tom set up the telescoping ramp that allowed easy access to the house through the garage. As she was pushed up the ramp and through the back door, Mom smiled with delight at faces that greeted her. Did she know that she was home?

Once Grandma arrived for Thanksgiving the grandkids bounced into action, providing her with refreshments and helping in the kitchen so we could serve the meal expeditiously. Our goal was to leisurely enjoy a meal together in the short time that she was with us. Grandkids took turns feeding her hefty servings of holiday fare. As usual, she ate slowly and chewed her food completely. (According to Aunt Max, the Young sisters were raised to aid their digestion in this manner.) Like a matriarch happily enjoying her family's interaction and laughter, she sat upright and quietly munched.

For Mom Thanksgiving ended when the van arrived to take her back to the nursing home. Thankful that she had been strong enough to make the trip, I considered the day a total success, until I heard disturbing news the following afternoon from a staff person.

"Don't tell anyone I told you, but I thought you should know, so it doesn't happen again," she began. According to my source, when Mom returned to third floor after Thanksgiving dinner, the van driver wheeled her into the dayroom and left her there with third-floor staff. What he didn't know was that Mom's aide was not one of those people. For three hours staff worked around Mom and allowed her to sit in her winter gear without assistance. No one took initiative to push her down the hall or to inform her aide that she had returned.

Although I appreciated being informed, the facts sickened me. What I equally despised was the atmosphere in which a concerned staff person could not communicate openly about a resident's care to the family without jeopardizing his or her job or relationship with other staff.

The experience taught me a lesson that I utilized after Christmas Eve dinner. Once Mom was loaded into the van for her return to the nursing home, I waited twenty minutes, called third floor and confirmed that she had returned and that her aide had been notified.

The following day, Angie and I visited Mom in the nursing home and helped her with Christmas Dinner. Christmas 2005 for Mom was an enjoyable holiday.

The day after Christmas, Angie and I arrived again, this time in the late afternoon. We brought Mom into the empty dining room and settled in for a treat of punch and chocolates while teenage employees set the tables for supper. Oblivious to our presence or perhaps just unconcerned, one loudly informed the other about the mishaps on Christmas Eve.

"Aides were havin' a social hour and didn't come back to the floor," one shared, obviously peeved that she had worked while others partied. "The only residents who got fed were the five who had families here."

Hoping the aide was exaggerating Angie rolled her eyes and mouthed quietly in my direction, "Do they not see us?" But the girls continued sharing workplace gossip about breaches in residents' care. The effect that the disturbing information might have had on family members totally escaped them.

No longer surprised by free-flowing gossip, I focused on Mom and Angie, thankful that on Christmas Eve Mom was home with us, and that Angie, visiting from California for a mini-vacation, chose to spend hours each day with her grandmother.

2006

O<small>N</small> J<small>ANUARY</small> 3, 2006, I<small>RONDALE</small> H<small>IGH</small> S<small>CHOOL</small> <small>REOPENED</small> after the holiday recess. Finals for first semester classes were less than three weeks away, and the sprint to the finish had begun.

No longer did I hop in my car and head directly over to the nursing home after I wrapped up each morning at Irondale. Instead, I headed home, changed clothes and took a quick walk with our border collie, Jasper. Still eager to stride out toward Freedom Park, he lumbered at a slower pace than in previous years and stopped often to rest. His life had accelerated through each stage at a rate seven times faster than the humans in his family. As he paused to lift his leg on a crusty snowbank, I converted dog years to human years and realized that our trusty twelve-year-old dog was approaching the age of my mother. Both had arrived at a stage in their lives when the simple things brought the most pleasure. For Jasper it was a short walk in the fresh air. For Mom it was companionship each afternoon. Often Mom was back in her bed for her afternoon nap by the time I arrived. She smiled when I appeared, and I convinced myself that she was comforted by our cozy, private time together.

While Mom slept, I wrote. Letters to my father often graced the pages of my journal. Months earlier I had been surprised when the words "Dear Dad" flowed out of the pen, yet my resulting monologue to my father had been comforting. It had provided an opportunity to bounce my inner thoughts off the standards of compassion and justice that he had framed by his example. During my private sessions with Mom, more letters addressed in this manner were finding a home in my journal.

Dear Dad,

Mom has just dozed off. I'm sitting in her favorite chair, the small wingback in the soft color of pistachios. This chair is built perfectly for her petite frame but not for my long-legged one, so I push it close and use the edge of her bed as my elevated footstool. There is something very comforting about sitting close to her as she relaxes and then naps. This is where you will find me most afternoons now, at least for an hour or two. We talk (I talk/she listens) for the first few minutes and then her eyes slowly close. Sometimes I bring my schoolwork, or my knitting, or, like today, my journal, and just settle into the rhythm of her breathing.

Peacefully she sleeps. I marvel at her smile and her beautiful unlined face. Where have her wrinkles gone? It is almost as if dementia has softened the world for her. Nothing to fret about anymore, I guess. Her worries have disappeared right along with her other connections to the outside world. Even asleep her lips curl up into a soft look of contentment. You married a beautiful woman, Dad.

Her weight has stabilized around 115 pounds. People around her get nervous whenever it drops a little. I try to explain that at her healthiest, 95 to 105 pounds was normal, but I get the feeling that having a resident lose weight is a no-no, even if the weight loss reflects a return to normal times. I find it interesting that a byproduct of her inactivity is a weight gain that has filled out most of her facial wrinkles, sort of like a series of Botox treatments. James feeds her at noon now, so on the days when he is working, I know that she is being well feed in my absence. He is such a gem. Jeanine still checks on Mom routinely later in the day, although sadly her caseload does not include Mom on a regular basis anymore. It is hard to keep up with all the staffing changes. Overall, I have been impressed, but James and Jeanine are still unmatched for their skill and genuine concern for Mom. Do they know how special they are? I try to tell them, but words seem so inadequate.

One characteristic that I sense as a common thread among the immigrant population of employees here is resiliency. I can't imagine leaving my country and my family and starting over in a foreign place where my education's value may be questioned and my cultural differences scrutinized.

Why are some people resilient beyond belief and others unable to adapt—rigid to the point that they snap? You and Mom were resilient. I loved your stories of "making do" during the Depression and of families coming together for mutual support during World War II. People just moved forward with hopes that better times were coming. What a generation of resilient people lived before me!

When I see the smile on Mom's face, I witness that same resilience. She is ready for whatever is next and is probably contemplating a wonderful reunion with you. Yet, death will mean a departure from the people that she loves here on earth, especially those cherished grandchildren. I wonder if she feels the pull.

At times I swear she seems to have a foot in each world. Those daily chats with the angels have become nonverbal ones now. She still stares up and nods in an approving manner to whatever/ whomever she is hearing/seeing, and if she is communicating in return, she is accomplishing it on a level beyond my comprehension. At other times she seems almost catatonic, but I attribute that to something entirely different, probably physiological. These episodes, though short, are quite disturbing, probably because they remind me that we are heading to the finish line of this marathon of diseases. Is it around the next bend, or do we have miles and miles and miles to go? I am so tired that I long for the end, but the end will be just that. Mom will leave us. The race will be over, and we will have all lost.

Love and miss you,

J

Dear Dad,

The quiet time that Mom and I are spending together in her room has definitely improved my disposition. It has been almost two months since I have rearranged my visits for later in the day. Now I can avoid the chaos of the dining room and focus on Mom during our private time together. On most days Mom's care is good. But, there are still those wildly awful days, like the morning when Kate walked through the dining room and found that Mom's arms were not in her sleeves—NOT IN HER SLEEVES!! Mom was hobbled by the confines of her knit top making her unable to move even her good arm. "Obviously, James is not on duty!" was Kate's comment to me. (How many times have I uttered that remark?) In her efficient style, Kate immediately righted the situation and reported the problem. I really miss Kate. She approached her job with eyes wide open, always advocating for those with no voice. Plus, she communicated openly and honestly with me. I so appreciated her honesty over the "Fine, everything's fine" communication by others who continually refuse to acknowledge problems (or just want to hide them from me). Kate's recent resignation is a great loss to the nursing home. You would have loved her, Dad. In many ways she reminds me of Krista—young, full of energy and enthusiasm. That infectious laugh! Her next employer will be very lucky. Right now she is not working, so I am hiring her as Mom's companion while we are away in February. We are heading back to your favorite place, Maui, with Lyn and Warren to B421 of the Maui Sunset, the condo you loved. Once Lyn and Warren conclude their vacation, Angie, Krista and Steve will join us, and we will stay until Steve's sister Holly weds Seth on the beach. It is pleasant to have some special things to look forward to.

The trip is a retirement celebration for Tom and me, too. For our family, 2006 will prove to be a year of change!

Love and miss you,

J

Dear Dad,

January 5, 2006—nine more days with students, then finals and semester grading. My career is wrapping up. It is official. I have notified my principal that I will not be returning. Tom and I are hoping to enjoy many years of retirement while we are both healthy. "Travel while you can," you told me, "while you are still healthy." We are, but for how long?

*Is dementia in my future, just like it was for Mom and Grandma
Young? The question is more than a little disturbing, especially when
I hesitate during word retrieval, or misplace something, or open up a
cupboard door without a clear thought of what I am searching for.
Stress? Fatigue? The onset of something more dire? I don't know, but
I haven't ended up in Rochester yet.*

*There will be many aspects of teaching that I will miss, especially
the interactions with kids. But I am so tired. Bone tired. Not from
the rigors of teaching, but from six plus years of mourning. I grieve
over Mom's terminal condition, the gradual slippage that has chiseled
away so much of the mother that I love, and the necessity to advocate
daily for her quality-of-life. Thank heavens for hospice! Mom's comfort is their top priority and...*

As if on cue the door opened and into Mom's room stepped Kaye and
Sarah, Mom's hospice nurse and social worker. Both had arrived to accompany
me to Mom's quarterly care conference. I closed my journal and together we
descended to a conference room and joined four members of my mother's nursing home care team. Together we discussed Mom's status. One question set
me back. Claire, the dietary technician, asked if I had ever thought of switching
my mother to a mechanical diet because it "takes so long for her to chew."

My stomach tightened. "Is the length of time a problem?" I asked,
trying to pinpoint the reason for this suggestion.

Claire sensed my angst. She back-pedaled by stating that she was concerned that Mom was not getting her full nutrition because she lost interest. "It takes her so long to chew her meat that she doesn't get to the rest
of her meal," she said.

"Mom has a full set of teeth and has no problem swallowing," I
replied. "She loves tossed salads, fresh veggies, desserts, much more than
meat. Why can't she be given those first, then if she loses interest, at least
she will have enjoyed her meal."

"Protein is important," Claire replied and then began to explain the
well-known facts about the need for protein in a healthy diet.

Thankfully, at this point hospice came to my rescue. Kaye described the hospice approach to comfort care. According to her, protein was no longer a concern. "Teen should be given what she enjoys eating," she explained, "and if that is salads and desserts, then staff should feed those items first."

Discussion about my mother's diet finally ended with an agreement to allow her to chew her food. No changes were made to mechanically grind her meals.

The rest of the care conference was uneventful. Kaye accompanied me back to Mom's room where I privately thanked her for advocating for my mother's best interest. After a quick check on Mom she left, and I returned to my journal entry to conclude my letter to Dad.

Do you know how sometimes the fog lifts, the curtain parts, or whatever cliché best describes clear vision of the obvious? Mom has lived here three and a half years and I finally realize why I have been at odds with the nursing home since day one.

While the nursing home prefers to keep Mom's weight up as an indication that she is well taken care of, I would be content to see her enjoy her meals. They want to add thick, milky supplements to replace calories she eats too slowly to attain at mealtime. My emphasis is on Mom's mealtime enjoyment, but that requires proper staffing so she can be fed unhurriedly and completely three meals a day, every day. If that is done and her weight drops, so be it.

While the nursing home wants Mom to wear the easiest outfit to place around her, I would rather see her warm and comfortable. Their answer is adaptive dresses that leave legs and backs exposed. My answer is stretchy outfits in bright colors that protect her modesty and retain her dignity.

While the nursing home instructs staff through Mom's care plan, I would like someone to simply offer her a drink of water for the simple enjoyment of it.

For three plus years I have been unsuccessfully attempting to recreate the harmony we left behind at the Gardens, and now I know why.

The nursing home and I have different agendas. Thank heaven for hospice!

Today's hospice order: feed salads and desserts first! Music to my ears! Resident-centered care at last!

Love and miss you,

J

Gratitudes

W RITING SETTLED MY SOUL. PURE AND SIMPLE! What started out almost four years earlier as a method of record-keeping, journaling had become a lifeline, attaching me to my roots, offering me a space to vomit up my pain and anger, and reflecting back the golden threads that appeared during introspective scribbling.

Each night I continued to type quick daily updates regarding Mom's care into my expanding computerized journal. The length of each entry usually inversely correlated with the competence of the day. Short entries recorded "good" days. Long entries recorded not only the state in which I found my mother, but also possible reasons for it and my emotional reactions to it. Brainstormed responses often found their way to the pages as well.

My portable journals, simple blank books, resided in various book bags and purses. At least one traveled with me throughout any given day. Available for short jottings, fleeting questions or pregnant thoughts, they became the depositories for contemplative entries. One afternoon while Mom dozed, I jotted random memories. Soon personified blessings reflected back from the pages of my journal as I recounted the thoughtfulness, compassion and humor of four special women:

I love how Virginia simply stated, "I want to visit Teen!" not "Do you want me to visit your mom?" Her statement refreshingly spoke of her desire to see her church friend. Such a gift to hear that someone wants to see Mom. I came early today to be present during their visit. Virginia arrived, immaculate and fresh, with a glorious, multicolored scarf around her neck. A few years younger than Mom and a few inches shorter (is that possible?) she reminds me of the Energizer bunny. No sign of pity in her eyes. Thank you, Virginia! Mom sat silently throughout the visit until it was time to return her to her room. Virginia walked alongside as I pushed Mom down the hall. A flicker of recognition, spurred by something only God knows, caused Mom to turn toward Virginia, focus, and with a genuine, warm smile greet her with a laugh, and an "Oh, my." Virginia responded, "I think she remembers me," but for Virginia it would have been just fine either way.

Speaking of scarves, Karen's Christmas gift to Mom was a beautiful scarf in muted tints and shades of aqua and green resembling impressionistically painted water. How often has Karen arrived at my doorstep with small, beautifully wrapped gift bags for my mother? "Put this under your Christmas tree," she would say, or "Here's a little something for your mom for . . ." (Christmas, Mother's Day, Spring, etc.) I doubt that she realizes how much her remembrance of Mom lightens my spirit!

I enjoyed a marathon breakfast with Carol today. We compared notes, now that both of us have mothers in nursing homes. (I couldn't recommend Mom's facility when Carol's family was searching for a place for her mother. How sad is that!) Time with Carol is a soothing balm. We remind each other that although advocating for a loved one is crazy work, we are not insane, and our stories are not unique. There are daughters (and sons, spouses, partners, friends) elsewhere traveling similar journeys, running into the same roadblocks, experiencing the same disappointments—failures in execution of care plans—lack of communication from one shift of caregivers to the next—understaffing on weekends, etc. Her mother's body is failing but her brain remains sharp; my mother's health is just the opposite—either way, frustration, fear, sadness. While I am worried about my mother's quality-of-life, Carol is worried about her mother's medications, blood sugar levels, medical procedures, and bumpy transitions back and forth from hospital to nursing home. Re-energized by our support for each other, we head to separate nursing homes, both of us holding fear at bay, not looking too far into the future—one day at a time . . .

Cheryll's a kindred spirit—a cousin with whom I share common ground, yet we operate apart as we deal with the demands of needy parents in opposite ends of the Twin Cities. Her folks, dear Uncle Wayne and Aunt Harriet, slide in and out of transitional care as their health fluctuates. Meanwhile, she juggles the demands of each emergency with responsibilities of job and family, all the while dealing with her own health issues. How does she keep her sense of humor?

"You wouldn't have believed it," she told me. "I asked the nursing home's social worker a question that started out 'When my father gets strong enough to leave here,' and she piped up, 'Oh, he'll never get strong enough to leave here!' So I told her, 'Oh, yes he will!' And, he did!" she said with a nod and a laugh, reminiscent of the dogged determination and wry humor often depicted by her father. Then she said, "I was scolded by the nursing home staff because my mother (walker and all) moved too fast down the hall, endangering other residents. So I told them, 'In her whole life, Harriet has never done anything slowly. So, just what do you want me to do exactly?'"

I can picture it all! Aunt Harriet darting down the hallway with speed exceeding nursing home limits.

I wish we were closer, Cheryll. We could be a team, supporting and spelling each other while we take care of our elders. Thanks for the laughter. Keep the stories coming.

Wax Stripping

My last day with students—January 19, 2006! The details of administering and correcting my final exam occupied the morning and by early afternoon with my grade book stuffed into my briefcase, I walked out of Irondale High School and headed to the nursing home.

I found Mom in bed, already napping. Pulling up a chair next to her, I fashioned a flat surface out of my briefcase, opened my grade book and spent the next hour averaging final grades as she snoozed away. Increasingly a strong, caustic odor seeped under the closed door, and I ventured out in the hall to identify its source. A large, round container sat in the hallway next to a long-handled scrapping tool that was balanced against the doorframe of the adjacent room. Two occupants of the room had been moved, beds and all, to the hallway for their afternoon naps. No screens or temporary accommodations for privacy separated them from the curious stares and noise of residents, staff and visitors who rounded the corner of the hallway and happened upon them.

I asked Mom's nurse about the strong odor. "It's a wax stripper," she told me, and then added, "It's harmless."

Harmless? Don't wax strippers come with directions to use in well-ventilated areas? And, why would stripping wax off the floors of residents' rooms be top priority in January, in Minnesota, when the frigid temperatures prohibit the opening of windows? I didn't even bother with the questions.

Disgusted, I returned to Mom's room, shut the door and stuffed a towel into the crack under it. An hour later I developed a sick headache and kissed Mom goodbye, feeling totally guilty for leaving her behind in the stench. Before I could leave the building, I had two small tasks to complete. First, I filled out a comment sheet with my concerns about the use of chemicals without proper ventilation. At the bottom I added a request to be informed when the floor in my mother's room was scheduled for wax stripping, so I could take her off the floor and not subject her to the indignity of sleeping in the hall. This was the first time that I had used the comment form, a recent addition in an attempt to improve communication. As I dropped it into the "comment" box, I had no way of knowing that this concern like so many others would disappear into a black hole, never to be discussed again.

Second, I stopped at the reception desk and asked for the "missing items" notebook, so I could document a missing lap quilt. Ironically, the "missing items" notebook was missing.

It wasn't until hours later that the strange timing for the winter wax stripping activity became apparent. According to the guidelines from the Centers for Medicare & Medicaid Services, state inspections of nursing home facilities are conducted every twelve to fifteen months. By my calculations, since the 2005 survey took place in January, the State surveyors were due back anytime between now and, at the latest, March. Again, it appeared that Riverside North was sprucing up for expected company.

Coincidentally, while I was busy with my student's grade reports, the Nursing Home Report Cards hit the newspapers. Riverside North scored twenty-nine out of a possible forty. I focused on the quality-of-life category that reflected the survey that was completed without input from the two families wishing to have their voices heard in regard to issues of security. Even without us the score in this critical category was a dismal two out of five, an assessment that was spot on, in my opinion, and a strong affirmation of all I had witnessed.

The next morning, my final day at Irondale High School arrived. Logging into the network I recorded grades and exited for the last time. After final goodbyes to my teaching partner and the front office staff, I carried my box of personal belongings out to my car.

I had little time to either mourn or savor the fact that this chapter of my life was concluding, because, once again, a thief in my mother's home had captured my attention. For the past month I had monitored the situation, and I was ready for action.

Since the administration's reaction to "missing" items could be summed up as pitifully unresponsive, this time I sidestepped them completely and spent my first week of retirement sleuthing and then writing about the whole experience. I entitled the resulting story, *Chocolates, anyone?* I brought it to my book group and read it to Helen, Margie, Joann and Nancy, four longtime friends who had not only offered endless emotional support as Mom slipped away, but also listened *ad nauseam* to my many sagas of the sweet/sour life behind nursing home walls.

Chocolates, Anyone?

I have been reduced to counting chocolates. As the old saying goes, who would have ever thought? But here I am in a room at the end of a long, nursing home corridor, sitting by the bedside of my dementia-stricken mother, counting Godiva chocolates, or should I say, finding no more to count.

This story began a few months earlier. On her eighty-eighth birthday Mom received two beautiful, gold boxes of Godiva chocolates from a dear friend, and I needed to find a secret hiding place for these treasures.

Hiding them was essential. Past experience had been my teacher. My lesson began one afternoon when I arrived later than usual and decided a mid-afternoon treat was in order.

"How about a chocolate, Mom?" I said as I popped open one of two boxes of Whitman's Samplers that were stacked on an open shelf of her TV stand. To my surprise, since Mom was incapable of helping herself to this treat, I discovered that the first layer of candy was picked over.

"Someone must be taking the time to feed you some of your chocolates," I said, smiling at the thought that a staff person took the effort to extend this bit of compassion. I raised the paper divider expecting to find a complete selection of mixed chocolates in the bottom row. To my amazement the entire second layer was devoid of candy with nothing remaining except empty white paper cups lined up in perfect rows. I turned my attention to the second box and was astonished to discover that the seal was broken on it as well. I opened it and found more white paper cups in both the top and bottom layers, but not one single chocolate remained. It was obvious that someone besides Mom was enjoying her candy, and whoever it was also attempted to cover up the loss by putting the few remaining pieces in the top row of the top box.

Did I report a chocolate thief? No. I thought about it, but if a hard-working staff member wanted a sweet now and again, I'm sure Mom would have graciously shared hers, if she could have spoken. I kept the discovery to myself and began my secret pastime as ace detective.

Just who was the chocoholic, I wondered? I searched through Mom's miscellaneous things until I uncovered another box of candy that I hadn't had the heart to throw away months, maybe even years, earlier. These chocolates were old, old, old—tinges of white streaked the chocolate exterior, and the inside nougats could shatter teeth. I counted the chocolates—seventeen. I placed the closed box on the open shelf of the TV stand where the Whitman's Samplers had previously sat. And every day when I visited, I counted chocolates—seventeen, seventeen, seventeen—for days the number stayed the same and I deduced that my dismal-looking chocolates did not entice the chocolate thief. But then a pattern developed. On one particular day seventeen dropped to thirteen, and then days went by until thirteen dropped to ten and several days later, ten to seven. It was as I suspected. The chocolate bandit was an occasional visitor and thankfully not one of Mom's regular aides.

So, when Mom's friend Zippy presented her with a present of not one, but two, beautiful, gold boxes of the very best—expensive, delectable Godiva truffles, I knew that I needed to hide them from the chocolate thief. I stashed both boxes in an inconspicuous, flat container and slid it on top of a plastic storage bin high on the closet shelf. Occasionally I retrieved the candy, a task requiring a folding chair and a balancing act. After Mom and I split one of the huge, delicious truffles, I climbed back up into the closet and hid the box again. One day I decided that I needed to find a handier hiding place. I took one candy box and placed it in a dresser drawer that was clearly marked for out-of-season clothes. No need for anyone to go into this drawer now that winter had arrived, I reasoned. I hid the box between folded, summer-weight knit tops. I looked around for a second hiding place. Finding none, I decided to take the second box home and store it there.

Several days later, like a mouse sniffing out cheese, the chocoholic struck again. I opened up the dresser drawer and found Mom's knit tops in disarray. I retrieved the Godiva box and discovered someone had been snooping—chocolates were missing and the elastic cord around the box was not as I had left it. But on that particular day I hurried my visit. Trying to muffle my sneezing and coughs, I quickly checked in on Mom and left without changing the box's location. After two days of nursing a cold, I returned to discover that not only were the rest of the truffles missing, but the gold box had disappeared as well.

Now it was time to report. Val, the floor's supervisor, stepped into Mom's room looking for a staff person. As she turned to leave, I asked if we could talk. She indicated that she was on a mission and would catch up to me later. I waited and then realized that she and others were at the far end of the floor engaged in a ritual of accompanying a deceased resident out to a waiting hearse. How important is a box of chocolates in comparison to the great loss at the other end of the floor? Without talking to Val I left the building and drove home.

But once home I stared at the second box of Godiva chocolates—the one I had removed for safekeeping. How ludicrous! Mom was lying in a bed miles away, and on my desk sat her chocolates. To ensure that they would not be stolen, must they be delivered to her one chocolate at a time? The absurdness of the situation overtook me. I opened the beautiful, gold box and stared at the chocolates. And then, in a fit of insanity, I grabbed a marker and scribbled "SMILE FOR THE CAMERA!!" on a notecard and placed it on top of the truffles before closing the box.

On Sunday I visited Mom and placed the box with the notecard in her dresser drawer between her knit tops where the first box had been. Will the chocolate thief return and read the note? Will he/she experience a moment of fear that the unethical theft of chocolate had been indelibly recorded on a granny-cam? But, most important, will he/she feel a tiny bit of remorse for pawing through personal belongings and stealing from a helpless resident?

Monday, the box appeared untouched. Tuesday, no change. But today, Wednesday, I discover that all the chocolates have disappeared from the gold box. The time to talk to Val has arrived. She accompanies me to Mom's room where I describe the scenario. She assures me that she will remind staff of the policy that forbids them from taking candy from a resident without being invited.

I stare at her incredulously. A policy reminder about chocolates?

"This isn't simply about chocolates," I want to rage. "This is about trust! This is about providing a safe, secure living arrangement for a vulnerable adult. Open your eyes!" But I can't get the words out. Bruised from three years of challenging the status quo, I fold, like the exhausted, disheartened person I have become. Val, appearing satisfied that she had placated one more disgruntled family member, leaves to attend to other duties.

So, here I sit, staring at a beautiful, gold box, now devoid of chocolates. This time, at least, the chocolate thief has left the box behind. I decide to use it for storage. On Mom's TV stand sits a stack of Christmas letters waiting to be filed away. They fit nicely into the empty box. I secure it with the elastic cord and tuck it away among Mom's other treasures.

Two days pass. I return. The pretty gold box and its contents, the Christmas letters, have disappeared. I crumple. Game over, I declare. The thief has won with the help of the nursing home system. I don't want to play anymore. Silently, I walk to the dayroom in search of empty boxes. As Mom naps I spend the remainder of the afternoon packing up the rest of Mom's "treasures" for their trip to their new home, my basement.

After the Chocolates

As ONLY TRIED-AND-TRUE FRIENDS CAN DO, Nancy, Helen, Margie, and Joann laughed and cried with me as I read my story and added additional details.

They listened as I shared one conversation that was not recorded in my chocolate episode. It occurred on the weekend of the final theft of the gold box with the enclosed Christmas cards. A nurse, who was acting as the building supervisor for the weekend (yes, it disappeared on a weekend) shared how frustrated she had become by the loss of oscillators when temporary staff were in the building.

"What are they doing with oscillators?" she had asked her husband, who promptly took her to the computer and showed her the $150 price tag for oscillators on E-bay. Chocolates, oscillators, credit cards, diamond engagement rings—from insignificant to precious—was anything safe?

I told my friends about a hidden camera positioned in Mom's room to catch the chocolate thief and how Julie had bought a box of Godiva chocolates and placed it in Mom's dresser as bait. But setup took weeks. The window of opportunity to snare the perpetrator had closed.

I told them about reorganizing Mom's room so that the framed pictures on the walls and a few comforting knick knacks on flat surfaces were all that remained of my mother's personal belongings. Like the set for a theater production, her "home" was now only skin deep. I had removed from her closet all the clothes that she would never wear and found homes for them. I cleared dresser drawers of sentimental objects. Nothing of value remained.

I told them about discovering in the process the disappearance of two of the three pairs of earrings that I had brought to the nursing home for Mom, even though they were in a tiny box within another box in the bottom drawer—only costume jewelry, but my mother's all the same.

I told them about the continuous struggle to assure that Mom was given a drink of water between meals and about my fear that the next UTI would kill her.

I told them things that they had heard a million times before, but good friends that they were, they listened as I ranted, and then they passed the tissues.

And, when I returned home exhausted and sad, Tom was there, and we decided that after our vacation we would investigate moving Mom to a hospice house, even though she would be significantly farther away. Words from a hospice nurse resonated: "There you won't have to worry about whether your mom gets simple comforts, like a drink of water."

...

As THE DEPARTURE DATE FOR OUR TRIP APPROACHED, worry and dread tempered my excitement. In early February, influenza hit the building. The outbreak not only placed my mother in jeopardy, but also threatened to scuttle our private arrangement with Kate to act as her companion during my absence. Pregnant, Kate would need to follow doctor's orders and avoid third floor if an outbreak occurred.

One morning I arrived to find Mom alone in the dining room. Her aide, obviously not James, had left her in front of her dinner while he delivered another resident to the dentist. Mom was slouched on her tailbone with her foot caught behind the footrest of her wheelchair. Her face was covered in food, yet her Jell-O, cookie, and liquids were untouched. Her sweatshirt was wet and cold from her midmorning shampoo at the beauty shop, so I returned her to her room and changed her clothes, only to discover that she lacked an undershirt and that her elbow pad had been placed on the wrong arm. Thankfully, the incompetence of my mother's morning aide was matched by the kindness of the hospice chaplain Greta, who arrived and, finding me distraught, ministered to me as well as Mom.

Three days before we were scheduled to leave on our vacation, a nurse tested Mom's urine and confirmed the dreaded news: Mom was suffering from another UTI.

Sunday, the day before our trip began, Kaye, the nurse from hospice, was unable to determine if the culture from Mom's urine specimen matched the antibiotic resistant bacteria of the previous year, because there was no history of Mom's previous UTIs in her chart. Those records had been moved downstairs but were unavailable because the staff person who could access them was on vacation.

Kaye also informed me that the nursing home staff had discontinued recording Mom's fluids as ordered weeks earlier by hospice. She assured me that she would reinstate the order. I was heartsick. The infection was raging, the nursing home staff had not been watching Mom's fluid intake as ordered, and we couldn't even get the records to see if we were dealing with the same bacteria that invaded her body a year earlier.

As a crowning touch, James had reported that after returning from several days off, he found food caked like cement on Mom's teeth. Kaye checked the charts. They indicated that my mother had been given oral care with Prevident, the prescription toothpaste, twice daily. This documentation did not jive with James's statements, the state of my mother's teeth, or the two, unused tubes of the toothpaste that I found in my mother's bathroom.

Individually these setbacks were little cracks in the road, but overlapping they created a crevice so wide that Mom once again disappeared.

After confirming that Kate had been given doctor's clearance to visit Mom (since third floor had avoided a flu outbreak), I finished the day by Mom's side. I talked to her, explained that I was going to Maui, and promised that I would be back if she needed me. Then I kissed her goodbye and returned home to pack for a trip that I was not sure I should be taking.

Maui and Back

THE AIRPORT WAS USUALLY ONE OF MY FAVORITE PLACES. I loved to ponder the private stories of those around me. Where was that serviceman going? Was he headed home for a joyful reunion or back to an assignment that placed him in harm's way? What about that couple descending the escalator with three, excited children, that elderly man and woman struggling to take off shoes at the security checkpoint, or that businesswoman multitasking with laptop and cell phone at the boarding gate?

However, the excitement of our trip to Maui was muted by the troubling onset of Mom's UTI and repeated vomiting. My concerns for her health overshadowed my curiosity about the stream of humanity in the airport's concourse. Tom assured me that returning from Maui was an option if emergencies arose, but even with contingency plans in place I found it difficult to enjoy the trip.

At our boarding gate we settled in for a forty-five-minute wait. I grabbed my cell phone and placed five phone calls. First, I received a report from a nurse that my mother had slept comfortably and was now back in her room after eating a decent breakfast. Krista, Zippy, Helen, and Kate, Mom's four guardian angels, each received the latest updates on her condition. Besides thanking everyone, there was nothing more to do.

We boarded the plane that took us to an island in the Pacific, so far away, and yet a place where I felt a unique closeness with my parents. They introduced Tom and me to their paradise during a vacation in 1973. Later when grandchildren arrived, Grandma and Grandpa relished the opportunity to pass along their love for the island to the next generation. After retirement Maui had become their winter home-away-from-home.

Leaving behind the Minnesota windchills and my daily nursing home routine, I arrived in Maui with a desire to rest and enjoy time with Tom and friends. We rendezvoused with Lyn and Warren and settled into B421 of the Maui Sunset in Kihei. Finally, my body began to relax into the calming peacefulness of a Hawaiian evening. Below our lanai, Tiki torches gently illumined the immaculate grounds of the Maui Sunset. Straight ahead the moon's rays reflected off the crests of mild ocean swells. Majestic palms, with fronds splayed in perfect symmetry, showed no crippling signs of the whipping they had endured from afternoon trade winds. The day was ending, and I felt "at home." Although it was only midnight in Maui, it was 4:00 a.m. Minnesota time, so exhausted, Tom and I slipped into bed.

Thanks to the four-hour time change, we awakened in the dark. With coffee cups in hand Tom and I relaxed on the lanai waiting for the sun to waken the island. As the first rays of sunshine spilled over Haleakala, a huge dormant volcano, the curtain of darkness slowly receded, and the Valley Island unfurled in all its tropical finery. Sunrise in Maui embodied the brilliance of creation punctuated by a feeling of certainty that something or someone greater than we could imagine was in control. We could relax, thanks to emails and phone communications with Krista, Helen, Kate and Zippy. Indications were encouraging. Mom's appetite was returning, and she seemed to be improving.

I sensed Mom and Dad's presence everywhere, as we walked the beaches that they had loved and as we honored the sunsets from the same lanai where they nightly had paused to appreciate God's handiwork. I picked up Dad's binoculars and scanned the ocean for whales and their babies, or if I was lucky, entire pods of humpbacks, wondering how many times he had stood in this very spot with binoculars in hand.

Lyn and Warren offered a therapeutic mixture of unconditional support and playful diversion as we enjoyed Maui together. My friendship with Lyn began back in the late 1960s at Concordia College in Moorhead where the two of us shared classes in the Home Economics Department, a stint in the Home Management House and eventually the same dorm room. I was delighted when, years later, she married Tom's friend Warren. Warren is so rock-solid that if anyone asked Krista and Angie how they should proceed if anything happened to Tom and me, "Call Warren" would be their first reply.

Lyn and Warren were well acquainted with Mom, her condition and her bumpy journey during the last few years. With no signs of annoyance at my repetitive blathering, they allowed me to pour out my frustrations and sadness. And when the time was right, they and Tom scheduled delightful diversions: a late afternoon whale watch where we enjoyed the antics of mothers and babies from a boat's close proximity; a visit to Lahaina with a leisurely walk down Front Street; and a drive upcountry to Pukalani and the home of close friends and Minnesota transplants, David and Colleen, who, along with Colleen's brother Rob, treated us with much aloha.

Maui was a prescription for respite. As the days stacked up, I found my energy returning as each day brought phone calls from Krista or Zippy and emails from Helen or Kate describing Mom's improvements.

Eight days into our trip, I recognized the ring tone of my cell phone and ran into the bedroom to answer it. The caller ID said "Riverside Homes." The pulse of my heart quickened as I answered and found Delores, Mom's nurse, on the other end. She started the conversation with a vague comment.

"There has been a change in your mother's condition," she said. Then she informed me that Mom was running a 101-degree fever. There was concern about possible pneumonia and she was ordering a chest X-ray.

I asked the only question that I could formulate. "Has hospice been notified?"

"Yes," she answered, and then stated something about someone she called by a name I did not recognize. "Vicki is here and she asked me to call you."

I didn't pursue the identity of "Vicki." Instead, I focused on the word *pneumonia*. The friend of the elderly, who arrives to take people out of their misery. The same visitor that shortened Dad's life at an alarming speed. Pneumonia!

I bumbled through the rest of the conversation, trying to digest what I was hearing and wondering what other questions I should be asking. I requested the results of the X-ray as soon as they became available, and the conversation ended.

"Pneumonia, Tom. They think she may have pneumonia," I said with a voice that edged on panic.

"Are they taking X-rays?" he asked.

"Yes, and they'll call with results. But she's running a fever of 101. How could things change so quickly? I should have asked if she'd aspirated—or what they are doing to comfort her. What happened?"

Tom's hug calmed me. "I'll check with Northwest Airlines and see what kind of availability there is just in case the X-rays aren't good."

I paced around wondering if I should start packing. Two minutes later I gave up and walked out to the living room where Tom was searching the NWA website for flight information.

"Tom, I need to go. I can't wait for the X-rays." Was I overreacting? I didn't care.

A flurry of activity began. Phone calls were made to Krista and Helen. Both were surprised at Mom's turn, a drastic change from what both had witnessed during their recent visits. Tom called the airlines and spoke directly to a NWA representative who miraculously found a vacant seat on the afternoon flight and offered it at a reasonable rate. Tom relayed the information and waited for my go-ahead, then booked me on a Hawaiian Airlines inter-island flight to Honolulu and a nonstop Northwest Airlines flight that was scheduled to deliver me to Minneapolis at 6 a.m. the next morning.

I returned to the bedroom to pack, flustered again by the task.

"Just take essentials," Tom said. "If your mom stabilizes you can return. And if you can't, I'll bring everything home when I come." His direction calmed me.

"What about Angie?" I asked. She was scheduled to arrive in Maui from San Francisco in three days. "You need to be here when she comes."

"We'll take it step by step. For now, just pack what you need."

Culling through my warm weather wardrobe, I grabbed the warmest outfit that I had: pants, long-sleeved tee, sweater and lightweight jacket. I changed into the tee shirt and pants and stuffed the others into my backpack, along with a few toiletries, cell phone, journal, wallet and key chain, and finally exchanged my sandals for socks and tennis shoes. I was packed.

As we neared the airport, my cell phone rang. It was Angie calling from San Francisco. "Krista called. What's happening?" she asked, before adding, "I need to see Grandma."

"We're not sure yet. I'm heading home. We'll call when we know more" was all I could offer.

"But I need to see Grandma," she repeated.

"I know." Clearly she was experiencing the same type of separation anxiety that was coursing through my body. "We're at the airport. Sorry, but I have to go. Dad will call you back," I promised as Tom dropped me off in front of Agricultural Inspection before heading back to the condo to coordinate communications and logistics from the ground.

Check-in was accomplished smoothly and quickly. The Hawaiian Airlines employee scrutinized me when she found out that I was flying one-way and had no luggage to check. More than likely those facts flagged my ticket because security personnel whisked me off to the side for a more thorough screening once I passed through the metal detector.

Finally, I arrived at the departure gate. There sitting like an angel in long pants was Rob, Colleen's brother. Coincidentally, I had been booked on his return flight to Minneapolis. His comforting presence was the work of fate or something more profound. Besides letting me use his cell phone (mine was woefully low on charge), he led me on a shortcut from the inter-island terminal to the main terminal once we arrived in Honolulu. Then as we waited to board our nonstop flight to Minneapolis, he helped me sort out the maze of problems resulting from the timing of Mom's deterioration.

"Why don't you work backwards," Rob suggested, helping me regain a measure of self-control. "Can Angie's ticket to Maui be pushed back a few days? If so, that would give her time to book a flight to Minneapolis and see her grandmother."

"Of course," I agreed. Work backwards. One thing at a time.

From a floral shop in the concourse next to the gate I purchased a fragrant plumeria lei and the sales woman wrapped it for travel. The final telephone call before boarding was to Helen. She had seen Mom and believed that she had stabilized. She also offered to pick me up at 6:00 a.m. outside the terminal in Minneapolis and to drive me directly over to North.

Although long, the flight was pleasantly uneventful. Relaxed vacationers sporting tanned bodies settled in for eight hours of travel. One by one the people around me dozed off, and I tried to do the same. Sleep came in snatches, and each time I awakened, I checked my watch and said a silent prayer for Mom. As Rob descended to baggage claim, I exited the terminal and spotted Helen next to her car at the curb. Handing me a winter jacket and a bottle of water, she welcomed me home, and we headed to the nursing home about twenty minutes away.

I saw no one as we exited the elevator on third floor and continued down the hallway to Mom's room. Holding my breath I entered. There she was. Resting comfortably. Eyes open. The only hint that something was wrong was the whistling rattle that emerged every time she breathed.

"Hi, Mom! It's Jackie. I'm here. And I brought you something from Maui."

I took the lei out of my backpack, unwrapped it and draped it across her pillow next to her head, then kissed her gently. The distinct, tropical scent of plumeria filled the room, and Mom smiled. With great relief I pulled up a chair next to her and talked to her about anything that came into my head—Maui, the condo, the whales, the trade winds, all things that she loved.

A nurse entered and inserted an instrument into Mom's ear.

"Ninety-seven degrees," she reported.

I called Tom. "Mom is lying next to me," I whispered. "Her fever is gone, but she is so unresponsive, and there is a rattle as she breathes, like there is phlegm that she can't clear."

He informed me that Angie's flight to Maui had been postponed and that she would be arriving in Minneapolis later in the day, and he gave me updates on his conversations with Krista. "She wants you to call her." Tom's cell phone in Maui had become communication central.

Zippy arrived. I began to explain what had happened, that Mom had taken a turn for the worse.

"I know," Zippy said. "I was the one who found her in distress. I don't know why, but for some reason I came over to check on Teen before work instead of waiting until after. When I got here, she was hyperventilating. She couldn't breathe. I asked a nurse to administer oxygen and then told them to call you."

"Oh, my gosh. You are 'Vicki!' Mom's nurse told me a Vicki had asked her to call me. At least I thought she said Vicki. It was you! Zippy, if you hadn't come, what would have happened?"

Neither of us could answer my question.

Later, Kaye from hospice arrived.

"How is she doing?" she asked as she approached Mom's bed.

"Her fever is gone," I responded, but my remark produced a quizzical look on Kaye's face. She placed her freshly disinfected hand on Mom's cheek and forehead and then took a thermometer out of her bag and placed it in Mom's armpit.

"One hundred and one. She still has her fever."

"But they took it in her ear not that long ago and it registered ninety-seven."

"Here, you keep this," she said, handing me the thermometer. "Track her temperature yourself. Take it under the arm. It's more accurate. Just add one degree." She listened to the congestion in Mom's lungs and then talked to her in a reassuring voice.

"What's happening?" I asked, and then I received the news that confirmed my internal need to fly over 4,500 miles. It was unlikely that Mom would survive this bout of pneumonia.

The vigil began.

The Vigil

I FLIPPED MOM'S WALL CALENDAR TO MARCH 2006. As I stared at the monthly grid of days I wonderer which of these dates would forever mark her passing.

Although shortened, my Maui vacation had been a much-needed respite, much like one my parents had been given before the end of my brother's life.

"We suggest that you consider spending a week at St. Joe's," Jim's hospice nurse had said. "Not because you need hospitalization right now, but because your parents need a respite to gather strength for the final days."

So, Jim spent a week on the hospice floor while Mom and Dad rested. Then he returned home, and they cared for him until he died.

Now I realized that I had been given a respite, and I was back for the last mile of Mom's race. She would cross the finish line, and, thankfully, she would be accompanied by a family member every step of the way. Although a bit sleep deprived from the overnight flight, I sensed a sweet calmness flowing through my body on this March 1 evening. My greatest fear would not materialize. Mom would not die alone.

Mom's room at the end of a long nursing home corridor became a gathering place for family and friends. Krista and Steve brought food and bottles of water. My friend Cindy delivered Angie from the airport and offered to help in any way that we needed her. Clay and Becky arrived. Now Mom was surrounded by her grandchildren. Most importantly, we made a pact: someone would always be with her. I breathed deeply and exhaled. Angie reclined on the bed next to her grandmother and slept. Krista stayed awake all night by her grandmother's bedside so I could go home, shower, sleep for the first time in forty-eight hours, and change into warmer clothes before heading back to the nursing home. All was well.

On Thursday, March 2, Kaye listened to Mom's lungs again and confirmed that she was now in a semi-coma. Answering my questions she explained that end of life was different for each individual, but people in Mom's condition rarely lived longer than twenty-four to forty-eight hours. Kaye described the physical changes that most likely would occur: the mottling of the skin from the extremities inward as circulation changed, the slowing of respiration.

I called Tom. With the end so near, any thoughts we had of his returning to Minnesota were discarded. For me, remaining in touch by telephone trumped a return trip that would place him out of contact for many hours.

Surprisingly, there was something truly comforting in knowing that this was Mom's last infection. She was nearing the time when her spirit could escape its dementia-ridden cage. The grandchildren and I watched and listened, but the skin on Mom's hands and feet remained a beautiful shade of ivory, and her rattled breathing continued in a steady, rhythmic pattern.

Once again Mom and her family were graced with visitors bearing special gifts of friendship. Kate arrived and described her visits with Mom while I was in Maui. We talked about her pregnancy and marveled at the circular nature of life. My friend Nancy brought hugs along with food, but most importantly, her infectious laugh.

Helen's spouse Perry arrived with hymnal in hand, and he and Zippy harmonized to one tune after another. The music acted as a magnet. Darlene, a resident and friend of Mom's from down the hall, asked if she could join us, and other residents ambled in and out of Mom's room to enjoy the music and to check in on their friend.

Later, I slipped out and updated Pearl, Mom's trusty friend and tablemate. This wonderful woman had experienced the loss of so many friends, and with each one she had to wonder when her time would come.

Later in the day Greta, the hospice chaplain, played her flute for Mom. Then she presented me with a comforting image.

"The family and friends that surround your mom remind me of a group of midwives," she said. "They have gathered to assist her in her rebirth. What a tribute to her!"

Rebirth. Not death. A visual that sustained me. Another hospice gift.

Krista and Angie returned to Krista's home for some sleep. Zippy stayed late into the night to keep me company. Hoping she heard our voices and felt our presence, we sat on either side of Mom and talked for hours with her between us. Finally, I encouraged Zippy to go home and get some rest. She was exhausted from juggling work, school, and trips to the nursing home. Zippy was a person that our family never would have met if Mom had not suffered from dementia. She had become a golden thread, a living sign of unexpected grace that accompanied tragedy.

Now alone with Mom I turned on the soothing sounds of the Healing Touch CD and adjusted the volume, loud enough to fill the lonely corners of the room, but soft enough to create a soothing lullaby. I picked up my journal and began to explore the strange juxtaposition of tucking in my own mother for the night. Being able to focus on my writing was testament to the serenity I felt in my heart. My mood tonight was nostalgic.

My mind drifted back five decades to simpler times when Mom was strong of mind and body, and I, at age five, was buffered from the hardships of life by childlike naivete and my parents' comforting presence. Soon, a real-life bedtime story, for no particular audience, streamed out of my pen.

"Tell me a Tommy story," I'd plead as Mom tucked the blankets around me and kissed me good night. My cousin Tommy expertly played the part of the precocious little preschooler, and his pranks made great fodder for bedtime stories. There was the story of Tommy gathering everyone's shoes, lining them up neatly on the back step and filling each one with sand. My favorite was a story of Tommy's disappearance after he somehow boarded a St. Paul streetcar and rode it back and forth all afternoon. Even though I knew their endings, these stories contained a measure of thrill, and I vicariously enjoyed the thought of Tommy's antics unfolding under the eyes of so many adults. Mom, thespian that she was, narrated "Tommy Stories" as if she were relating them for the first time, complete with dialectal inflections and perfect timing. Jim, lying in the lofted bunk bed, completed the receptive audience for Mom's magical storytelling.

Perhaps the reason I loved "real life" bedtime stories, over the fantastical, once-upon-a-time, fairytale variety was because the Tommy stories connected me to my father's relatives who lived three hundred miles away in the Twin Cities.

In spite of being separated from extended family, Dad loved Crookston. As a parole agent, he traveled around the northwest quadrant of the state and soon became well respected by law enforcement in neighboring towns as well as by the parolees who appreciated the help he offered with job placement and counseling. One exception, however, created a "real life" tale that Mom never incorporated in her repertoire of bedtime stories. One parolee, a man diagnosed as psychopathic, threatened Dad's life as well as the lives of the rest of his family. Eventually the man was committed to a state hospital, but until that time Mom expanded her bedtime ritual. On nights when Dad was working out of town, she tucked my brother and me into bed with a bedtime story, kissed us goodnight and turned out the lights. Unknown to us, after we fell asleep, she reentered the room, barricaded the door by sliding the wooden dresser in front of it, and climbed into the lower bunk with me. There she slept until dawn when she rose and returned the dresser to its original position before we awoke. Years later, well after the threat had passed, Dad was the one who shared with Jim and me the story of this unsettling time and the extent of our mother's actions to keep us safe and oblivious to the threat.

Now, it is your family's turn to keep you safe, Mom.

I closed my journal and gazed at Mom, who appeared comfortable and yet so fragile. A small rattle from her throat was the only clue that the infection persisted. Her petite frame occupied little space in the bed. I drew the bed sheet back and checked her hands and feet—smooth, beautiful, ivory skin.

Friday, March 3, another day had come. Accompanying a loved one through the actively dying process can be a spiritual gift. I experienced it along with my parents sixteen years earlier when Jim succumbed to his insidious brain cancer. Now Mom's granddaughters and grandson were feeling the comfort that comes from being present both physically and emotionally during a loved one's final days. Their gentle, gutsy little grandma had epitomized unconditional love since before their earliest memories. Now, each of them was traveling a separate path through the grieving process. Soon she would leave her defective body behind, and her survivors would seek out memories of pre-dementia times to comfort us in our grief.

After sunrise, activity increased in Mom's room. The aides and nurses on each shift were now accustomed to the presence of family members and friends gathered in the room. Although Delores had been absent since I returned from Maui, other third-floor nurses, three of whom were male, sensed the fragility of Mom's condition and brought the finest level of compassion to her care. Nursing assistants, James, Jeanine and Eric, tenderly cared for and repositioned my mother's tiny body, while many other aides, who had worked with Mom in the past, found moments to pop in for quiet visits with Mom and her family. Theresa, although no longer the nurse assigned to my mother's care, checked in often. Each visitor was a concrete reminder of the many wonderful people that worked on third floor.

When Sharon, another hospice nurse, checked Mom's vitals and listens to her lungs she downgraded her condition from "semi-coma" to "coma," but also communicated a measure of surprise that Mom was hanging on.

True to her compassionate reputation Rebecca, the third-floor receptionist, anticipated the needs of the family. Thanks to her, a rollaway bed was wheeled into the room, even before the family realized what a tiring vigil Mom's last days would require. Rebecca checked on Mom's progress often. She spent snatches of time with Mom, and extended thoughtful gestures of support to our exhausted family. She delivered a traveling basket of spiritual books and tapes and other items of comfort for the family and asked if we were in need of meals.

Lyn and Warren surprised us with a visit. Blurry-eyed from their overnight return flight from Maui, they delivered a fresh flower lei to Mom, and we replaced the highly fragrant, but short-lived plumeria. I found it incomprehensible that so much had happened since I had last seen them in Maui three days earlier.

Years of losing a loved one to dementia had given me time to process much of my grief. By phone I shared with Tom the latest hospice message: Mom could pass at any moment. Strangely, I was comforted by the fact that he was still in Maui. His presence there confirmed that after the vigil was over, I would return to this tranquil island. I explained that in his absence the grandchildren had stepped up. He assured me that he was being tended to by our Maui friends Colleen and David. Now my only regret was that he would not have the opportunity to experience firsthand the blessings of support from those who had crossed the threshold of Mom's room. As if on cue, Helen arrived again, this time with soup.

The revolving door ushered in family members of other third-floor residents, a wife of one, a daughter of another. All of us had been traveling parallel journeys with our loved ones, and they offered words of support and condolence. Shortly, my journey would end, and theirs would continue until it was time for their final goodbyes.

The weekend began. The staff person assigned to supervise the building during the night shift stepped into Mom's room, introduced herself to me and reminded me that the nursing home was "on skeleton staff."

"Would you like me to contact the chaplain?" she asked.

I simply answered, "Thank you, no. We are being wonderfully ministered to by a hospice chaplain."

The question jolted me into the realization of a critical absence during the past three days. Outside of a quick check-in by the third-floor clinical coordinator, no Monday-Friday staff, including other members of Mom's care team, the chaplain, or any building administrators, were included in the list of nursing home staff who had entered Mom's room to share a few special moments with her or the family. Perhaps they were on vacation, or ill. Perhaps they did not know that someone on the floor was dying. Perhaps they did not want to answer any of my questions about Mom's sudden change in condition. Perhaps it was not in their job descriptions. Now, they had all left the building for the weekend. It was what I had come to expect, but it saddened me all the same.

One person who did stop by to see Mom before leaving for the weekend was Theresa, who was currently nursing on another floor. She was leaving for the weekend. I offered a special goodbye and included our family's thanks, just in case the vigil would end before she returned on Monday morning.

Once the night shift was underway, I realized how eerily quiet third floor became on a Friday night. I was especially thankful that Mom had a private room, so the grandchildren and I could close the door and talk into the wee hours of the morning without disturbing other residents. As the evening progressed, Krista, Angie, Clay, and Becky gathered, and laughing and storytelling stretched into the night. I curled up on the rollaway bed and drifted off for a few hours of sleep.

At 4:00 a.m. March 4, I awoke for the day and took my turn as vigil keeper. The kids either went home or swapped a chair for a spot on the rollaway for a nap, and the room became quiet again. Maureen, the third nurse from hospice to check on Mom, was surprised at her strength but alerted us that she might pass soon. Like I had done often over the last four days, I called Tom. Each time he expected to hear that Mom was gone. "The kids continue to be incredible," I told him. "All is well here," I assured him again. But I missed him, and I knew that it was difficult for him to be so far away.

The pastor from our church visited briefly, and the family picked a date for Mom's memorial service. Since her wishes for cremation had been established years before the onset of her dementia, an immediate service would not be necessary. Thankfully, overwhelming funeral preparations did not dominate our thoughts. We simply chose a date, April 9, Palm Sunday, for an afternoon memorial service with the burial the day before. Krista passed the information on to extended family, while I concentrated on being present with Mom.

"Midwives" encircled Mom throughout the day. Only the faces changed, as friends exchanged places for extended visits. Helen and Perry arrived. Book group friends Joann and Nancy returned, this time bringing a special surprise, my dear friend Barb from Grand Marais. Storytelling began in earnest once more. Laughter. Hugs. Mom continued her steady breathing as friends and grandkids came and went. We hypothesized that perhaps Mom sensed that this party was just too much fun to leave. By now all of us believed that she was holding out until the next day, March 5, the anniversary of Dad's death.

Sunday, March 5. In the early hours I drove quickly home for my daily shower and change of clothes, while Krista stood guard with cell phone in hand in case Mom's breathing changed. The morning was calm and quiet. Hospice nurse Maureen examined Mom. Again we were told that the end was near. Once Margie arrived with Nancy, all of my book group, the supportive women who through the years had patiently listened to my mother's story, had occupied a place in the circle. Each had become an integral part of this the final, redeeming chapter.

The grandkids sensed that this would be the last day of their grandmother's life. They took turns privately spending time with her and telling her anything that they wanted spoken before she took her final breath.

James tenderly cared for Mom throughout his morning shift, and before he left for the day announced that he was off until Tuesday. In my heart I knew that Mom would not survive until then so I gave him a hug, and with tears streaking my cheeks I thanked him for being such a compassionate caregiver, my mother's hero. Around 10:30 p.m. Jeanine checked in right after her shift ended. She assured us that she would be returning in less than eight hours to work a double shift. Although she would not be assigned to Mom, she would be close by if we needed her. Once more, hugs, tears. Another hero.

Scuttlebutt hinted that the state surveyors would most likely show up for their visit in the morning. It had been nearly fifteen months since their last survey, so their appearance was inevitable sometime in the next three weeks. "Just in case," one nursing assistant whispered, "strong staffing has been scheduled for tomorrow morning."

How I wish the state would arrive tonight!

The night shift began and the floor became eerily quiet. The night's designated facility supervisor entered Mom's room. She informed me that the highest-ranking staff person working on Mom's floor that night was a TMA, a trained medications aide.

"There is no nurse?" I asked.

"Not tonight. Only two of the four floors have been assigned nurses tonight. I'm a nurse, so if you need me talk to the TMA. She will know how to contact me."

She rattled on, mentioning something about being occupied on the opposite end of the complex with paperwork relating to falls. I half listened, because I was stuck on the incredulous fact that two floors of over 100 nursing home residents had no nurse readily available to oversee their care. Once she departed, I fully realized how thankful I was that Mom was not alone and that she did not require skilled nursing care.

The evening ebbed by, and about 11:00 p.m. I left Krista, Angie and Clay with their grandma and took a walk down to the first-floor commons area to stretch my legs. In the few minutes that I was gone, Mom's breathing changed, and I was quickly summoned back. Once more, steady breathing resumed, and we sat, quietly talking until the clock ticked away the last remaining minutes of March 5, disproving our prediction of Mom's departure. No one was inclined to leave, so the four of us hunkered down for the rest of the night. Taking turns, two of us listened to Mom's breathing from bedside chairs while the other two napped on the rollaway bed.

On Monday, March 6, the dirty remnants of winter slowly receded as the morning sun attacked the remaining snow. Ice crystals melted into rivulets that traveled the least restrictive path down the sidewalk and into the spongy earth. Mom would not experience the rebirth of spring. No more trips around the kidney-shaped pond in her wheelchair to watch the antics of the baby waterfowl. No Easter dinner at our house. No inhalation of fragrant lilacs. Not for Mom.

I turned away from the window and centered on the activity in the room. Mom had survived the night, but the end was near, according to Kaye, who arrived from hospice. She handed me her stethoscope, and I listened to

Mom's lungs. I heard what sounded like dried, rustling leaves. Kaye was amazed that Mom was still hanging on.

"Has everyone said goodbye? Have you given her permission to leave?" she asked.

"I think so" was my feeble reply.

Before Kaye left, she reminded us to ask the nurse on duty to call her when Mom passed. This was likely the last visit from hospice. She commended our family for surrounding Mom with love. My verbal thank-you for the weeks of compassionate care sounded woefully inadequate.

As Eric, Mom's morning aide, a gentle bear of a man, cleansed and gently repositioned her, the grandkids stood outside the room and discussed Kaye's questions.

Had we all said goodbye? Yes.

In addition, I had told Mom that along with taking care of her granddaughters, I would look after Clay, a responsibility she and Dad had gladly undertaken after Jim died. Clay had told his grandmother that he would take care of me, as had Krista and Angie. We chuckled as we compared notes. Obviously, we would all be taking great care of each other. What could she be waiting for? We telephoned Tom and put the cell phone to Mom's ear so she could hear his goodbye, too. We told her again that it was okay to go. Had we covered everything? We thought we had, so we simply waited.

The eerie quiet of the night and weekend was exchanged for a flurry of Monday morning activity around third floor. Eleanor, Mom's social worker, caught me in the hallway. She verbalized surprise at Mom's condition. Her comment saddened me. Didn't she realize that Mom's vigil was now in its sixth day?

"Would you like the procession of honor for your Mom?" she asked referring to the new protocol for exiting deceased residents out the front door with a procession of staff and residents. I remembered the words of the director of nursing at a family meeting months earlier as he described this new protocol. I liked the idea of honoring the resident in this manner, until he explained the timing for the change. "Because of remodeling the back doors will be blocked by construction," he had said.

"No, thank you," I simply answered. *Those who have visited Mom these last few days have honored her.*

"Would you like the chaplain to come up and say a prayer?"

"Yes, that would be nice," I said and excused myself so I could return to Mom's room.

Eric's kindness extended to the family as he wheeled in a cart with four lunch trays of lasagna, side dishes and enticing iced beverages and encouraged us to eat. My friend Ruth quietly talked to me as the grandkids circled the bed with their chairs. I encouraged them to eat some lunch or at least drink something. Finally, they rose almost in unison and reached for glasses of water. As if their retreat from her bedside provided the impetus she needed to head to the light, Mom's breathing changed.

"She's not breathing." It was Ruth's voice that reached me first, then Clay's with the same message.

We circled again. Two short breaths and then a pause. Two more short breaths. Another pause. A long breath. And then she was gone. The glowing whiteness of her skin confirmed her passing. It was 12:34 p.m.

We had been expecting this moment, but once it arrived the finality of Mom's departure crushed us. My first instinct was to call Tom. But first, the grandchildren and I paused, each in our own private grief.

Similar to my brother's passing, I felt an immediate detachment to the body, the shell that remains after the soul departs. Finally, Mom was free of the disease that had crippled her. I hesitated to notify the nursing staff. I feared that once I informed the nurse on duty that Mom was no longer breathing, our privacy would evaporate. So I purposefully waited until calls to Tom, Zippy, and Helen were completed and Ruth departed with a list of friends to notify. Then the nurse was summoned, and once she confirmed that Mom's heart was no longer beating, she called hospice.

From that point, the announcement of Mom's passing spread throughout the floor. Floodgates opened and an onslaught of people, both residents and members of Mom's care team, crowded into her room for a final prayer. We uncomfortably waited for the chaplain until finally in his absence Val, the third-floor clinical coordinator, asked us to join hands and say the Lord's Prayer together. Then she followed it with a thoughtful prayer of her own. At that point members of Mom's care team turned to the grandchildren and offered hugs and condolences before they exited.

"Who were those people?" asked Clay referring to the ones who had just hugged him and were now on to other business, "and why didn't they visit Grandma when she was alive?"

I could answer the first question, but not the second.

Again the room was quiet, and we were alone.

"Whoa, that was strange." Krista followed up her comment with an intuitive analogy. "That felt a bit like being in a restaurant when someone called out for wait staff to gather and sing 'Happy Birthday'." We nodded in agreement.

In a grief-filled fog we proceeded.

Leaving Clay and Angie in the room, Krista and I located Pearl, described Mom's peaceful passing and said goodbye. Sarah arrived with condolences, answers to my questions, and assurances that hospice would be in contact with the family in the days ahead.

Shortly, a nurse informed me that she had the Cremation Society on the phone.

"They would like to know how soon you would like them to come for your mother. They will wait until others have a chance to pay respects if you would like," she added.

"Please tell them to come right away."

Shortly, Zippy arrived, and we shared tears and hugs.

While I am talking to Clay in the hallway, a gray-haired woman sped past us and ducked into my mother's room. A minute later Krista ran out and called to me, "Mom, quick, come in. The chaplain is saying a prayer."

I reentered the room with Krista and found Zippy alone with a woman who was by this time midway through her prayer. After the "amen" she explained that she had been called in as a sub for the chaplain, but without introductions she exited as swiftly as she appeared. Who was she? I didn't know. Did she know that the deceased was my mother? Or that the people in the hallway were grandchildren? The moment for communication had passed.

Perhaps accentuated by a strange combination of sleep deprivation and grief, the intrusive, sanctimonious gestures of the last few minutes heightened my internal anxiety. Fearing the grandchildren were experiencing the same, I gathered them and suggested that they all go home. I wanted nothing else to blemish the quiet, spiritual passing of their grandmother. In addition, Clay had yet to talk to Becky, Krista was exhausted and running a fever, and Angie was visibly distraught. They all needed to get away from the building.

Just as they left, the representative from the Cremation Society arrived. Before he gently wrapped Mom's body and placed her on the gurney, he asked if I would like the Hawaiian flower lei to accompany her.

"That would be nice" were all the words I could get out.

Helen arrived at the nursing home and waited for the elevator. Perfectly timed the doors opened; inside was the gurney.

"Is that Teen Johnson?" she asked. Upon confirmations, she kissed her hand and placed it gently upon the covering, and then Mom's body exited the building for the final time.

Eager to also leave the building, I hesitated, only because I knew that once I left, I would not want to return to clean out Mom's few remaining belongings.

"We can move things now," said Zippy. "Don't leave anything of value here."

"There is little of value left," I explained.

"Then it won't take us long to pack up," Helen added.

Lyn entered not realizing that Mom had passed. So, instead of assisting with the vigil she helped with the packing. With lightening speed Zippy removed pictures off the wall, while Lyn and Helen wrapped photo frames and trinkets in fleecewear. I sought out Rebecca who scrounged up boxes. In record time the packing was completed. We loaded the boxes onto a flatbed and balanced trash bags filled with clothing on top. When we closed the door, we left behind only four items: an empty dresser, a plant stand, a TV cart, and Mom's wingback chair. With perfect timing, Steve phoned and offered to return the following morning with his cousin Tommy to claim the furniture. We transferred Mom's personal belongings to my car and to Helen's, and I turned my attention to Zippy, who was expressing her grief outwardly and honestly, characteristic of her heritage. I feebly expressed my indebtedness to her. How differently the end of Mom's life might have unfolded had Zippy not found Mom in distress. Thanks to her, Mom had not died alone.

Helen and I caravanned home, with my car in the lead. On one residential street I glanced at the speedometer and realized I was driving twenty miles per hour over the speed limit. Breathe! Breathe! I lessened the force on the gas pedal. Mile after mile I separated myself farther from the red brick building, and thanks to Helen, Lyn, Zippy, Steve and Tommy, there would be no need to return.

Carried Along

Mom had passed, and I experienced the strange sensation of being, for the first time, an orphan, albeit a fifty-eight-year-old one. The only survivor of my family of origin. No parents. No siblings. The reality of this condition startled me and gave me greater empathy for my daughters, who were given up by birth mothers in a country on the other side of the world. Now I understood the holes in their hearts, even though they were surrounded with love.

March 8, 2006

A Northwest Airlines jet is carrying me back to Tom. Actually, I have been "carried" ever since Mom left us. For the last two days a tag-team of friends and family has not let my feet touch the ground, thanks to simple, yet overwhelmingly supportive gestures: phone calls from girlfriends with offers of help, Helen's comforting presence at the Cremation Society (thank heaven for Mom's preplanning), Dick's bear hugs and airport taxi service for Angie, Steve's and Tommy's furniture moving, Clay's evening visit to lessen the quiet of an empty house, Cindy's upbeat conversation while she chauffeurs me to the airport, etc. Although life has changed, my golden threads are all around me—strong, flexible reeds that weave a basket of support, a safe nest in which to rest.

A conversation with Helen reminded me that I am still able to grow new shoots on my family tree. We talked about the intersection of our lives and our closeness. Like sisters, we agreed. A comforting thought for someone who has lost the final member of her family of origin!

In less than five hours I will be landing in Kahului, and Tom will be waiting. I'm so incredibly tired. All the people I know and love are safe. No worries right now.

I closed my journal and stowed it in my backpack then quickly relaxed into a deep sleep. Awake again, I peered out the window of the plane. Off to the south the peaks of Mauna Kea and Mauna Loa, the volcanoes of the Big Island, protruded through a cover of clouds. The plane continued past them. Eventually, the ocean below gave way to lush, green fields of sugar cane. As the setting sun disappeared into the Pacific, the jet landed on the tarmac and taxied to the gate. Finally, I pulled out my cell phone and placed the call.

"Tom, I'm here!" So was he, just beyond security. We located each other easily in the small airport. A homecoming! With no luggage to collect, we quickly headed out to the car. An inhalation of tropical freshness cleansed me of any remnants of anxiety. Now with Tom next to me, I felt like I had finally completed the incredible journey of parenting my parents.

Before heading back to the condo, we decided to detour to Koho's, a local eatery, for a bite of dinner and a long conversation. At the first stoplight my cell phone rang.

"Hi, Mom!" It was Krista. "Just calling to make sure your plane landed safely."

"It did, and I'm with your dad." We talked briefly.

Finally, we arrived at the condo in Kihei. I stood in the bedroom and recalled all the worry and confusion attached to the day I left. Had it only been eight days?

It was not until the next morning, after a walk along the beach and the purchase of a Maui newspaper, that Tom and I were shaken by the headlines. An air ambulance scheduled to land at the Maui airport had crashed into a car dealership at 7:08 p.m. the preceding evening. I grabbed my cell phone and checked the time of Krista's call: 7:05 p.m. We had just changed course to head to Koho's when the phone had rung. Had we continued straight to the condo, we would have passed the car dealership and perhaps witnessed like so many others the fiery crash that took the lives of the medical crew aboard. The newspaper story was a horrific reminder that death does not always come slowly and gently. It was with grateful hearts that Tom and I gathered Angie, Krista and Steve safely together at the end of the week.

No longer worried about Mom, cell phones were turned off during walks on the beach and heart-to heart conversations with Karen, a dear friend from my past who lived three blocks from the Maui Sunset. She asked about the date and time of the memorial service, so she could simultaneously honor my mother by scattering tropical flowers into the surf.

On the final weekend of our stay we gathered on the beach for Holly and Seth's wedding, complete with flower leis and Hawaiian wedding chants. New beginnings!

Now, for the fourth time in one month I was crossing the Pacific. This time I was heading home to plan a memorial service for Mom, one that would help us reclaim our memories of the vibrant, articulate woman that all of us loved so much.

Moving On

MANY PEOPLE SAY FUNERALS PROVIDE CLOSURE, a time to truly accept the passing of a loved one. In our family's case, those that loved my mother had been saying goodbye to her for years. As her disease insidiously gnawed away at her ability to function in her world, we had grieved each loss with heartbreaking sadness.

No, for me acceptance of Mom's passing arrived on March 6, 2006, the moment her soul departed her body along with her final breath. With that exhalation, dementia lost its power to commandeer Mom's core. Free at last, her spirit soared, and the burial and memorial service, with strokes of love and support from extended family and friends, supplied the exclamation points that celebrated this passage.

Indelible impressions marked the burial of Mom's ashes on a Saturday morning and the celebration of her life the following Sunday afternoon: an eagle overseeing the activity at the cemetery on a crisp, sunlit morning—family members gathering around an urn and bouquet of white daisies—simple prayers—the Young and the Johnson branches of the family tree enjoying an old-fashioned turkey dinner together—storytelling, laughter, hugs—Palm Sunday afternoon, Peace United Methodist Church—photographs of Mom in every stage of her life—her portrait and a bouquet of tropical flowers on an altar draped in soft, colorful fabrics—comforting music—and especially, Tom's spoken words that helped those in attendance reclaim our memories of a vital, healthy mother, grandmother, sister, aunt and friend.

...

TOO SOON AUNT BETTY AND AUNT MAX, Mom's wildly wonderful sisters, along with cousins from the Young branches of the family tree flew home with commitments to reunite for events other than funerals. Again, a visit with extended family had been unbelievably therapeutic. My aunts' tales of sisterly interactions, complete with human foibles, invoked healing laughter and helped me resist the temptation to elevate my mother to any level of sainthood. She would have hated that designation. Instead, with humanity fully restored, she became again the tiny dynamo, lover of life and fun and family.

With Tom's help, I went about the business of tying up all the loose ends that a trustee is assigned to do when a death occurs. I settled Mom's finances, sorted through her personal belongings, and sent memorial contributions to her favorite places: Hamline University Class of '39 Scholarship Fund and Children's Home Society of Minnesota. The hospice program so appreciated by the family was added to the list.

No longer trekking over to the nursing home for daily visits, I spent afternoons writing notes of thanks for random acts of compassion. Modest, yet profoundly supportive gestures from individual healthcare workers were acknowledged: spending a few minutes with Mom after a work shift; talking with her even though she was technically "comatose"; turning her gently or repositioning the flower lei on her pillow so she could still see and smell it. The list was long.

• • •

UNFORTUNATELY, FROM THE MOMENT WE RETURNED FROM MAUI, Corporate continued to haunt me, even though Mom's ashes were in the ground.

"Here's a letter from the nursing home," said Tom as he sorted the mail that awaited us after our return. Half expecting to find a condolence letter, I opened the envelope and discovered a bill for the entire month of March, even though Mom had passed on March 6.

I initiated a call to the business office to inform them of Mom's death.

"I guess you would like a new bill" was the only response.

"Yes" was all I could muster, disappointed once more in the impersonality of my mother's final home.

A second letter arrived a few days later from corporate headquarters. It was a fundraising letter, beautifully printed and complete with return envelope, encouraging us to honor our loved ones, or to memorialize them "when the time comes" with gifts to Riverside North. We were not targeted because Mom had died, but simply because we were on the list. It was a form letter with the unfortunate arrival preceding any message of condolence.

The third letter arrived on Friday, May 12, over nine weeks after Mom's passing. This time the letter was one of condolence from the head of Riverside North. It was followed by a second letter that arrived on the following Monday, May 15, with the invitation to a memorial service on Wednesday, May 23, for the fourteen people from third floor who had died over the winter. I was stunned that nearly a quarter of the sixty residents of the floor would not see summer. I found the words of the letter, describing Mom as a sadly missed member of the "family" of the nursing home, ringing a bit hollow when they arrived nine weeks after she had passed. Cynically, I hypothesized the reason for the belatedness of the message. Condolence letters must be quarterly mass mailings. Mom just happened to have died early in the cycle.

As I entered the date of the memorial service into my day planner, I realized that Wednesday was not May 23 but May 24, so I called North to confirm. There was a mistake in the letter, I was told. The service was Tuesday, May 23.

Although this service was a simple formality for the staff, done quarterly on each floor, families experienced it only once, and I was disheartened that we were given less than two week's notice with a confusion in dates.

On Tuesday, May 23, I returned to North. Once Tom and I joined Clay, Krista, and friends Helen and Margie for the memorial service, we received good news as we approached the elevators. Because of noise from jackhammers, the memorial service was being moved from the third-floor dayroom to the chapel. A quiet, respectful ambiance greeted us as we entered and took our seats with other family members and a few residents from third floor who had been transported down.

To honor each deceased resident, a personal history from the information provided at his or her admission was read, followed by the lighting of a candle. Unfortunately, there was a mix-up, and the tribute to one resident, thankfully not Mom, was skipped. Discounting this omission, the service was a respectful conclusion.

Krista had one request before she left. She wanted to speak to James. We located him in the staff dining room, exchanged hugs and offered final words of thanks before we exited the building for the last time.

After the service images of special residents in attendance haunted me: the normally vivacious little lady, over 100-years-old, who had seemed so uncharacteristically detached during the service (possibly because she had been delivered to the chapel without her hearing aides); one of Mom's neighbors, only sixty-seven-years-old, valiantly struggling before the service to advocate for another resident who needed attention; and, of course, dear Pearl. They remained within the red brick building.

Communicating with Corporate

THE SUMMER OF 2006 BROUGHT ASSURANCES THAT LIFE GOES ON. Lawns greened up, trees leafed out and flowers budded. Days lengthened so that by mid-June a walk with Jasper could still be accomplished in the cooler hours of the evening without the risk of running out of daylight. Jasper and I headed out, just the two of us, for a quiet amble around the neighborhood. Although still an eager companion, he plodded along, investigating each tree, bush, and mailbox along our path. With no desire to stride at aerobic pace I relaxed and drifted into reflections on the circle of life.

Over the course of Jasper's lifetime and in a mode that resembled fast-forward, I had witnessed his passage through all but the final stage of the life cycle. Had it been only thirteen years ago this spring that he joined our family as a curious and adorable black-and-white puppy, complete with silky fur, a pink spot on his nose, and a white blaze down the center of his face? Quickly he grew long and lean and established his position as herder of the family. He was always most happy when everyone, especially his mistress, Angie, was safely home. Eventually, his youthful leanness gave way to the muscle and bulk of adulthood. Still, he maintained his desire to be a lap dog, creating a comical picture when he plopped himself on top of whomever was seated on the couch. A much-loved and elder member of the family, he needed special considerations for his senior stage of life, such as a boost from behind as he navigated a flight of stairs. Sometime in the not too distant future, perhaps a few months from now, we would find ourselves saying goodbye to this trusty friend. Mortality, the nature of all living things.

My mind returned, as it so often did during introspective moments, to my parents and the exemplary lives they had led and the people they had touched. My blessings included the simple fact that Dad and Mom lived to be eighty-two and eighty-eight years old, respectively. They were not snatched by death at a young age or by acute heart attacks or fatal car crashes that left no time for saying goodbye. They lived long and productive lives that included years of opportunities to delight in their grandchildren. Dad understood the inevitability of death and the probability that Mom would outlive him. She was his greatest concern.

"Thank you, hospice," I said out loud to no one but Jasper, as we circled the neighborhood. I thought about the promise I made to my father. "I'll take care of Mom," I had said. Hospice had helped me do that. Still, I could not shake the sadness and frustration of the three years before the hospice team arrived. Truly, the nursing home experience would forever be a monumental disappointment.

Arriving back home, I settled in front of my computer and located *A Daughter's Promise*, my essay written month's earlier on our family's experience with eldercare. As my essay stated, Mom's dementia "has led her and her family on a journey that none of us wanted to take, through a care system inspired by the best of intentions, brilliant in the beginning but disappointing as we neared the end. We don't know when that end will come, but in the meantime, I'll remember my promise to Dad and travel alongside Mom through her journey."

I had experienced the final "when" and my journey was over. An end to the essay could be written. I updated it with a three paragraph postscript describing the enhancement of Mom's last months by the compassionate care provided by hospice; the announcement of her death following a six-day, family vigil; and a statement of consternation that on Mom's last night on earth, no nurse had been assigned to work on her floor.

Yet, even with the finality of the postscript, I experienced the gnawing of unfinished business as I saved the file, shut down the computer and climbed into bed.

The following morning, I printed a copy of my essay. During the next few days, I shared it with family and friends. Results were varied. Some people were saddened by what they read; some were outraged. Some felt I was too light-handed because I had not named the nonprofit corporation responsible for my mother's care or written specifics about the poison pen note or the administration's tepid reaction to thievery within the building. Yet, all encouraged me to share the story.

Tentative, I balked at suggestions to send it to elected officials, but I assembled a list of recipients that included the administrators of the three facilities in which my parents lived, Mom's hospice team, and advocates for the elderly. To the list I added the CEO of Riverside Homes and the chairman of the board of directors for Mom's nursing home, whose name I did not know. In an attempt to get that information I picked up the phone and dialed corporate headquarters. When I asked the person at the other end of the line for the name of the chairperson of the board, I was forwarded to the voice mailbox of the executive assistant of the CEO. I left my request for this information along with my phone number and waited for a return call. Hours later the phone rang, but the resulting conversation was so bizarre that I immediately sat down at my computer and reconstructed it to the best of my recollection:

> *EA (executive assistant): I'd like to speak to Jackie Herron.*
> *J (Jackie/me): Speaking*
> *EA: This is (her name) from Riverside Homes. You had a question?*
> *J: Thanks for returning my call. I am interested in sending something to the chairperson of the board of directors of Riverside North, and I am needing his or her name and address.*
> *EA: Why do you want to know that?*
> *J: Because I want to send the chair something?*
> *EA: Where are you from?*
> *J: Excuse me?*
> *EA: Are you from The Mad Hatter (pseudo name)?*
> *J: What? No.*
> *EA: So where are you from?*
> *J: I had a mother at Riverside North who died recently. And, I'd like to send something to the chair of the board, so, if I could please have that person's name.*

EA: *What are you sending?*

J: *Something that I wish to send directly to the chairperson?*

EA: *What is it?*

J: *I need the name of the chair so I can send it to HIM or HER. Is there a chairman of the board?*

EA: *I work with the board. You can send it to me. I'll make sure they get it.*

J: *I would like to send it directly. May I please have his or her name?*

EA: *I can't give you that information.*

J: *You can't give me that information? Isn't it public record?*

EA: *Yes, but I can't help you.*

J: *Why not?*

EA: *We've been having some trouble and we have to be careful.*

J: *(pause) What is The Mad Hatter?*

EA: *(response was indefinite and incoherent)*

J: *So you won't give me the name of the board chair?*

EA: *You can send anything to me, (and she gave me her name) with attention to the chair of the board, and I will see that it gets passed along.*

Bizarre! Shaking my head at the reconstructed script of the phone conversation, I was stunned at what the conversation revealed.

First, I was shocked at my own unwillingness to openly explain to this woman what I would be sending. Her repeated insistence at knowing about the contents of my correspondence with the chairman of the board triggered an even greater reluctance on my part to give her any information at all about my essay. Why was I so guarded? Did I fear retribution? Was I still nursing wounds inflicted by previous acts of whistleblowing? Could I muster the fortitude to deal with any fallout that followed the telling of our story?

"She's a gatekeeper," said my friend Lyle, when I described my conversation with the executive secretary. Then he enlightened me on the use of this tactic in business.

Gatekeeping—an intentional impediment—a strange concept for this public school teacher whose school district expected and encouraged open communication.

Confused, I did what I often do in confusing situations. I began to list what I knew for sure.

First, I knew that my mother's safety was no longer a factor. That thought was freeing, since fear of retribution had prevented me from seeking assistance outside of my mother's facility while she was alive.

I knew that the elusive name of the chairperson of the board could be tracked down through the State Attorney General's Office.

I knew that when I figured out who that person was, I would send a copy of my essay to him or her and to the CEO of Riverside Homes. Furthermore, the envelopes that contained these copies would be addressed to their private residences away from corporate America.

I knew that I was going on a quest to find out more about the Mad Hatter.

I knew that the executive assistant of the corporation that held the responsibility to oversee my mother's nursing home had gifted me in a rather bizarre way with impetus to continue sharing our family's story. Thanks to her, I was motivated to jump the gate.

Sharing A Daughter's Promise

JULY 17, 2006, WAS A BUSY SATURDAY. Clay and Becky were both running in Grandma's Marathon in Duluth, Minnesota. It would be Becky's first attempt at long-distance running, and I marveled at her ease with this challenge. She and Clay had dedicated themselves to their training regimen, and I eagerly awaited news that they had crossed the finish line. While they ran, I busied myself with the finishing touches of *A Daughter's Promise* and the necessary preparations for mailing. I wrote a one-page preface that accomplished two objectives. First, to give authenticity to my story I named the corporation and the facilities that provided my mother's care. Then I added a paragraph highlighting a book that was so critical in my understanding of eldercare: *It Shouldn't Be This Way: The Failure of Long-Term Care* by Robert L. Kane, M.D. (Professor and Director of the Center on Aging, University of Minnesota) and Joan C. West.

I ended the preface with my name, slipped it between the title page and the body of my essay and transported the entire work over to Kinko's to be copied, collated and stapled. Once home with essays in hand, I stuffed each into an addressed envelope along with a personalized cover letter, complete with contact information, that encouraged the recipient to read our family's story and to continue advocacy for vulnerable people needing long-term care.

Dr. Robert L. Kane, the person I referenced in the preface of my article, would be receiving a copy. I had never met Dr. Kane, and I was sure that he was totally unaware of the lifeline that he held out to me several months before Mom died. I had just completed my rough draft of *A Daughter's Promise* and had filed it away hoping that the cathartic process of recording our family's experience would give me some peace. Still, I was overwhelmed with feelings of inadequacy. No matter how hard I had tried or what method I had used, I had not been able to institute consistent improvements in my mother's care. At that point I was questioning both my thinking and my emotional response.

Then one morning I turned on Minnesota Public Radio to an interview in progress about the failures of long-term care. It took me a few minutes to grasp that the interviewee had written a book with his sister about the challenges the two of them had faced as advocates for their mother. I stopped puttering in the kitchen and turned full attention to the story that was unfolding. It was as if he were reading from *A Daughter's Promise*. His story was my story in so many ways. Different mothers in different facilities in different states, yet parallel experiences, similar challenges, the same shocking disappointments.

The interviewee was Dr. Robert Kane. His book validated everything that had been twisting in my gut. What reassurance there was in knowing that our family's experience was not simply an aberration, something to be brushed aside as Murphy's Law. How comforting to realize that I shared common frustrations and disappointments with a renowned, highly educated and well-positioned authority.

A strong measure of hopelessness, however, accompanied this relief. No, it shouldn't be this way. Yet, it was. I had been witnessing this failure for years, and what I heard with resounding firmness from my kitchen radio added clear confirmation. Furthermore, hearing someone speak about the realities of long-term care heightened my anxiety, especially since at that moment Mom was still living in that reality. Yet, on that morning as Dr. Kane enlightened the radio's audience, he also nurtured the doggedness in my core, and I was spurred on to continue my daily advocacy for my mother.

Two other envelopes, addressed to the co-chairs of the board of directors of Mom's nursing home, lay in the stack of essays ready for the mail. Attorney General Mike Hatch's staff had expeditiously fulfilled my quest for information of public record—the same information that the office of the corporation that had charged my mother over a quarter of a million dollars for nursing home care had been unwilling to share.

The CEO of Riverside Homes would receive his own copy. I would like to imagine him as a caring person who would be sincerely interested in the story of one family who moved through his care system. Yet, I realized that my only image of him was a postage-sized photo in a promotional brochure.

Finally, each envelope was weighed, stamped and sent. I had done what I could do. I had given voice, perhaps meekly, to our story, and voice alone was all I had to offer.

I welcomed Clay's call confirming that both he and Becky had successfully crossed the finish line of Grandma's Marathon.

Then, I wondered if I could declare my marathon finished.

State Reports and Complaints, 2006

Fully retired, healthy, and ready to enjoy days no longer filled with nursing home visits or care-related strategy sessions, I turned attention to shelved hobbies. Now the brick buildings that I frequented were Ramsey County branch libraries, and my strategy sessions involved fascinating people like the lavender-haired saleswoman at Borealis Yarns who helped me match beautiful yarns to an array of knitting patterns.

Laughter lightened my spirit during lunch dates with friends. Even thoughts of Riverside Homes brought a smile to my face when a friend told me about a thrift shop called the Mad Hatter that was having difficulty with its landlord in addressing a rodent problem. The consignment shop was in a strip mall, near the corporate headquarters of Mom's care system, and the landlord of the property, she informed me, was none other than the corporation itself. Corporate! Could four legged critters be one of the "problems" the executive assistant referred to in our phone conversation? Then smiles turned to laughter when I pictured one more scenario. Did the executive secretary fear that the item I wished to send to the board chair was something more disgusting than simple correspondence? Could that assumption be her reason for asking if I was "from the Mad Hatter"?

Probably the most freeing realization was my understanding that answers to such questions were unnecessary. The suppositions were simply entertaining possibilities. Yes, I had lightened up.

Holidays were enjoyable again. I no longer equated them with high-alert times when nursing home visits required hyper-vigilance. Shortly after July Fourth an email alert from the Minnesota Department of Health notified me that new state survey results had been posted online. I checked the listing of facilities with new postings and located the name of my mother's nursing home. When I opened the link to the facility's latest survey, a lengthy report greeted me. From these pages I gleaned that the road to re-certification had been long and difficult. The survey began seven days after Mom died. At that time the facility was found:

> *"Not in substantial compliance"* with *"widespread deficiencies that constituted no actual harm with potential for more than minimal harm (Level F) but not immediate jeopardy to resident health or safety."*[(5)]

More disturbing was the length of time that passed before deficiencies were corrected to the satisfaction of the surveyors. During that time the Department of Health imposed a state monitoring remedy. On the critical three-month mark from the initial survey, mandatory denial of payment for new Medicare and Medicaid admissions became effective. Finally, after repeated visits by the surveyors the facility was judged to be in compliance, re-certification was granted and remedies were discontinued.

I scrolled further into the document and located the details of the deficiencies, knowing that each represented an actual resident whose care was considered sub-par by State surveyors. As I read through the failures, several struck a familiar chord. The facility failed to follow the care plan for five of eighteen residents . . . failure to reposition residents in a timely manner . . . failure to brush teeth with Prevident . . . it was Mom's story all over again, especially when I read the following:

> *Resident #11 . . . The resident's care plan directed the staff to "elevate right arm" and to apply a "sling to right arm when up."*
>
> *At 4:30 p.m. the resident was observed sitting in a wheelchair in the day room. The resident's right arm was not elevated and there was not a sling on the right arm.*
>
> *At 6:00 a.m. the resident was observed to be asleep in the bed. The resident's right arm was not elevated.*
>
> *At 7:50 a.m. the resident was observed in the dining room. The resident was sitting at the table and did not have a sling on the right arm.*[(6)]

The report provided striking similarity to the breach in protocol for Mom's battered wrist when I found her in the dayroom with no splint, cushion, or ice. Resident #11, however, was neglected by all three shifts of caregivers. And, if this neglect took place under the eyes of watchful state surveyors, what about run-of-the-mill days with no overseers?

I read the column of information on the right of each page that contained the facility's plan of correction for each deficiency:

> *Resident #11 . . . plan of care was reviewed and updated, along with the nursing assistant's assignment sheets. Sling was only ordered for comfort care and used at resident's request . . . Clinical administrator to audit.*"[7]

Inaccurate assignment sheets, not neglect, the paragraph seemed to indicate. Yet, wasn't the failure to follow the care plan a neglect issue, whether the sheets were updated or not? And why were the assignment sheets inaccurate in the first place? And weren't "audits" the accountability tool that I found so shockingly and repeatedly ineffective?

With each question my anxiety rose. As I read each deficiency, I shook my head in disappointment that the same issues were revisited from the prior year with no sustained change for the better.

I adjusted my printer to fast mode, pressed "print" and watched the pages slowly pile up in the output tray. In the meantime I grabbed an empty 3-ring notebook and labeled the spine "Resources: Eldercare/Nursing Homes" and filed the report inside.

Why was I doing this? Couldn't I be done? Couldn't I close the door on the last four years and just move on?

Corporate Silence

As I WAFFLED ABOUT, SICK OF EXPLORING THE REALITY OF ELDERCARE beyond my mother's experience, two happenings pushed me off my pedestal of complacency. Rather, I should say one happening, and one non-event.

The happening involved a complaint filed against my mother's nursing home. In the past I had avoided this link on the Minnesota Department of Health website. However, curiosity, stirred by my emotional reaction to the State survey report, got the best of me, and I followed the links until a recent complaint appeared on my monitor. This complaint investigated allegations of neglect that were detailed in a long paragraph. Investigative findings and a conclusion that "evidence of neglect was inconclusive" filled two more pages. I read the allegations carefully. Medication errors, inadequate assistance with eating and range of motion exercises, falsification of medication records, and lack of supervision resulting in one head injury and neglect of a second resident were alleged. I read the investigative findings that were summarized after interviews with staff, observations of meal service and the distribution of medication, and reviews of records and reports. All allegations, except one, were judged "unsubstantiated." One deficiency was issued because of a two-day delay of medication.[8]

The debate inside my head began. Here was the appropriate place to complain, but I never did. "Call the State," I had been advised by well-meaning friends when I described my concerns about my mother's care. I chose to work within the facility, hoping for a cooperative approach. However, I looked at the allegations in the complaint and realized the striking similarities to problems with my mother's care. I should have called when I found her arm dangling with no splint—when I found her back in her room without lunch—when doctor's orders or hospice orders were not followed—when a prescription was not administered but records indicated that it was. I could have been the one to help substantiate the breaches reported in this complaint.

Yet, how can families report without fear of retaliation? They can't. They wait until their loved ones are no longer vulnerable. They wait until death arrives. Then it is too late.

Our family's story about my parents' experiences within eldercare facilities, especially the disappointing nursing home, however, struck some chords. The envelopes containing *A Daughter's Promise* reached their destinations, and timely and encouraging feedback arrived by email and telephone. Requests were made and permission granted to share the story to a wider audience. Yet, weeks passed with no response from the administrator, CEO or board chairs overseeing my mother's nursing home.

Finally, two months after mailing *A Daughter's Promise*, Beverly Pierce called and acknowledged receipt of my essay. She had "read it several times and shared it with staff." One of Corporate's goals, according to her, was to improve the nursing home end of the continuum of care—to make facilities more person-centered. Yet, she acknowledged that the present "community model" was staff-focused and needed to be altered to better meet the needs of residents. Defensively, she unnecessarily reminded me that the problems delineated in my essay occurred in other nursing homes as well. Our conversation was brief and cordial. As I hung up the phone I recalled how excited I had been when I had met her at our first-ever meeting of third-floor families. I had such hope that things would change.

Response from the co-chairs of the board and the CEO of the corporation was the non-event. They ignored my story. Apparently they had no interest in speaking with me, offering feedback or widening my perspective by sharing their own. I was disappointed, but not surprised, which was disappointing by itself. Perhaps they just wanted me to go away.

Instead, their dismissal of my concerns motivated me to move forward. I dug out a copy of *A Daughter's Promise* and addressed it to the unit supervisor of the Licensing and Certification Program whose signature concluded the state's survey report. In a cover letter I thanked her for her work advocating for nursing home residents and pleaded for continued diligence. Then I drove over to the New Brighton Post Office once more.

Minnesota Culture Change Coalition

W EEKS LATER, A MIDMORNING TELEPHONE call brightened the day. The unit supervisor from the Licensing and Certification Program of the Minnesota Department of Health and Human Services, thanked me for sending her our family's story. Our conversation was filled with questions for each other, plus a sharing of perspective.

We talked about the bumpy road to compliance taken by my mother's nursing home during the latest survey.

We talked about the reasoning behind the state's reluctance to begin surprise visits on the weekends. (Since skeletal staffing was generally the rule on the weekend, residents would further suffer because surveyors required staff assistance during surveys.)

We talked about issues regarding my mother's care that paralleled issues of non-compliance recorded in the state report.

And, we talked about my reluctance to ask for assistance from the State Department of Health. I tried to adequately explain my feelings of vulnerability intertwined with fear of retaliation that erupted anytime I remotely considered filing a complaint.

Our conversation was unhurried. Most importantly, she listened in a non-patronizing way, and as the phone conversation ended, I felt a rush of sadness that I had not reached out to her, for direction if nothing else, earlier in Mom's journey.

Now, I had heard from all the recipients of A Daughter's Promise in one way or another, if I discounted those at the corporate level of Riverside Homes. I concluded that silence was all I could expect from the CEO and the board of directors. It was amazingly sad that those who chose not to respond were the people I trusted to make wise decisions for my mother.

They were the ones who established the value system and set the standards within it. They were the people who I had hoped would become Mom's voice when she needed her final home to attend to the simple requests that she was unable to articulate: a drink of water, a change of position, an unhurried meal, a feeling of safety. Simple, gentle things! The requests that were drowned out by other voices—voices concerned about staffing, funding and impressing State surveyors—voices from Corporate who spoke not a word to me except through marketing brochures and fundraising letters.

Who became Mom's voice when she could no longer speak? Who looked in her eyes and searched for the messages they communicated in her unspoken language? Who never overlooked her? Who never forgot her? The list of heroes and angels was lengthy. Family, friends, caregivers, residents, those people shared a common purpose. They all honored my mother by never allowing her disease to overshadow the essence of her humanity. They never lost sight of the woman behind the disease.

Other caregivers ignored Mom when her simple needs dropped off their busy radars. Others ignored me as I tried to tell her story.

"You sound angry." The comment came from Clay in an attempt to pinpoint the emotion that kept me writing about his grandmother's final years.

His comment jolted me. I had always considered anger in negative terms. Yet, finally I saw anger as a friend, an ally. My anger had protected me. Without it I would have been tempted to continue to hide behind a veil of denial, or worse, to dissolve into mind-numbing depression. Instead, anger had been the fire that had ignited a passion to shed the blinders, observe, listen, and question. Now, all that was left was to write, write, write. I thanked my anger and tucked it aside, assured that if needed, it would rise again.

However, there was a movement afoot that required no angry rants to draw attention to the need for overhaul of long-term care. A newspaper headline captured my attention and steered me to the Internet for links to innumerable websites that revealed an exciting, comforting discovery. Organizations, both familiar and unfamiliar, all stakeholders in long-term care, had banded together into the Minnesota Culture Change Coalition that described its unified mission: "Supporting dignity, respect, choice and self determination in long-term care."[9]

They understood the realities, and they were advocating for positive changes for both those who lived and those who worked in long-term care. Excitedly I signed up for the Partnering for Person-Centered Care Summit, scheduled for March 23, 2007, and hosted by the Minnesota Culture Change Coalition.

People converged on RiverCentre in St. Paul for the one-day care summit. Sitting elbow to elbow around tables with nursing home administrators, State Department personnel, coalition representatives and family members, I immediately focused on the two goals that were bulleted on the day's agenda:

• Learn why we should and how we can change nursing homes for the better.

• Discover how we can work together to make it happen.

Relief flooded over me as I read the two simple statements. Right there in black and white was common ground. Yes, there should be a change; and yes, it could occur. The coalition understood. No convincing required. Residual anger melted into puddles of thankfulness with the realization that the day's discussions would center on the need for change rather than the arguments for why things couldn't.

As the day progressed, presenters, videos, and group activities led participants to greater understanding of the benefits of individualized care over institutionalized care for both the person receiving and the person giving the care. What seemed like an expensive change was shown to save money as risk prevention increased. Everyone, even nursing home corporations, could benefit. Teamwork was encouraged. Everyone won. What a refreshing concept!

An administrator of an Iowan nursing home sat at my table and shared the story of the conversion of his nursing home to one reflecting the new model. "We started with the tub room," he described. "Totally lacking in privacy, we turned it into a comfortable bathing room, complete with dressing area, with the emphasis on preserving the dignity of the residents and offering them a pleasurable experience." Then he explained other changes, many re-quiring little or no additional cost, like renaming the tub room "the spa," as-signing staff according to the flow of work instead of following an inflexible work schedule, and incorporating input from residents into decisions regard-ing bedtimes and menus. *How do I make my reservation for sometime in the fu-ture?*

One particularly revealing activity centered on the case study of a man who entered a care facility for rehabilitation following a hospital stay. Nursing home personnel who arranged his schedule ignored his desire to stay up late and his reaction to alarms (due to his occupation as a fire-fighter). Instead, he was forced to fit into the long-term facility's schedule of early bedtimes. That led to a downward spiral of his general condition. When he arose and wandered late at night, he set off an alarm. The alarm triggered agitation. To counteract his emotional state, he was given a calm-ing medication. Side effects of the medication created wooziness and in-stability. In this condition, he attempted to walk to the bathroom when no one responded to his call light. Walking unassisted, he fell and broke a hip. Fear of further injury prompted him to cut back on his fluid intake, so he wouldn't have to get up and go to the bathroom in the middle of the night. Lack of fluids resulted in urinary tract infections. His body weakened and eventually, his temporary stay in the facility became a permanent one.

The moral of the case study, as I saw it, was that institutional care created many of its own problems. Time and attention to individual needs at the front end of a long-term stay could increase the success of rehabili-tation for the individual and decrease the cost of care.

I thought of Mom with the mention of the dreaded UTI. On a lighter note, I saw tables and tables of people huddling and discussing the possi-bilities of person-centered care. Furthermore, I was heartened to see an ad-ministrator from the Gardens, who introduced me to another attendee, a representative from North. The din rose into waves of possibility, muted at times by an occasional skeptic. At the conclusion of the summit, I re-turned home, relieved and thankful that a coalition was at work, giving voice to people in vulnerable stages of their lives—people just like Mom—people still living behind red brick walls.

The Story Continues

V ALENTINE'S DAY 2009! A day to honor loving, human relationships.

I dedicated the winter to writing, to organizing all my journals, notes and resources. My goal was to share our family's journey through the writing of a memoir, a story that hopefully would speak for Mom by telling her story. At times the process was overwhelming, and I found it difficult to "show up at the page" each day as more experienced writers had encouraged me to do. Perhaps improvements in eldercare had taken place and my mother's story was passe, outdated, out-of-touch. In less than a month we would arrive at the third anniversary of her passing.

Writing was on my agenda for the day, but a second cup of hot coffee with Tom in our cozy, four-season porch caused me to tarry, until he picked up the morning's newspaper.

"Jac, look at this," he said. But instead of passing me the paper, he summarized the article. "Your mother's nursing home has been faulted for the death of a resident."

"What?" was all that I could manage.

"North has been faulted for maltreatment because a resident suffered a severe neck injury while under the home's care—poor lady, she died. The home wasn't cited for any formal violations of state or federal nursing care standards," he continued, "because according to this article it thoroughly investigated the incident and retrained its workers in the required reporting procedures."

"Thoroughly investigated?" I interrupted sarcastically.

"Now the nursing home believes that it is being treated unfairly because the state can't pinpoint the incident or rule out an accident," he said.

Tom passed the paper over to me, and I read every word.

"Can't pinpoint the incident? If no one admits to seeing something, it didn't happen, right?" I heard my voice escalating as I threw out my hypothetical question to Tom, Corporate, the state and the wind.

His was the only response. "Sounds familiar."

"But in this woman's case somebody had to have attended to her after her trauma! Someone had to have helped her up, if nothing else," I added. "Why is no one willing to consider that perhaps the system failed? Just an ethical response and an apology, for starters."

Without waiting for a reply I moved into the computer room and logged onto the Minnesota Department of Health website and searched for the link to "nursing home incident reporting."

I clicked on "view file" and gained access to the written report in full. My stomach churned as I read the details of a woman's suffering shift after shift, day after day; staff interviews; varied responses and suppositions.

I read about the internal investigation and the inability to identify the cause of the injury along with the facility's response: retraining of staff. Finally, I focused on interviews with family members who described the horrific injury and their loved one's screams of pain.

Two aspects of the report, probably minor in nature to other readers, screamed at me from the computer screen. Both resonated with eerie familiarity. Staff interviews suggested an impossible scenario: that the resident might have accidentally caused her own injury and then returned herself to bed without informing staff. When in doubt, blame the victim. I had heard it before. I was also taken aback by the family's reluctance to divulge the name of a staff person who shared a rumor regarding "an incident in the bathroom" that resulted in the injuries. "Consequently, the investigators were unable to follow-up on the information," the report stated. [10]

How many times had conscientious staff members, frustrated by the lack of response when concerns were voiced through the correct channels, shared information with me about Mom's care? I, too, never divulged their names, because I knew that their jobs would be jeopardized for sharing negative information with the family. Instead, I attempted to address those concerns at care conferences or third-floor family meetings, only to become frustrated, depressed and distrustful of a broken system. The conspiracy of silence—I was a party to it by not taking my concerns to agencies outside the nursing home.

Eventually Mom's nursing home would restore its good name when the state amended its decision and ruled that *maltreatment is inconclusive as it relates to Resident #1's injuries. Although information gathered during the investigation supports the fact that trauma was the cause . . . the investigation was unable to determine whether or not the trauma was the result of maltreatment. Therefore, there is less than a preponderance of evidence to show that maltreatment did or did not occur.* [11]

To me the ruling was disappointing and frustrating, but not surprising. How could an act of maltreatment be proven when the victim was unable to speak and staff members with information chose silence?

I was fully aware that accidents happen and often cannot be avoided, even with the best of care. However, for the resident with the neck injury, even if maltreatment could not be confirmed, shouldn't someone be asking additional questions? What happened after the accident? What breaches in quality care took place during the days between her accident and her ambulance ride to the hospital?

Documentation of the resident's experience offered insight into systemic failures of nursing home care. Shift after shift of nursing home caregivers seemed unfamiliar with the cause, timing and extent of her injury. Some were unresponsive to her cries of pain. Others, although conscientious, were rendered helpless, caught like single cogs in a huge and broken system of eldercare. While family members sought explanations, the facility requested a reconsideration of the maltreatment finding.

I clipped the newspaper article and taped it to the wall behind my computer. It joined a hodgepodge of clippings about nursing home abuse and neglect in the Twin Cities, Minnesota and America. The stories were doubly tragic because many of the abused and neglected residents also suffered from Alzheimer's disease and other forms of dementia. Victims without voices. People needing advocates!

Mom had passed on, but the nursing home story continued. Motivation restored, I returned again to the computer and began to type.

Endnotes

(1) Minnesota Department of Health, 22 April 2005. Web. 17 July 2005

(2) Minnesota Department of Health, 22 April 2005. Web. 17 July 2005.

(3) Minnesota Department of Health, 22 April 2005. Web. 17 July 2005.

(4) Ibid.

(5) Minnesota Department of Health, 7 July 2006. Web. 7 July 2006.

(6) Minnesota Department of Health, 7 July 2006. Web. 7 July 2006.

(7) Minnesota Department of Health, 7 July 2006. Web. 7 July 2006.

(8) Minnesota Department of Health, 7 July 2006. Web. 1 August 2006.

(9) Minnesota Culture Change Coalition, n.d. Web. 16 February 2007.

(10) Minnesota Department of Health, 14 February 2009. Web. 14 February 2009.

(11) Minnesota Department of Health, 8 May, 2009. Web. 20 May, 2009.

Questions for Discussion

1. What aspects of Teen's story most affected you? Who in the book did you most identify with and why?

2. According to the author, denial can be a veil that people hide behind. What truths were denied by the author? What circumstances in your life are you choosing to camouflage behind a veil of denial? Why?

3. As resident-centered care fell away so did Teen's quality-of-life. What systemic ills of nursing home care currently exist? What immediate steps should be taken to improve lives of nursing home resident? What long-range changes would you like to see take place?

4. The author referred to the "blindness" of some nursing home staff. What causes this type of blindness? What can be done to restore sight?

5. When the author capitalized the word Corporate, this faceless entity became a character in the story. How was this character portrayed? What life experiences give you empathy for the plight of the author and/or the corporation?

6. The author chose to work with nursing home personnel when crises arose. Why was she reluctant to involve outside regulators? How would you handle issues of theft and neglect of a loved one in the nursing home?

7. When evaluating a potential care facility for your loved ones, what factors have been or would be important to you?

8. How was death portrayed in the book? What is your concept of death? If you have been present during the death of a loved one, how did that experience affect you?

9. During debates over healthcare policies and funding, who represents the people without voices? How might you add your voice to the choir of advocates?

More questions are available at www.jaclynnherron.com

Acknowledgments

W HEN MY MOTHER'S VOICE SPOKE CLEARLY, she advised me, "Do all that you are capable of doing, and when that isn't enough, await angels." Then she reminded me to be attentive, because angels often arrive in earthly attire. She was right.

Thank you, Dr. Robert L. Kane, for your radio message in 2005 when you talked about long-term care and how it "shouldn't be this way." You validated all that I was experiencing as my mother's advocate. Unknowingly you prompted me to keep writing. Thank you for your continued support, including your willingness to read drafts of this memoir and to offer helpful suggestions.

I am indebted to the teachers and students of the Loft Literary Center who encouraged and nurtured the telling of this story. I especially wish to thank Nancy Raeburn, who discovered the nuggets of a memoir within my early writings and fostered their expansion.

I appreciate Seal Dwyer, Corinne Dwyer and North Star Press for believing in the worthiness of my mother's story and for bringing it to print.

Many thanks to Dr. Rosemary Chapin for the early review and to Steve Aanenson for his expertise with website development.

Names of organizations, facilities and people have been changed to preserve the privacy of residents, family members and staff of the buildings in which my parents lived. However, it is my hope that many will recognize within the story their personal acts of advocacy for my mother. I am especially grateful for the members of my mother's hospice care team. Each member personified compassion and taught Teen's family what person-centered care for the ill and elderly really looks like.

With appreciation, I thank extended family members and friends whose first names appear in the text: Lyle Baker, Diana Berndt, Barbara

Bottger, Dorothy Ann and Fred Deziel, Betty Ebersviller, Nan Fisher, Deb Hanchar, Rob Hand, Dick Heiser, Donna Herron, Cheryll Johnson, Holly and Seth Krachmer, Tommy Launderville, Perry Nelson, Karen Peterson, Virginia Reynolds, Ruth Rose, Allison Simpson, Colleen and David Welty, Maxine Williams, and Warren Wollenberg. I remember with gratitude those who along with Mom have passed on: Linda Cunningham, John Fisher, and Wayne and Harriet Johnson.

Margie Baker, Carol Christie, Sue Foster, Joann Heiser, Helen Nelson, Lynette Kopperud, Karen Lake, Nancy Olson, and Cindy Phair, from the beginning you lived this story alongside me. You encouraged me to write, read manuscripts at different stages, and offered reflections and insights. You support me still. Many thanks. Nancy, thanks so much for being the first to describe my mother's journey as a time when our family was "singing solo."

Zipporah Onwonga, wonderful Zippy, you never lost sight of your friend Teen, even after dementia tried to hide her away. Thank you for allowing me to share the strand of your life story that intertwines with my mother's.

Arleen Rutten, thanks for sharing old photos that capture special Johnson family moments and for your enthusiastic support.

Clay and Becky Johnson, Krista and Steve Freier and Angie Herron, you enriched your grandparents' lives, and you continue to bless mine. Many thanks not only for allowing me to share our family's very personal tale, but also for your encouragement. I look forward to years of watching you bestow the legacy of your grandparents' love onto the next generation: Mia and Zoe Johnson and Baby Freier (due shortly before the birth of this memoir).

And finally, my best friend and beloved husband Tom, you are my rock. Thanks to your love and support, serenity fills my soul and hope inspires our future.

About the Author

JacLynn Herron, MOTHER OF TWO ADULT DAUGHTERS, lives in New Brighton, Minnesota, with her husband Tom. A graduate of Concordia College in Moorhead, Minnesota, she is a retired secondary school educator who, because of her mother's experience, has become a passionate advocate for person-centered care for the ill and elderly. Additional information about the author, eldercare/advocacy resources and the essay *A Daughter's Promise: Taking Care of Mom in the Twenty-First Century* can be found at www.jaclynnherron.com